KU-756-791

# Blackstone's Statutes on

# Evidence

15th edition

*edited by*

## Phil Huxley

LLB, LLM
*Former Principal Lecturer at Nottingham Law School,*
*Nottingham Trent University*

UNIVERSITY OF BRADFORD
WITHDRAWN AND DISCARDED
LIBRARY

## OXFORD
UNIVERSITY PRESS

BD 040015983 7

# OXFORD
## UNIVERSITY PRESS

Great Clarendon Street, Oxford, OX2 6DP,
United Kingdom

Oxford University Press is a department of the University of Oxford.
It furthers the University's objective of excellence in research, scholarship,
and education by publishing worldwide. Oxford is a registered trade mark of
Oxford University Press in the UK and in certain other countries

This selection © Phil Huxley 2018

The moral rights of the author have been asserted

First published by Blackstone Press 1991

Twelfth edition 2012
Thirteenth edition 2014
Fourteenth edition 2016
Fifteenth edition 2018

Impression: 1

All rights reserved. No part of this publication may be reproduced, stored in
a retrieval system, or transmitted, in any form or by any means, without the
prior permission in writing of Oxford University Press, or as expressly permitted
by law, by licence or under terms agreed with the appropriate reprographics
rights organization. Enquiries concerning reproduction outside the scope of the
above should be sent to the Rights Department, Oxford University Press, at the
address above

You must not circulate this work in any other form
and you must impose this same condition on any acquirer

Public sector information reproduced under Open Government Licence v3.0
(http://www.nationalarchives.gov.uk/doc/open-government-licence/open-government-licence.htm)

Published in the United States of America by Oxford University Press
198 Madison Avenue, New York, NY 10016, United States of America

British Library Cataloguing in Publication Data
Data available

ISBN 978-0-19-881858-8

Printed in Italy by L.E.G.O. S.p.A.

Links to third party websites are provided by Oxford in good faith and
for information only. Oxford disclaims any responsibility for the materials
contained in any third party website referenced in this work.

Oxford University Press is committed to using paper from sustainable and ethical sources.

# Contents

# Alphabetical contents

# Chronological contents

# Editor's preface

The UK government has for almost all of the last two years been preoccupied (some commentators have used the word 'paralysed') with the consequences of the UK referendum vote on membership of the European Union. What with extended parliamentary recesses, party conferences, and other time-hungry activities, major legislation has been in relatively short supply. The only major legislative changes relevant to the current edition of this book have been brought about by the Police and Crime Act 2017 which, in this context, has meant a number of changes to the Police and Criminal Evidence Act 1984. This edition has benefited from suggestions from colleagues teaching Evidence in Law Schools in England and Wales and I thank them. The book no longer carries the Protection of Children Act 1978, Part 1 of PACE 1984, or the Crime (International Co-operation) Act 2003. The revised Codes C and D of the PACE Codes of Practice are included as are the updated Criminal Procedure Rules of 2015 to cover the changes brought about by SI 2018 No 132.

The first edition of this book was published in 1991. It was inspired by my colleague and friend Michael O'Connell who was instrumental in fashioning the content. Michael hung up his word processor in 2006 and I have decided that the time has come for me to the do the same. I wish to thank everyone at OUP for their courtesy and patience in the preparation of this as well as earlier editions. Their attention to detail has contributed in no small way to the success of the series.

The law is stated as on St David's Day 2018.

*Phil Huxley*

# New to this edition

The fifteenth edition of *Blackstone's Statutes on Evidence* has been fully revised and updated with all relevant legislation through to 1 March 2018 including:
- Amendments to PACE 1984 by the Police and Crime Act 2017
- New Codes C and D of the Codes of Practice under PACE 1984
- Updated Criminal Procedure Rules

# Blackstone's Statutes
## Unsurpassed in authority, reliability, and accuracy

The titles in the Blackstone's Statutes series are a collection of carefully reviewed and selected unannotated legislative material and official documents.

We make every effort to ensure titles in the series meet the needs of their target market. They are reviewed by lecturers to match university courses closely and are expertly edited to be manageable in size, whilst retaining their comprehensive coverage.

The editors only include material from legislation that will be valuable to students and lecturers and it is therefore abridged where necessary.

### Conventions used in *Blackstone's Statutes on Evidence*
An ellipsis symbol . . . indicates text that has not been included in this edition.

The material in this book is reproduced in its most up-to-date form. Supplementary notes and details of amending provisions are generally not included.

All statutes have been enacted but some very recent legislation may not yet be in force.

 Visit **www.oup.com/uk/statutes** for accompanying online resources including video guides to reading and interpreting statutes, exam tips, and an interactive sample Act of Parliament.

# Part I

# Criminal Proceedings—Statutes

## Criminal Procedure Act 1865

(1865, c. 18)

### 3   How far witnesses may be discredited by the party producing

A party producing a witness shall not be allowed to impeach his credit by general evidence of bad character; but he may, in case the witness shall in the opinion of the judge prove adverse, contradict him by other evidence, or, by leave of the judge, prove that he has made at other times a statement inconsistent with his present testimony; but before such last-mentioned proof can be given the circumstances of the supposed statement, sufficient to designate the particular occasion, must be mentioned to the witness, and he must be asked whether or not he has made such statement.

### 4   As to proof of contradictory statements of adverse witness

If a witness, upon cross-examination as to a former statement made by him relative to the subject matter of the indictment or proceeding, and inconsistent with his present testimony, does not distinctly admit that he has made such statement, proof may be given that he did in fact make it; but before such proof can be given the circumstances of the supposed statement, sufficient to designate the particular occasion, must be mentioned to the witness, and he must be asked whether or not he has made such statement.

### 5   Cross-examinations as to previous statements in writing

A witness may be cross-examined as to previous statements made by him in writing, or reduced into writing, relative to the subject matter of the indictment or proceeding, without such writing being shown to him; but if it is intended to contradict such witness by the writing, his attention must, before such contradictory proof can be given, be called to those parts of the writing which are to be used for the purpose of so contradicting him: Provided always, that it shall be competent for the judge, at any time during the trial, to require the production of the writing for his inspection, and he may thereupon make such use of it for the purposes of the trial as he may think fit.

### 6   Proof of conviction of witness may be given

(1) If upon a witness being lawfully questioned as to whether he has been convicted he either denies or does not admit the fact, or refuses to answer, it shall be lawful for the cross examining party to prove such conviction; and a certificate containing the substance and effect only (omitting the formal part) of the indictment and conviction for such offence, purporting to be signed by the proper officer of the court where the offender was convicted having the custody of the records of the court where the offender was convicted, or by the deputy of such clerk of officer, (for which certificate a fee of (25p) and no more shall be demanded or taken), shall upon proof of the identity of the person, be sufficient evidence of the said conviction, without proof of the signature or official character of the person appearing to have signed the same.

(2) In subsection (1) 'proper officer' means—

(a) in relation to a magistrates' court in England and Wales, the designated officer for the court; and

(b) in relation to any other court, the clerk of the court or other officer having the custody of the records of the court, or the deputy of such clerk or other officer.

# Criminal Evidence Act 1898

(1898, c. 36)

## 1   Competency of witnesses in criminal cases

(1) A person charged in criminal proceedings shall not be called as a witness in the proceedings except upon his own application.

(2) Subject to section 101 of the Criminal Justice Act 2003 (admissibility of evidence of defendant's bad character), a person charged in criminal proceedings who is called as a witness in the proceedings may be asked any question in cross-examination notwithstanding that it would tend to criminate him as to any offence with which he is charged in the proceedings.

(3) . . .

(4) Every person charged in criminal proceedings who is called as a witness in the proceedings shall, unless otherwise ordered by the court, give his evidence from the witness box or other place from which the other witnesses give their evidence.

## 2   Evidence of person charged

Where the only witness to the facts of the case called by the defence is the person charged, he shall be called as a witness immediately after the close of the evidence for the prosecution.

## 3   Right of reply

The fact that the person charged has been called as a witness shall not of itself confer on the prosecution the right of reply.

# Perjury Act 1911

(1911, c. 6)

## 13   Corroboration

A person shall not be liable to be convicted of any offence against this Act, or of any offence declared by any other Act to be perjury or subornation of perjury, or to be punishable as perjury or subornation of perjury, solely upon the evidence of one witness as to the falsity of any statement alleged to be false.

## 14   Proof of certain proceedings on which perjury is assigned

On a prosecution—

(a) for perjury alleged to have been committed on the trial of an indictment . . .; or

(b) for procuring or suborning the commission of perjury on any such trial,

the fact of the former trial shall be sufficiently proved by the production of a certificate containing the substance and effect (omitting the formal parts) of the indictment and trial purporting to be signed by the clerk of the court, or other person having the custody of the records of the court where the indictment was tried, or by the deputy of that clerk or other person, without proof of the signature or official character of the clerk or person appearing to have signed the certificate.

# Prevention of Crime Act 1953

(1953, c. 14)

## 1  Prohibition of the carrying of offensive weapons without lawful authority or reasonable excuse

(1)  Any person who without lawful authority or reasonable excuse, the proof whereof shall lie on him, has with him in any public place any offensive weapon shall be guilty of an offence, and shall be liable—

(a)  on summary conviction, to imprisonment for a term not exceeding six months or a fine not exceeding the prescribed sum or both;

(b)  on conviction on indictment, to imprisonment for a term not exceeding four years or a fine . . . or both.

(2)  Where any person is convicted of an offence under subsection (1) of this section the court may make an order for the forfeiture or disposal of any weapon in respect of which the offence was committed.

(3)  . . .

(4)  In this section 'public place' includes any highway and any other premises or place to which at the material time the public have or are permitted to have access, whether on payment or otherwise; and 'offensive weapon' means any article made or adapted for use for causing injury to the person, or intended by the person having it with him for such use by him or by some other person.

# Homicide Act 1957

(1957, c. 11)

## 2  Persons suffering from diminished responsibility

(1)  A person ('D') who kills or is a party to the killing of another is not to be convicted of murder if D was suffering from an abnormality of mental functioning which—

(a)  arose from a recognised medical condition,

(b)  substantially impaired D's ability to do one or more of the things mentioned in subsection (1A), and

(c)  provides an explanation for D's acts and omissions in doing or being a party to the killing.

(1A)  Those things are—

(a)  to understand the nature of D's conduct;

(b)  to form a rational judgment;

(c)  to exercise self-control.

(1B)  For the purposes of subsection (1)(c), an abnormality of mental functioning provides an explanation for D's conduct if it causes, or is a significant contributory factor in causing, D to carry out that conduct.

(2)  On a charge of murder, it shall be for the defence to prove that the person charged is by virtue of this section not liable to be convicted of murder.

(3)  A person who but for this section would be liable, whether as principal or as accessory, to be convicted of murder shall be liable instead to be convicted of manslaughter.

(4)  The fact that one party to a killing is by virtue of this section not liable to be convicted of murder shall not affect the question whether the killing amounted to murder in the case of any other party to it.

# Criminal Justice Act 1967

(1967, c. 80)

## 9 Proof by written statement

(1) In any criminal proceedings, a written statement by any person shall, if such of the conditions mentioned in the next following subsection as are applicable are satisfied, be admissible as evidence to the like extent as oral evidence to the like effect by that person.

(2) The said conditions are—

(a) the statement purports to be signed by the person who made it;

(b) the statement contains a declaration by the person to the effect that it is true to the best of his knowledge and belief and that he made the statement knowing that, if it were tendered in evidence, he would be liable to prosecution if he wilfully stated in it anything which he knew to be false or did not believe to be true;

(c) before the hearing at which the statement is tendered in evidence, a copy of the statement is served, by or on behalf of the party proposing to tender it, on each of the other parties to the proceedings; and

(d) none of the other parties or their solicitors, within the relevant period serves a notice on the party so proposing objecting to the statement being tendered in evidence under this section:

Provided that the conditions mentioned in paragraphs (c) and (d) of this subsection shall not apply if the parties agree before or during the hearing that the statement shall be so tendered.

(2A) For the purposes of subsection (2)(d), 'the relevant period' is—

(a) such number of days, which may not be less than seven, from the service of the copy of the statement as may be prescribed by Criminal Procedure Rules, or

(b) if no such number is prescribed, seven days from the service of the copy of the statement.

(3) The following provisions shall also have effect in relation to any written statement tendered in evidence under this section, that is to say—

(a) if the statement is made by a person under the age of eighteen, it shall give his age;

(b) if it is made by a person who cannot read it, it shall be read to him before he signs it and shall be accompanied by a declaration by the person who so read the statement to the effect that it was so read; and

(c) if it refers to any other document as an exhibit, the copy served on any other party to the proceedings under paragraph (c) of the last foregoing subsection shall be accompanied by a copy of that document or by such information as may be necessary in order to enable the party on whom it is served to inspect that document or a copy thereof.

(3A) In the case of a statement which indicates in pursuance of subsection (3)(a) of this section that the person making it has not attained the age of 14, subsection (2)(b) of this section shall have effect as if for the words from 'made' onwards there were substituted the words 'understands the importance of telling the truth in it'.

(4) Notwithstanding that a written statement made by any person may be admissible as evidence by virtue of this section—

(a) the party by whom or on whose behalf a copy of the statement was served may call that person to give evidence; and

(b) the court may, of its own motion or on the application of any party to the proceedings, require that person to attend before the court and give evidence.

(5) An application under paragraph (b) of the last foregoing subsection to a court other than a magistrates' court may be made before the hearing and on any such application the powers of the court shall be exercisable by a puisne judge of the High Court, a Circuit judge or Recorder sitting alone.

(8) A document required by this section to be served on any person may be served—

(a) by delivering it to him or to his solicitor; or

(b) by addressing it to him and leaving it at his usual or last known place of abode or place of business or by addressing it to his solicitor and leaving it at his office; or

(c) by sending it in a registered letter or by the recorded delivery service or by first class post addressed to him at his usual or last known place of abode or place of business or addressed to his solicitor at his office; or

(d) in the case of a body corporate, by delivering it to the secretary or clerk of the body at its registered or principal office or sending it in a registered letter or by the recorded delivery service or by first class post addressed to the secretary or clerk of that body at that office;

and in paragraph (d) of this subsection references to the secretary, in relation to a limited liability partnership, are to any designated member of the limited liability partnership.

## 10    Proof by formal admission

(1) Subject to the provisions of this section, any fact of which oral evidence may be given in any criminal proceedings may be admitted for the purpose of those proceedings by or on behalf of the prosecutor or defendant, and the admission by any party of any such fact under this section shall as against that party be conclusive evidence in those proceedings of the fact admitted.

(2) An admission under this section—

(a) may be made before or at the proceedings;

(b) if made otherwise than in court, shall be in writing;

(c) if made in writing by an individual, shall purport to be signed by the person making it and, if so made by a body corporate, shall purport to be signed by a director or manager, or the secretary or clerk, or some other similar officer of the body corporate;

(d) if made on behalf of a defendant who is an individual, shall be made by his counsel or solicitor;

(e) if made at any stage before the trial by a defendant who is an individual, must be approved by his counsel or solicitor (whether at the time it was made or subsequently) before or at the proceedings in question.

(3) An admission under this section for the purpose of proceedings relating to any matter shall be treated as an admission for the purpose of any subsequent criminal proceedings relating to that matter (including any appeal or retrial).

(4) An admission under this section may with the leave of the court be withdrawn in the proceedings for the purpose of which it is made or any subsequent criminal proceedings relating to the same matter.

# Criminal Appeal Act 1968

(1968, c. 19)

# PART I  APPEAL TO COURT OF APPEAL IN CRIMINAL CASES

*Appeal against conviction on indictment*

## 1    Right of appeal

(1) Subject to subsection (3) below a person convicted of an offence on indictment may appeal to the Court of Appeal against his conviction.

(2) An appeal under this section lies only—

(a) with the leave of the Court of Appeal; or

(b) if, within 28 days of the date of conviction, the judge of the court of trial grants a certificate that the case is fit for appeal.

(3) Where a person is convicted before the Crown Court of a scheduled offence it shall not be open to him to appeal to the Court of Appeal against the conviction on the ground that the decision of the court which sent him to the Crown Court for trial as to the value involved was mistaken.

(4) In subsection (3) above 'scheduled offence' and 'the value involved' have the same meanings as they have in section 22 of the Magistrates' Courts Act 1980 (certain offences against property to be tried summarily if value of property or damage is small).

### 23   Evidence

(1)  For the purposes of an appeal, or on an application for leave to appeal, under this Part of this Act the Court of Appeal may, if they think it necessary or expedient in the interests of justice—

    (a)  order the production of any document, exhibit or other thing connected with the proceedings, the production of which appears to them necessary for the determination of the case;

    (b)  order any witness to attend for examination and be examined before the Court (whether or not he was called in the proceedings from which the appeal lies); and

    (c)  receive any evidence which was not adduced in the proceedings from which the appeal lies.

(1A)  The power conferred by subsection (1)(a) may be exercised so as to require the production of any document, exhibit or other thing mentioned in that subsection to—

    (a)  the Court;

    (b)  the appellant;

    (c)  the respondent.

(2)  The Court of Appeal shall, in considering whether to receive any evidence, have regard in particular to—

    (a)  whether the evidence appears to the Court to be capable of belief;

    (b)  whether it appears to the Court that the evidence may afford any ground for allowing the appeal;

    (c)  whether the evidence would have been admissible in the proceedings from which the appeal lies on an issue which is the subject of the appeal; and

    (d)  whether there is a reasonable explanation for the failure to adduce the evidence in those proceedings.

(3)  Subsection (1)(c) above applies to evidence of a witness (including the appellant) who is competent but not compellable.

(4)  For the purposes of an appeal, or an application for leave to appeal, under this Part of this Act, the Court of Appeal may, if they think it necessary or expedient in the interests of justice, order the examination of any witness whose attendance might be required under subsection (1)(b) above to be conducted, in manner provided by rules of court, before any judge or officer of the Court or other person appointed by the Court for the purpose, and allow the admission of any depositions so taken as evidence before the Court.

(5)  A live link direction under section 22(4) does not apply to the giving of oral evidence by the appellant at any hearing unless that direction, or any subsequent direction of the court, provides expressly for the giving of such evidence through a live link.

(6)  In this section, 'respondent' includes a person who will be a respondent if leave to appeal is granted.

# Theft Act 1968

(1968, c. 60)

### 22   Handling stolen goods

(1)  A person handles stolen goods if (otherwise than in the course of the stealing) knowing or believing them to be stolen goods he dishonestly receives the goods, or dishonestly undertakes or assists in their retention, removal, disposal or realisation by or for the benefit of another person, or if he arranges to do so.

(2)  A person guilty of handling stolen goods shall on conviction on indictment be liable to imprisonment for a term not exceeding fourteen years.

### 25   Going equipped for stealing, etc.

(1)  A person shall be guilty of an offence if, when not at his place of abode, he has with him any article for use in the course of or in connection with any burglary or theft.

(2)  A person guilty of an offence under this section shall on conviction on indictment be liable to imprisonment for a term not exceeding three years.

(3)  Where a person is charged with an offence under this section, proof that he had with him any article made or adapted for use in committing a burglary or theft shall be evidence that he had it with him for such use.

(5)  For purposes of this section an offence under section 12(1) of this Act of taking a conveyance shall be treated as theft.

## 27    Evidence and procedure on charge of theft or handling stolen goods

(1)  Any number of persons may be charged in one indictment, with reference to the same theft, with having at different times or at the same time handled all or any of the stolen goods, and the persons so charged may be tried together.

(2)  On the trial of two or more persons indicted for jointly handling any stolen goods the jury may find any of the accused guilty if the jury are satisfied that he handled all or any of the stolen goods, whether or not he did so jointly with the other accused or any of them.

(3)  Where a person is being proceeded against for handling stolen goods (but not for any offence other than handling stolen goods), then at any stage of the proceedings, if evidence has been given of his having or arranging to have in his possession the goods the subject of the charge, or of his undertaking or assisting in, or arranging to undertake or assist in, their retention, removal, disposal or realisation, the following evidence shall be admissible for the purpose of proving that he knew or believed the goods to be stolen goods:—

    (a)  evidence that he has had in his possession, or has undertaken or assisted in the retention, removal, disposal or realisation of, stolen goods from any theft taking place not earlier than twelve months before the offence charged; and

    (b)  (provided that seven days' notice in writing has been given to him of the intention to prove the conviction) evidence that he has within the five years preceding the date of the offence charged been convicted of theft or of handling stolen goods.

(4)  In any proceedings for the theft of anything in the course of transmission (whether by post or otherwise), or for handling stolen goods from such a theft, a statutory declaration made by any person that he despatched or received or failed to receive any goods or postal packet, or that any goods or postal packet when despatched or received by him were in a particular state or condition, shall be admissible as evidence of the facts stated in the declaration, subject to the following conditions:—

    (a)  a statutory declaration shall only be admissible where and to the extent to which oral evidence to the like effect would have been admissible in the proceedings; and

    (b)  a statutory declaration shall only be admissible if at least seven days before the hearing or trial a copy of it has been given to the person charged, and he has not, at least three days before the hearing or trial or within such further time as the court may in special circumstances allow, given the prosecutor written notice requiring the attendance at the hearing or trial of the person making the declaration.

(5)  This section is to be construed in accordance with section 24 of this Act; and in subsection (3)(b) above the reference to handling stolen goods shall include any corresponding offence committed before the commencement of this Act.

## 30    Spouses and civil partners

(1)  This Act shall apply in relation to the parties to a marriage, and to property belonging to the wife or husband whether or not by reason of an interest derived from the marriage, as it would apply if they were not married and any such interest subsisted independently of the marriage.

(2)  Subject to subsection (4) below, a person shall have the same right to bring proceedings against that person's wife or husband for any offence (whether under this Act or otherwise), as if they were not married and a person bringing any such proceedings shall be competent to give evidence for the prosecution at every stage of the proceedings.

(4)  Proceedings shall not be instituted against a person for any offence of stealing or doing unlawful damage to property which at the time of the offence belongs to that person's wife or husband or civil partner, or for any attempt, incitement or conspiracy to commit such an offence, unless the proceedings are instituted by or with the consent of the Director of Public Prosecutions:

Provided that—

(a) this subsection shall not apply to proceedings against a person for an offence—

    (i) if that person is charged with committing the offence jointly with the wife or husband or civil partner; or

    (ii) if by virtue of any judicial decree or order (wherever made) that person and the wife or husband are at the time of the offence under no obligation to cohabit; and

    (iii) an order (wherever made) is in force providing for the separation of that person and his or her civil partner.

(5) Notwithstanding section 6 of the Prosecution of Offences Act 1979 subsection (4) of this section shall apply—

(a) to an arrest (if without warrant) made by the wife or husband or civil partner, and

(b) to a warrant of arrest issued on an information laid by the wife or husband or civil partner.

## 31    Effect on civil proceedings and rights

(1) A person shall not be excused, by reason that to do so may incriminate that person or the spouse or civil partner of that person of an offence under this Act—

(a) from answering any question put to that person in proceedings for the recovery or administration of any property, for the execution of any trust or for an account of any property or dealings with property; or

(b) from complying with any order made in any such proceedings;

but no statement or admission made by a person in answering a question put or complying with an order made as aforesaid shall, in proceedings for an offence under this Act, be admissible in evidence against that person or (unless they married or became civil partners after the making of the statement of admission) against the spouse or civil partner of that person.

(2) Notwithstanding any enactment to the contrary, where property has been stolen or obtained by fraud or other wrongful means, the title to that or any other property shall not be affected by reason only of the conviction of the offender.

# Misuse of Drugs Act 1971

(1971, c. 38)

## 5    Restriction of possession of controlled drugs

(1) Subject to any regulations under section 7 of this Act for the time being in force, it shall not be lawful for a person to have a controlled drug in his possession.

(2) Subject to section 28 of this Act and to subsection (4) below, it is an offence for a person to have a controlled drug in his possession in contravention of subsection (1) above.

(2A) Subsections (1) and (2) do not apply in relation to a temporary class drug.

(3) Subject to section 28 of this Act, it is an offence for a person to have a controlled drug in his possession, whether lawfully or not, with intent to supply it to another in contravention of section 4(1) of this Act.

(4) In any proceedings for an offence under subsection (2) above in which it is proved that the accused had a controlled drug in his possession, it shall be a defence for him to prove—

(a) that, knowing or suspecting it to be a controlled drug, he took possession of it for the purpose of preventing another from committing or continuing to commit an offence in connection with that drug and that as soon as possible after taking possession of it he took all such steps as were reasonably open to him to destroy the drug or to deliver it into the custody of a person lawfully entitled to take custody of it; or

(b) that, knowing or suspecting it to be a controlled drug, he took possession of it for the purpose of delivering it into the custody of a person lawfully entitled to take custody of it and that as soon as possible after taking possession of it he took all such steps as were reasonably open to him to deliver it into the custody of such a person.

(5) . . .

(6) Nothing in subsection (4) . . . above shall prejudice any defence which it is open to a person charged with an offence under this section to raise apart from that subsection.

## 28    Proof of lack of knowledge etc. to be a defence in proceedings for certain offences

(1) This section applies to offences under any of the following provisions of this Act, that is to say section 4(2) and (3), section 5(2) and (3), section 6(2) and section 9.

(2) Subject to subsection (3) below, in any proceedings for an offence to which this section applies it shall be a defence for the accused to prove that he neither knew of nor suspected nor had reason to suspect the existence of some fact alleged by the prosecution which it is necessary for the prosecution to prove if he is to be convicted of the offence charged.

(3) Where in any proceedings for an offence to which this section applies it is necessary, if the accused is to be convicted of the offence charged, for the prosecution to prove that some substance or product involved in the alleged offence was the controlled drug which the prosecution alleges it to have been, and it is proved that the substance or product in question was that controlled drug, the accused—

    (a) shall not be acquitted of the offence charged by reason only of proving that he neither knew nor suspected nor had reason to suspect that the substance or product in question was the particular controlled drug alleged; but

    (b) shall be acquitted thereof—

        (i) if he proves that he neither believed nor suspected nor had reason to suspect that the substance or product in question was a controlled drug; or

        (ii) if he proves that he believed the substance or product in question to be a controlled drug, or a controlled drug of a description, such that, if it had in fact been that controlled drug or a controlled drug of that description, he would not at the material time have been committing any offence to which this section applies.

(4) Nothing in this section shall prejudice any defence which it is open to a person charged with an offence to which this section applies to raise apart from this section.

# Magistrates' Courts Act 1980

(1980, c. 43)

## 98    Evidence on oath

Subject to the provisions of any enactment or rule of law authorising the reception of unsworn evidence, evidence given before a magistrates' court shall be given on oath.

## 101    Onus of proving exceptions, etc.

Where the defendant to an information or complaint relies for his defence on any exception, exemption, proviso, excuse or qualification, whether or not it accompanies the description of the offence or matter of complaint in the enactment creating the offence or on which the complaint is founded, the burden of proving the exception, exemption, proviso, excuse or qualification shall be on him; and this notwithstanding that the information or complaint contains an allegation negativing the exception, exemption, proviso, excuse or qualification.

## 104    Proof of previous convictions

Where a person is convicted of a summary offence by a magistrates' court, other than a youth court, and—

    (a) it is proved to the satisfaction of the court, on oath or in such other manner as may be prescribed, that not less than 7 days previously a notice was served on the accused in the prescribed form and manner specifying any alleged previous conviction of the accused of a summary offence proposed to be brought to the notice of the court in the event of his conviction of the offence charged; and

    (b) the accused is not present in person before the court, the court may take account of any such previous conviction so specified as if the accused had appeared and admitted it.

### 107   False statements in declaration proving service, etc.

If, in any solemn declaration, certificate or other writing made or given for the purpose of its being used in pursuance of rules of court as evidence of the service of any document or the handwriting or seal of any person, a person makes a statement that he knows to be false in a material particular, or recklessly makes any statement that is false in a material particular, he shall be liable on summary conviction to imprisonment for a term not exceeding 6 months or a fine not exceeding level 3 on the standard scale or both.

## Criminal Justice Act 1982

**(1982, c. 48)**

### *Unsworn statements*

### 72   Abolition of right of accused to make unsworn statement

    (1) Subject to subsections (2) and (3) below, in any criminal proceedings the accused shall not be entitled to make a statement without being sworn, and accordingly, if he gives evidence, he shall do so (subject to sections 55 and 56 of the Youth Justice and Criminal Evidence Act 1999) on oath and be liable to cross-examination; but this section shall not affect the right of the accused, if not represented by counsel or a solicitor, to address the court or jury otherwise than on oath on any matter on which, if he were so represented, counsel or a solicitor could address the court or jury on his behalf.

    (2) Nothing in subsection (1) above shall prevent the accused making a statement without being sworn—

      (a) if it is one which he is required by law to make personally; or

      (b) if he makes it by way of mitigation before the court passes sentence upon him.

## Police and Criminal Evidence Act 1984

**(1984, c. 60)**

## PART II   POWERS OF ENTRY, SEARCH AND SEIZURE

### *Search warrants*

### 8   Power of justice of the peace to authorise entry and search of premises

    (1) If on an application made by a constable a justice of the peace is satisfied that there are reasonable grounds for believing—

      (a) that an indictable offence has been committed; and

      (b) that there is material on premises mentioned in subsection (1A) below which is likely to be of substantial value (whether by itself or together with other material) to the investigation of the offence; and

      (c) that the material is likely to be relevant evidence; and

      (d) that it does not consist of or include items subject to legal privilege, excluded material or special procedure material; and

      (e) that any of the conditions specified in subsection (3) below applies in relation to each set of premises specified in the application,

he may issue a warrant authorising a constable to enter and search the premises.

    (1A) The premises referred to in subsection (1)(b) above are—

(a) one or more sets of premises specified in the application (in which case the application is for a 'specific premises warrant'); or

(b) any premises occupied or controlled by a person specified in the application, including such sets of premises as are so specified (in which case the application is for an 'all premises warrant').

(1B) If the application is for an all premises warrant, the justice of the peace must also be satisfied—

(a) that because of the particulars of the offence referred to in paragraph (a) of subsection (1) above, there are reasonable grounds for believing that it is necessary to search premises occupied or controlled by the person in question which are not specified in the application in order to find the material referred to in paragraph (b) of that subsection; and

(b) that it is not reasonably practicable to specify in the application all the premises which he occupies or controls and which might need to be searched.

(1C) The warrant may authorise entry to and search of premises on more than one occasion if, on the application, the justice of the peace is satisfied that it is necessary to authorise multiple entries in order to achieve the purpose for which he issues the warrant.

(1D) If it authorises multiple entries, the number of entries authorised may be unlimited, or limited to a maximum.

(2) A constable may seize and retain anything for which a search has been authorised under subsection (1) above.

(3) The conditions mentioned in subsection (1)(e) above are—

(a) that it is not practicable to communicate with any person entitled to grant entry to the premises;

(b) that it is practicable to communicate with a person entitled to grant entry to the premises but it is not practicable to communicate with any person entitled to grant access to the evidence;

(c) that entry to the premises will not be granted unless a warrant is produced;

(d) that the purpose of a search may be frustrated or seriously prejudiced unless a constable arriving at the premises can secure immediate entry to them.

(4) In this Act 'relevant evidence', in relation to an offence, means anything that would be admissible in evidence at a trial for the offence.

(5) The power to issue a warrant conferred by this section is in addition to any such power otherwise conferred.

(6) This section applies in relation to a relevant offence (as defined in section 28D(4) of the Immigration Act 1971) as it applies to an indictable offence.

(7) ...*

## 9  Special provisions as to access

(1) A constable may obtain access to excluded material or special procedure material for the purposes of a criminal investigation by making an application under Schedule 1 below and in accordance with that Schedule.

(2) Any Act (including a local Act) passed before this Act under which a search of premises for the purposes of a criminal investigation could be authorised by the issue of a warrant to a constable shall cease to have effect so far as it relates to the authorisation of searches—

(a) for items subject to legal privilege; or

(b) for excluded material; or

(c) for special procedure material consisting of documents or records other than documents.

(2A) ...**

---

* **Editor's Note:** Execution of process of English courts in Scotland.
** **Editor's Note:** Execution of process of English courts in Scotland and Northern Ireland.

### 10    Meaning of 'items subject to legal privilege'

(1)  Subject to subsection (2) below, in this Act 'items subject to legal privilege' means—

    (a) communications between a professional legal adviser and his client or any person representing his client made in connection with the giving of legal advice to the client;

    (b) communications between a professional legal adviser and his client or any person representing his client or between such an adviser or his client or any such representative and any other person made in connection with or in contemplation of legal proceedings and for the purpose of such proceedings; and

    (c) items enclosed with or referred to in such communications and made—

        (i) in connection with the giving of legal advice; or

        (ii) in connection with or in contemplation of legal proceedings and for the purposes of such proceedings,

when they are in the possession of a person who is entitled to possession of them.

(2)  Items held with the intention of furthering a criminal purpose are not items subject to legal privilege.

### 11    Meaning of 'excluded material'

(1)  Subject to the following provisions of this section, in this Act 'excluded material' means—

    (a) personal records which a person has acquired or created in the course of any trade, business, profession or other occupation or for the purposes of any paid or unpaid office and which he holds in confidence;

    (b) human tissue or tissue fluid which has been taken for the purposes of diagnosis or medical treatment and which a person holds in confidence;

    (c) journalistic material which a person holds in confidence and which consists—

        (i) of documents; or

        (ii) of records other than documents.

(2)  A person holds material other than journalistic material in confidence for the purposes of this section if he holds it subject—

    (a) to an express or implied undertaking to hold it in confidence; or

    (b) to a restriction on disclosure or an obligation of secrecy contained in any enactment, including an enactment contained in an Act passed after this Act.

(3)  A person holds journalistic material in confidence for the purposes of this section if—

    (a) he holds it subject to such an undertaking, restriction or obligation; and

    (b) it has been continuously held (by one or more persons) subject to such an undertaking, restriction or obligation since it was first acquired or created for the purposes of journalism.

### 12    Meaning of 'personal records'

In this Part of this Act 'personal records' means documentary and other records concerning an individual (whether living or dead) who can be identified from them and relating—

    (a) to his physical or mental health;

    (b) to spiritual counselling or assistance given or to be given to him; or

    (c) to counselling or assistance given or to be given to him, for the purposes of his personal welfare, by any voluntary organisation or by any individual who—

        (i) by reason of his office or occupation has responsibilities for his personal welfare; or

        (ii) by reason of an order of a court has responsibilities for his supervision.

### 13    Meaning of 'journalistic material'

(1)  Subject to subsection (2) below, in this Act 'journalistic material' means material acquired or created for the purposes of journalism.

(2)  Material is only journalistic material for the purposes of this Act if it is in the possession of a person who acquired or created it for the purposes of journalism.

(3)  A person who receives material from someone who intends that the recipient shall use it for the purposes of journalism is to be taken to have acquired it for those purposes.

### 14 Meaning of 'special procedure material'

(1) In this Act 'special procedure material' means—

(a) material to which subsection (2) below applies; and

(b) journalistic material, other than excluded material.

(2) Subject to the following provisions of this section, this subsection applies to material, other than items subject to legal privilege and excluded material, in the possession of a person who—

(a) acquired or created it in the course of any trade, business, profession or other occupation or for the purpose of any paid or unpaid office; and

(b) holds it subject—

(i) to an express or implied undertaking to hold it in confidence; or

(ii) to a restriction or obligation such as is mentioned in section 11(2)(b) above.

(3) Where material is acquired—

(a) by an employee from his employer and in the course of his employment; or

(b) by a company from an associated company,

it is only special procedure material if it was special procedure material immediately before the acquisition.

(4) Where material is created by an employee in the course of his employment, it is only special procedure material if it would have been special procedure material had his employer created it.

(5) Where material is created by a company on behalf of an associated company, it is only special procedure material if it would have been special procedure material had the associated company created it.

(6) A company is to be treated as another's associated company for the purposes of this section if it would be so treated under section 449 of the Corporation Taxes Act 2010.

### 15 Search warrants—safeguards

(1) This section and section 16 below have effect in relation to the issue to constables under any enactment, including an enactment contained in an Act passed after this Act, of warrants to enter and search premises; and an entry on or search of premises under a warrant is unlawful unless it complies with this section and section 16 below.

(2) Where a constable applies for any such warrant, it shall be his duty—

(a) to state—

(i) the ground on which he makes the application;

(ii) the enactment under which the warrant would be issued; and

(iii) if the application is for a warrant authorising entry and search on more than one occasion, the ground on which he applies for such a warrant, and whether he seeks a warrant authorising an unlimited number of entries, or (if not) the maximum number of entries desired;

(b) to specify the matters set out in subsection (2A) below; and

(c) to identify, so far as is practicable, the articles or persons to be sought.

(2A) The matters which must be specified pursuant to subsection (2)(b) above are—

(a) if the application relates to one or more sets of premises specified in the application, each set of premises which it is desired to enter and search;

(b) if the application relates to any premises occupied or controlled by a person specified in the application—

(i) as many sets of premises which it is desired to enter and search as it is reasonably practicable to specify;

(ii) the person who is in occupation or control of those premises and any others which it is desired to enter and search;

(iii) why it is necessary to search more premises than those specified under sub-paragraph (i); and

(iv) why it is not reasonably practicable to specify all the premises which it is desired to enter and search.

(3) An application for such a warrant shall be made ex parte and supported by an information in writing.

(4) The constable shall answer on oath any question that the justice of the peace or judge hearing the application asks him.

(5) A warrant shall authorise an entry on one occasion only unless it specifies that it authorises multiple entries.

(5A) If it specifies that it authorises multiple entries, it must also specify whether the number of entries authorised is unlimited, or limited to a specified maximum.

(6) A warrant—
  (a) shall specify—
    (i)   the name of the person who applies for it;
    (ii)  the date on which it is issued;
    (iii) the enactment under which it is issued; and
    (iv) each set of premises to be searched, or (in the case of an all premises warrant) the person who is in occupation or control of premises to be searched, together with any premises under his occupation or control which can be specified and which are to be searched; and
  (b) shall identify, so far as is practicable, the articles or persons to be sought.

(7) Two copies shall be made of a warrant which specifies only one set of premises and does not authorise multiple entries; and as many copies as are reasonably required may be made of any other kind of warrant.

(8) The copies shall be clearly certified as copies.

## 16    Execution of warrants

(1) A warrant to enter and search premises may be executed by any constable.

(2) Such a warrant may authorise persons to accompany any constable who is executing it.

(2A) A person so authorised has the same powers as the constable whom he accompanies in respect of—
  (a) the execution of the warrant, and
  (b) the seizure or detention of anything to which the warrant relates.

(2B) But he may exercise those powers only in the company, and under the supervision, of a constable.

(3) Entry and search under a warrant must be within three months from the date of its issue.

(3A) If the warrant is an all premises warrant, no premises which are not specified in it may be entered or searched unless a police officer of at least the rank of inspector has in writing authorised them to be entered.

(3B) No premises may be entered or searched for the second or any subsequent time under a warrant which authorises multiple entries unless a police officer of at least the rank of inspector has in writing authorised that entry to those premises.

(4) Entry and search under a warrant must be at a reasonable hour unless it appears to the constable executing it that the purpose of a search may be frustrated on an entry at a reasonable hour.

(5) Where the occupier of premises which are to be entered and searched is present at the time when a constable seeks to execute a warrant to enter and search them, the constable—
  (a) shall identify himself to the occupier and, if not in uniform, shall produce to him documentary evidence that he is a constable;
  (b) shall produce a warrant to him; and
  (c) shall supply him with a copy of it.

(6) Where—
  (a) the occupier of such premises is not present at the time when a constable seeks to execute such a warrant; but
  (b) some other person who appears to the constable to be in charge of the premises is present,

subsection (5) above shall have effect as if any reference to the occupier were a reference to that other person.

(7) If there is no person present who appears to the constable to be in charge of the premises, he shall leave a copy of the warrant in a prominent place on the premises.

(8) A search under a warrant may only be a search to the extent required for the purpose for which the warrant was issued.

(9) A constable executing a warrant shall make an endorsement on it stating—

(a) whether the articles or persons sought were found; and

(b) whether any articles were seized, other than articles which were sought

and, unless the warrant is a warrant specifying one set of premises only, he shall do so separately in respect of each set of premises entered and searched, which he shall in each case state in the endorsement.

(10) A warrant shall be returned to the appropriate person mentioned in subsection (10A) below—

(a) when it has been executed; or

(b) in the case of a specific premises warrant which has not been executed, or an all premises warrant, or any warrant authorising multiple entries, upon the expiry of the period of three months referred to in subsection (3) above or sooner.

(10A) The appropriate person is—

(a) if the warrant was issued by a justice of the peace, the designated officer for the local justice area in which the justice was acting when he issued the warrant;

(b) if it was issued by a judge, the appropriate officer of the court from which he issued it.

(11) A warrant which is returned under subsection (10) above shall be retained for 12 months from its return—

(a) by the designated officer for the local justice area, if it was returned under paragraph (i) of that subsection; and

(b) by the appropriate officer, if it was returned under paragraph (ii).

(12) If during the period for which a warrant is to be retained the occupier of premises to which it relates asks to inspect it, he shall be allowed to do so.

*Entry and search without search warrant*

## 17   Entry for purpose of arrest etc.

(1) Subject to the following provisions of this section, and without prejudice to any other enactment, a constable may enter and search any premises for the purpose—

(a)   of executing—

(i)    a warrant of arrest issued in connection with or arising out of criminal proceedings; or

(ii)   a warrant of commitment issued under section 76 of the Magistrates' Courts Act 1980;

(b)   of arresting a person for an indictable offence;

(c)   of arresting a person for an offence under—

(i)    section 1 (prohibition of uniforms in connection with political objects), of the Public Order Act 1936;

(ii)   any enactment contained in sections 6 to 8 or 10 of the Criminal Law Act 1977 (offences relating to entering and remaining on property);

(iii)  section 4 of the Public Order Act 1986 (fear or provocation of violence);

(iiia) section 4 (driving etc. when under influence of drink or drugs) or 163 (failure to stop when required to do so by constable in uniform) of the Road Traffic Act 1988;

(iiib) section 27 of the Transport and Works Act 1992 (which relates to offences involving drink or drugs);

(iv)   section 76 of the Criminal Justice and Public Order Act 1994 (failure to comply with interim possession order);

(v)    any of the sections 4, 5, 6(1) and (2), 7 and 8(1) and (2) of the Animal Welfare Act 2006 (offences relating to the prevention of harm to animals);

(vi)    section 144 of the Legal Aid, Sentencing and Punishment of Offenders Act 2012 (squatting in a residential building);

(ca)    of arresting, in pursuance of section 32(1A) of the Children and Young Persons Act 1969, any child or young person who has been remanded to local authority accommodation or youth detention accommodation under section 91 of the Legal Aid, Sentencing and Punishment of Offenders Act 2012;

(caa)    of arresting a person for an offence to which section 61 of the Animal Health Act 1981 applies;

(cb)    of recapturing any person who is, or is deemed for any purpose to be, unlawfully at large while liable to be detained—

(i)    in a prison, young offender institution, secure training centre or secure college, or

(ii)    in pursuance of section 92 of the Powers of Criminal Courts (Sentencing) Act 2000 (dealing with children and young persons guilty of grave crimes), in any other place.

(d)    of recapturing any person whatever who is unlawfully at large and whom he is pursuing; or

(e)    of saving life or limb or preventing serious damage to property.

(2)   Except for the purpose specified in paragraph (e) of subsection (1) above, the powers of entry and search conferred by this section—

(a)    are only exercisable if the constable has reasonable grounds for believing that the person whom he is seeking is on the premises; and

(b)    are limited, in relation to premises consisting of two or more separate dwellings, to powers to enter and search—

(i)    any parts of the premises which the occupiers of any dwelling comprised in the premises use in common with the occupiers of any other such dwelling; and

(ii)    any such dwelling in which the constable has reasonable grounds for believing that the person whom he is seeking may be.

(3)   The powers of entry and search conferred by this section are only exercisable for the purposes specified in subsection (1)(c)(ii) (iv) or (vi) above by a constable in uniform.

(4)   The power of search conferred by this section is only a power to search to the extent that is reasonably required for the purpose for which the power of entry is exercised.

(5)   Subject to subsection (6) below, all the rules of common law under which a constable has power to enter premises without a warrant are hereby abolished.

(6)   Nothing in subsection (5) above affects any power of entry to deal with or prevent a breach of the peace.

## 18   Entry and search after arrest

(1)   Subject to the following provisions of this section, a constable may enter and search any premises occupied or controlled by a person who is under arrest for an indictable offence, if he has reasonable grounds for suspecting that there is on the premises evidence, other than items subject to legal privilege, that relates—

(a)   to that offence; or

(b)   to some other indictable offence which is connected with or similar to that offence.

(2)   A constable may seize and retain anything for which he may search under subsection (1) above.

(3)   The power to search conferred by subsection (1) above is only a power to search to the extent that is reasonably required for the purpose of discovering such evidence.

(4)   Subject to subsection (5) below, the powers conferred by this section may not be exercised unless an officer of the rank of inspector or above has authorised them in writing.

(5)   A constable may conduct a search under subsection (1)—

(a)   before the person is taken to a police station or released under section 30A, and

(b)   without obtaining an authorisation under subsection (4), if the condition in subsection (5A) is satisfied.

(5A) The condition is that the presence of the person at a place (other than a police station) is necessary for the effective investigation of the offence.

(6) If a constable conducts a search by virtue of subsection (5) above, he shall inform an officer of the rank of inspector or above that he has made the search as soon as practicable after he has made it.

(7) An officer who—

(a) authorises a search; or

(b) is informed of a search under subsection (6) above,

shall make a record in writing—

(i) of the grounds for the search; and

(ii) of the nature of the evidence that was sought.

(8) If the person who was in occupation or control of the premises at the time of the search is in police detention at the time the record is to be made, the officer shall make the record as part of his custody record.

*Seizure etc.*

## 19  General power of seizure etc.

(1) The powers conferred by subsections (2), (3) and (4) below are exercisable by a constable who is lawfully on any premises.

(2) The constable may seize anything which is on the premises if he has reasonable grounds for believing—

(a) that it has been obtained in consequence of the commission of an offence; and

(b) that it is necessary to seize it in order to prevent it being concealed, lost, damaged, altered or destroyed.

(3) The constable may seize anything which is on the premises if he has reasonable grounds for believing—

(a) that it is evidence in relation to an offence which he is investigating or any other offence; and

(b) that it is necessary to seize it in order to prevent it being concealed, lost, altered or destroyed.

(4) The constable may require any information which is stored in any electronic form and is accessible from the premises to be produced in a form in which it can be taken away and in which it is visible and legible or from which it can readily be produced in a visible and legible form if he has reasonable grounds for believing—

(a) that—

(i) it is evidence in relation to an offence which he is investigating or any other offence; or

(ii) it has been obtained in consequence of the commission of an offence; and

(b) that it is necessary to do so in order to prevent it being concealed, lost, tampered with or destroyed.

(5) The powers conferred by this section are in addition to any power otherwise conferred.

(6) No power of seizure conferred on a constable under any enactment (including an enactment contained in an Act passed after this Act) is to be taken to authorise the seizure of an item which the constable exercising the power has reasonable grounds for believing to be subject to legal privilege.

## 20  Extension of powers of seizure to computerised information

(1) Every power of seizure which is conferred by an enactment to which this section applies on a constable who has entered premises in the exercise of a power conferred by an enactment shall be construed as including a power to require any information stored in any electronic form and accessible from the premises to be produced in a form in which it can be taken away and in which it is visible and legible or from which it can readily be produced in a visible and legible form.

(2) This section applies—

    (a) to any enactment contained in an Act passed before this Act;

    (b) to sections 8 and 18 above;

    (c) to paragraph 13 of Schedule 1 to this Act; and

    (d) to any enactment contained in an Act passed after this Act.

## 21   Access and copying

(1) A constable who seizes anything in the exercise of a power conferred by any enactment, including an enactment contained in an Act passed after this Act, shall, if so requested by a person showing himself—

    (a) to be the occupier of premises on which it was seized; or

    (b) to have had custody or control of it immediately before the seizure,

provide that person with a record of what he seized.

(2) The officer shall provide the record within a reasonable time from the making of the request for it.

(3) Subject to subsection (8) below, if a request for permission to be granted access to anything which—

    (a) has been seized by a constable; and

    (b) is retained by the police for the purpose of investigating an offence,

is made to the officer in charge of the investigation by a person who had custody or control of the thing immediately before it was so seized or by someone acting on behalf of such a person, the officer shall allow the person who made the request access to it under the supervision of a constable.

(4) Subject to subsection (8) below, if a request for a photograph or copy of any such thing is made to the officer in charge of the investigation by a person who had custody or control of the thing immediately before it was so seized, or by someone acting on behalf of such a person, the officer shall—

    (a) allow the person who made the request access to it under the supervision of a constable for the purpose of photographing or copying it; or

    (b) photograph or copy it, or cause it to be photographed or copied.

(5) A constable may also photograph or copy, or have photographed or copied, anything which he has power to seize, without a request being made under subsection (4) above.

(6) Where anything is photographed or copied under subsection (4)(b) above, the photograph or copy shall be supplied to the person who made the request.

(7) The photograph or copy shall be so supplied within a reasonable time from the making of the request.

(8) There is no duty under this section to grant access to, or to supply a photograph or copy of, anything if the officer in charge of the investigation for the purposes of which it was seized has reasonable grounds for believing that to do so would prejudice—

    (a) that investigation;

    (b) the investigation of an offence other than the offence for the purposes of investigating which the thing was seized; or

    (c) any criminal proceedings which may be brought as a result of—

        (i) the investigation of which he is in charge; or

        (ii) any such investigation as is mentioned in paragraph (b) above.

(9) The references to a constable in subsections (1), (2), (3)(a) and (5) include a person authorised under section 16(2) to accompany a constable executing a warrant.

(10) The references to a constable in subsections (1) and (2) do not include a constable who has seized a thing under paragraph 19ZE of Schedule 3 to the Police Reform Act 2002.

## 22   Retention

(1) Subject to subsection (4) below, anything which has been seized by a constable or taken away by a constable following a requirement made by virtue of section 19 or 20 above may be retained so long as is necessary in all the circumstances.

(2) Without prejudice to the generality of subsection (1) above—

    (a) anything seized for the purposes of a criminal investigation may be retained, except as provided by subsection (4) below,—

        (i)   for use as evidence at a trial for an offence; or

        (ii)  for forensic examination or for investigation in connection with an offence; and

    (b) anything may be retained in order to establish its lawful owner, where there are reasonable grounds for believing that it has been obtained in consequence of the commission of an offence.

(3) Nothing seized on the ground that it may be used—

    (a) to cause physical injury to any person;

    (b) to damage property;

    (c) to interfere with evidence; or

    (d) to assist in escape from police detention or lawful custody,

may be retained when the person from whom it was seized is no longer in police detention or the custody of a court or is in the custody of a court but has been released on bail.

(4) Nothing may be retained for either of the purposes mentioned in subsection (2)(a) above if a photograph or copy would be sufficient for that purpose.

(5) Nothing in this section affects any power of a court to make an order under section 1 of the Police (Property) Act 1897.

(6) This section also applies to anything retained by the police under section 28H(5) of the Immigration Act 1971.

(7) The reference in subsection (1) to anything seized by a constable includes anything seized by a person authorised under section 16(2) to accompany a constable executing a warrant.

*Supplementary*

### 23   Meaning of 'premises' etc.

In this Act—

    'premises' includes any place and, in particular, includes—

        (a)   any vehicle, vessel, aircraft or hovercraft;

        (b)   any offshore installation;

        (ba)  any renewable energy installation;

        (c)   any tent or movable structure.

    'offshore installation' has the meaning given to it by section 1 of the Mineral Workings (Offshore Installations) Act 1971.

    'renewable energy installation' has the same meaning as in Chapter 2 of Part 2 of the Energy Act 2004.

# PART III   ARREST

### 24   Arrest without warrant: constables

(1) A constable may arrest without a warrant—

    (a) anyone who is about to commit an offence;

    (b) anyone who is in the act of committing an offence;

    (c) anyone whom he has reasonable grounds for suspecting to be about to commit an offence;

    (d) anyone whom he has reasonable grounds for suspecting to be committing an offence.

(2) If a constable has reasonable grounds for suspecting that an offence has been committed, he may arrest without a warrant anyone whom he has reasonable grounds to suspect of being guilty of it.

(3)  If an offence has been committed, a constable may arrest without a warrant—

    (a)  anyone who is guilty of the offence;

    (b)  anyone whom he has reasonable grounds for suspecting to be guilty of it.

(4)  But the power of summary arrest conferred by subsection (1), (2) or (3) is exercisable only if the constable has reasonable grounds for believing that for any of the reasons mentioned in subsection (5) it is necessary to arrest the person in question.

(5)  The reasons are—

    (a)  to enable the name of the person in question to be ascertained (in the case where the constable does not know, and cannot readily ascertain, the person's name, or has reasonable grounds for doubting whether a name given by the person as his name is his real name);

    (b)  correspondingly as regards the person's address;

    (c)  to prevent the person in question—

        (i)   causing physical injury to himself or any other person;

        (ii)  suffering physical injury;

        (iii) causing loss of or damage to property;

        (iv)  committing an offence against public decency (subject to subsection (6)); or

        (v)   causing an unlawful obstruction of the highway;

    (d)  to protect a child or other vulnerable person from the person in question;

    (e)  to allow the prompt and effective investigation of the offence or of the conduct of the person in question;

    (f)  to prevent any prosecution for the offence from being hindered by the disappearance of the person in question.

(6)  Subsection (5)(c)(iv) applies only where members of the public going about their normal business cannot reasonably be expected to avoid the person in question.

### 24A  Arrest without warrant: other persons*

(1)  A person other than a constable may arrest without a warrant—

    (a)  anyone who is in the act of committing an indictable offence;

    (b)  anyone whom he has reasonable grounds for suspecting to be committing an indictable offence.

(2)  Where an indictable offence has been committed, a person other than a constable may arrest without a warrant—

    (a)  anyone who is guilty of the offence;

    (b)  anyone whom he has reasonable grounds for suspecting to be guilty of it.

(3)  But the power of summary arrest conferred by subsection (1) or (2) is exercisable only if—

    (a)  the person making the arrest has reasonable grounds for believing that for any of the reasons mentioned in subsection (4) it is necessary to arrest the person in question; and

    (b)  it appears to the person making the arrest that it is not reasonably practicable for a constable to make it instead.

(4)  The reasons are to prevent the person in question—

    (a)  causing physical injury to himself or any other person;

    (b)  suffering physical injury;

    (c)  causing loss of or damage to property; or

    (d)  making off before a constable can assume responsibility for him.

(5)  This section does not apply in relation to an offence under Part 3 or 3A of the Public Order Act 1986.

### 26  Repeal of statutory powers of arrest without warrant or order

(1)  Subject to subsection (2) below, so much of any Act (including a local Act) passed before this Act as enables a constable—

---

* **Editor's Note:** The operation of this section is restricted by the provisions of SI 2012 No 1917.

(a) to arrest a person for an offence without a warrant; or

(b) to arrest a person otherwise than for an offence without a warrant or an order of a court,

shall cease to have effect.

(2) Nothing in subsection (1) above affects the enactments specified in Schedule 2 to this Act.

### 27  Fingerprinting of certain offenders

(4) The Secretary of State may by regulations make provision for recording in national police records convictions for such offences as are specified in the regulations.

(4A) In subsection (4) 'conviction' includes—

(a) a caution within the meaning of Part 5 of the Police Act 1997; and

(b) a reprimand or warning given under section 65 of the Crime and Disorder Act 1998.

(5) Regulations under this section shall be made by statutory instrument and shall be subject to annulment in pursuance of a resolution of either House of Parliament.

### 28  Information to be given on arrest

(1) Subject to subsection (5) below, where a person is arrested, otherwise than by being informed that he is under arrest, the arrest is not lawful unless the person arrested is informed that he is under arrest as soon as is practicable after his arrest.

(2) Where a person is arrested by a constable, subsection (1) above applies regardless of whether the fact of the arrest is obvious.

(3) Subject to subsection (5) below, no arrest is lawful unless the person arrested is informed of the ground for the arrest at the time of, or as soon as is practicable after, the arrest.

(4) Where a person is arrested by a constable, subsection (3) above applies regardless of whether the ground for the arrest is obvious.

(5) Nothing in this section is to be taken to require a person to be informed—

(a) that he is under arrest; or

(b) of the ground for the arrest,

if it was not reasonably practicable for him to be so informed by reason of his having escaped from arrest before the information could be given.

### 29  Voluntary attendance at police station etc.

Where for the purpose of assisting with an investigation a person attends voluntarily at a police station or at any other place where a constable is present or accompanies a constable to a police station or any such other place without having been arrested—

(a) he shall be entitled to leave at will unless he is placed under arrest;

(b) he shall be informed at once that he is under arrest if a decision is taken by a constable to prevent him from leaving at will.

### 30  Arrest elsewhere than at police station

(1) Subsection (1A) applies where a person is, at any place other than a police station—

(a) arrested by a constable for an offence, or

(b) taken into custody by a constable after being arrested for an offence by a person other than a constable.

(1A) The person must be taken by a constable to a police station as soon as practicable after the arrest.

(1B) Subsection (1A) has effect subject to section 30A (release of a person arrested elsewhere than at police station) and subsection (7) (release without bail).

(2) Subject to subsections (3) and (5) below, the police station to which an arrested person is taken under subsection (1A) above shall be a designated police station.

(3) A constable to whom this subsection applies may take an arrested person to any police station unless it appears to the constable that it may be necessary to keep the arrested person in police detention for more than six hours.

(4) Subsection (3) above applies—

   (a) to a constable who is working in a locality covered by a police station which is not a designated police station; and

   (b) to a constable belonging to a body of constables maintained by an authority other than a local policing body.

(5) Any constable may take an arrested person to any police station if—

   (a) either of the following conditions is satisfied—

     (i)  the constable has arrested him without the assistance of any other constable and no other constable is available to assist him;

     (ii) the constable has taken him into custody from a person other than a constable without the assistance of any other constable and no other constable is available to assist him; and

   (b) it appears to the constable that he will be unable to take the arrested person to a designated police station without the arrested person injuring himself, the constable or some other person.

(6) If the first police station to which an arrested person is taken after his arrest is not a designated police station, he shall be taken to a designated police station not more than six hours after his arrival at the first police station unless he is released previously.

(7) A person arrested by a constable at any place other than a police station must be released without bail if the condition in subsection (7A) is satisfied.

(7A) The condition is that, at any time before the person arrested reaches a police station, a constable is satisfied that there are no grounds for keeping him under arrest.

(8) A constable who releases a person under subsection (7) above shall record the fact that he has done so.

(9) The constable shall make the record as soon as is practicable after the release.

(10) Nothing in subsection (1A) or in section 30A prevents a constable delaying taking a person to a police station or releasing him under section 30A if the condition in subsection (10A) is satisfied.

(10A) The condition is that the presence of the person at a place (other than a police station) is necessary in order to carry out such investigations as it is reasonable to carry out immediately.

(11) Where there is any such delay the reasons for the delay must be recorded when the person first arrives at the police station or (as the case may be) is released under section 30A.

(12) Nothing in subsection (1A) or section 30A above shall be taken to affect—

   (a) paragraphs 16(3) or 18(1) of Schedule 2 to the Immigration Act 1971;

   (b) section 34(1) of the Criminal Justice Act 1972; or

   (c) any provision of the Terrorism Act 2000.

(13) Nothing in subsection (10) above shall be taken to affect paragraph 18(3) of Schedule 2 to the Immigration Act 1971.

## 30A  Bail elsewhere than at police station

(1) A constable may release on bail a person who is arrested or taken into custody in the circumstances mentioned in section 30(1).

(2) A person may be released on bail under subsection (1) at any time before he arrives at a police station.

(3) A person released on bail under subsection (1) must be required to attend a police station.

(3A) Where a constable releases a person on bail under subsection (1)—

   (a) no recognizance for the person's surrender to custody shall be taken from the person,

   (b) no security for the person's surrender to custody shall be taken from the person or from anyone else on the person's behalf,

   (c) the person shall not be required to provide a surety or sureties for his surrender to custody, and

   (d) no requirement to reside in a bail hostel may be imposed as a condition of bail.

(3B) Subject to subsection (3A), where a constable releases a person on bail under subsection (1) the constable may impose, as conditions of the bail, such requirements as appear to the constable to be necessary—

    (a) to secure that the person surrenders to custody,

    (b) to secure that the person does not commit an offence while on bail,

    (c) to secure that the person does not interfere with witnesses or otherwise obstruct the course of justice, whether in relation to himself or any other person, or

    (d) for the person's own protection or, if the person is under the age of 17, for the person's own welfare or in the person's own interests.

(4) Where a person is released on bail under subsection (1), a requirement may be imposed on the person as a condition of bail only under the preceding provisions of this section.

(5) The police station which the person is required to attend may be any police station.

## 30B    Section 30A: notices

(1) Where a constable releases a person under section 30A, he must give that person a notice in writing before he is released.

(2) The notice must state—

    (a) the offence for which he was arrested,

    (b) the ground on which he was arrested, and

    (c) whether the person is being released without bail or on bail.

(3) A notice given to a person who is released on bail must inform him that he is required to attend a police station.

(4) It may also specify the police station which he is required to attend and the time when he is required to attend.

(4A) If the person is granted bail subject to conditions under section 30A(3B), the notice also—

    (a) must specify the requirements imposed by those conditions,

    (b) must explain the opportunities under sections 30CA(1) and 30CB(1) for variation of those conditions, and

    (c) if it does not specify the police station at which the person is required to attend, must specify a police station at which the person may make a request under section 30CA(1)(b).

(5) If the notice does not include the information mentioned in subsection (4), the person must subsequently be given a further notice in writing which contains that information.

(6) The person may be required to attend a different police station from that specified in the notice under subsection (1) or (5) or to attend at a different time.

(7) He must be given notice in writing of any such change as is mentioned in subsection (6) but more than one such notice may be given to him.

## 30C    Section 30A: supplemental

(1) A person who has been required to attend a police station is not required to do so if he is given notice in writing that his attendance is no longer required.

(2) If a person is required to attend a police station which is not a designated police station he must be—

    (a) released, or

    (b) taken to a designated police station,

not more than six hours after his arrival.

(3) Nothing in the Bail Act 1976 applies in relation to bail under section 30A.

(4) Nothing in section 30A or 30B or in this section prevents the re-arrest without a warrant of a person released under section 30A if new evidence justifying a further arrest has come to light since his release.

## 30CA    Bail under section 30A: variation of conditions by police

(1) Where a person released on bail under section 30A(1) is on bail subject to conditions—

    (a) a relevant officer at the police station at which the person is required to attend, or

(b) where no notice under section 30B specifying that police station has been given to the person, a relevant officer at the police station specified under section 30B(4A)(c),

may, at the request of the person but subject to subsection (2), vary the conditions.

(2) On any subsequent request made in respect of the same grant of bail, subsection (1) confers power to vary the conditions of the bail only if the request is based on information that, in the case of the previous request or each previous request, was not available to the relevant officer considering that previous request when he was considering it.

(3) Where conditions of bail granted to a person under section 30A(1) are varied under subsection (1)—

    (a) paragraphs (a) to (d) of section 30A(3A) apply,

    (b) requirements imposed by the conditions as so varied must be requirements that appear to the relevant officer varying the conditions to be necessary for any of the purposes mentioned in paragraphs (a) to (d) of section 30A(3B), and

    (c) the relevant officer who varies the conditions must give the person notice in writing of the variation.

(4) Power under subsection (1) to vary conditions is, subject to subsection (3)(a) and (b), power—

    (a) to vary or rescind any of the conditions, and

    (b) to impose further conditions.

(5) In this section 'relevant officer', in relation to a designated police station, means a custody officer but, in relation to any other police station—

    (a) means a constable who is not involved in the investigation of the offence for which the person making the request under subsection (1) was under arrest when granted bail under section 30A(1), if such a constable is readily available, and

    (b) if no such constable is readily available—

        (i) means a constable other than the one who granted bail to the person, if such a constable is readily available, and

        (ii) if no such constable is readily available, means the constable who granted bail.

**30CB     Bail under section 30A: variation of conditions by court**

(1) Where a person released on bail under section 30A(1) is on bail subject to conditions, a magistrates' court may, on an application by or on behalf of the person, vary the conditions if—

    (a) the conditions have been varied under section 30CA(1) since being imposed under section 30A(3B),

    (b) a request for variation under section 30CA(1) of the conditions has been made and refused, or

    (c) a request for variation under section 30CA(1) of the conditions has been made and the period of 48 hours beginning with the day when the request was made has expired without the request having been withdrawn or the conditions having been varied in response to the request.

(2) In proceedings on an application for a variation under subsection (1), a ground may not be relied upon unless—

    (a) in a case falling within subsection (1)(a), the ground was relied upon in the request in response to which the conditions were varied under section 30CA(1), or

    (b) in a case falling within paragraph (b) or (c) of subsection (1), the ground was relied upon in the request mentioned in that paragraph,

but this does not prevent the court, when deciding the application, from considering different grounds arising out of a change in circumstances that has occurred since the making of the application.

(3) Where conditions of bail granted to a person under section 30A(1) are varied under subsection (1)—

    (a) paragraphs (a) to (d) of section 30A(3A) apply,

    (b) requirements imposed by the conditions as so varied must be requirements that appear to the court varying the conditions to be necessary for any of the purposes mentioned in paragraphs (a) to (d) of section 30A(3B), and

    (c) that bail shall not lapse but shall continue subject to the conditions as so varied.

(4)  Power under subsection (1) to vary conditions is, subject to subsection (3)(a) and (b), power—

    (a)  to vary or rescind any of the conditions, and

    (b)  to impose further conditions.

## 30D  Failure to answer to bail under section 30A

(1)  A constable may arrest without a warrant a person who—

    (a)  has been released on bail under section 30A subject to a requirement to attend a specified police station, but

    (b)  fails to attend the police station at the specified time.

(2)  A person arrested under subsection (1) must be taken to a police station (which may be the specified police station or any other police station) as soon as practicable after the arrest.

(2A)  A person who has been released on bail under section 30A may be arrested without a warrant by a constable if the constable has reasonable grounds for suspecting that the person has broken any of the conditions of bail.

(2B)  A person arrested under subsection (2A) must be taken to a police station (which may be the specified police station mentioned in subsection (1) or any other police station) as soon as practicable after the arrest.

(3)  In subsection (1), 'specified' means specified in a notice under subsection (1) or (5) of section 30B or, if notice of change has been given under subsection (7) of that section, in that notice.

(4)  For the purposes of—

    (a)  section 30 (subject to the obligation in subsection (2)), and

    (b)  section 31,

an arrest under this section is to be treated as an arrest for an offence.

## 31  Arrest for further offence

Where—

    (a)  a person—

        (i)   has been arrested for an offence; and

        (ii)  is at a police station in consequence of that arrest; and

    (b)  it appears to a constable that, if he were released from that arrest, he would be liable to arrest for some other offence,

he shall be arrested for that other offence.

## 32  Search upon arrest

(1)  A constable may search an arrested person, in any case where the person to be searched has been arrested at a place other than a police station, if the constable has reasonable grounds for believing that the arrested person may present a danger to himself or others.

(2)  Subject to subsections (3) to (5) below, a constable shall also have power in any such case—

    (a)  to search the arrested person for anything—

        (i)   which he might use to assist him to escape from lawful custody; or

        (ii)  which might be evidence relating to an offence; and

    (b)  if the offence for which he has been arrested is an indictable offence, to enter and search any premises in which he was when arrested or immediately before he was arrested for evidence relating to the offence.

(3)  The power to search conferred by subsection (2) above is only a power to search to the extent that is reasonably required for the purpose of discovering any such thing or any such evidence.

(4)  The powers conferred by this section to search a person are not to be construed as authorising a constable to require a person to remove any of his clothing in public other than an outer coat, jacket or gloves but they do authorise a search of a person's mouth.

(5)  A constable may not search a person in the exercise of the power conferred by subsection (2)(a) above unless he has reasonable grounds for believing that the person to be searched may have concealed on him anything for which a search is permitted under that paragraph.

(6)  A constable may not search premises in the exercise of the power conferred by subsection (2)(b) above unless he has reasonable grounds for believing that there is evidence for which a search is permitted under that paragraph on the premises.

(7)  In so far as the power of search conferred by subsection (2)(b) above relates to premises consisting of two or more separate dwellings, it is limited to a power to search—

    (a)  any dwelling in which the arrest took place or in which the person arrested was immediately before his arrest; and

    (b)  any parts of the premises which the occupier of any such dwelling uses in common with the occupiers of any other dwellings comprised in the premises.

(8)  A constable searching a person in the exercise of the power conferred by subsection (1) above may seize and retain anything he finds, if he has reasonable grounds for believing that the person searched might use it to cause physical injury to himself or to any other person.

(9)  A constable searching a person in the exercise of the power conferred by subsection (2)(a) above may seize and retain anything he finds, other than an item subject to legal privilege, if he has reasonable grounds for believing—

    (a)  that he might use it to assist him to escape from lawful custody; or

    (b)  that it is evidence of an offence or has been obtained in consequence of the commission of an offence.

(10)  Nothing in this section shall be taken to affect the power conferred by section 43 of the Terrorism Act 2000.

. . .

# PART IV  DETENTION

*Detention—conditions and duration*

## 34    Limitations on police detention

(1)  A person arrested for an offence shall not be kept in police detention except in accordance with the provisions of this Part of this Act.

(2)  Subject to subsection (3) below, if at any time a custody officer—

    (a)  becomes aware, in relation to any person in police detention, that the grounds for the detention of that person have ceased to apply and

    (b)  is not aware of any other grounds on which the continued detention of that person could be justified under the provisions of this Part of this Act,

it shall be the duty of the custody officer, subject to subsection (4) below, to order his immediate release from custody.

(3)  No person in police detention shall be released except on the authority of a custody officer at the police station where his detention was authorised, or if it was authorised at more than one station, a custody officer at the station where it was last authorised.

(4)  A person who appears to the custody officer to have been unlawfully at large when he was arrested is not to be released under subsection (2) above.

(5)  A person whose release is ordered under subsection (2) above shall be released

    (a)  without bail unless subsection (5A) applies, or

    (b)  on bail if subsection (5A) applies.

(5A)  This subsection applies if—

    (a)  it appears to the custody officer—

        (i)   that there is need for further investigation of any matter in connection with which the person was detained at any time during the period of the person's detention, or

        (ii)  that, in respect of any such matter, proceedings may be taken against the person or the person may be given a youth caution under section 66ZA of the Crime and Disorder Act 1998, and

    (b)  the pre-conditions for bail are satisfied.

(5B)  Subsection (5C) applies where—

    (a)  a person is released under subsection (5), and

    (b)  the custody officer determines that—

        (i)    there is not sufficient evidence to charge the person with an offence, or

        (ii)   there is sufficient evidence to charge the person with an offence but the person should not be charged with an offence or given a caution in respect of an offence.

(5C)  The custody officer must give the person notice in writing that the person is not to be prosecuted.

(5D)  Subsection (5C) does not prevent the prosecution of the person for an offence if new evidence comes to light after the notice was given.

(5E)  In this Part 'caution' includes—

    (a)  a conditional caution within the meaning of Part 3 of the Criminal Justice Act 2003;

    (b)  a youth conditional caution within the meaning of Chapter 1 of Part 4 of the Crime and Disorder Act 1998;

    (c)  a youth caution under section 66ZA of that Act.

(6)  For the purposes of this Part of this Act a person arrested under section 6(5) of the Road Traffic Act 1988 or section 30(2) of the Transport and Works Act 1992 is arrested for an offence.

(7)  For the purposes of this Part a person who—

    (a)  attends a police station to answer to bail granted under section 30A,

    (b)  returns to a police station to answer to bail granted under this Part, or

    (c)  is arrested under section 30D or 46A,

is to be treated as arrested for an offence and that offence is the offence in connection with which he was granted bail. But this subsection is subject to section 47(6) (which provides for the calculation of certain periods, where a person has been granted bail under this Part, by reference to time when the person is in police detention only).

(8)  Subsection (7) does not apply in relation to a person who is granted bail subject to the duty mentioned in section 47(3)(b) and who either—

    (a)  attends a police station to answer to such bail, or

    (b)  is arrested under section 46A for failing to do so,

(provision as to the treatment of such persons for the purposes of this Part being made by section 46ZA).

## 35  Designated police stations

(1)  The chief officer of police for each police area shall designate the police stations in his area which, subject to sections 30(3) and (5), 30A(5) and 30D(2) above, are to be the stations in that area to be used for the purpose of detaining arrested persons.

(2)  A chief officer's duty under subsection (1) above is to designate police stations appearing to him to provide enough accommodation for that purpose.

(2A)  The Chief Constable of the British Transport Police Force may designate police stations which (in addition to those designated under subsection (1) above) may be used for the purpose of detaining arrested persons.

(3)  Without prejudice to section 12 of the Interpretation Act 1978 (continuity of duties) a chief officer—

    (a)  may designate a station which was not previously designated; and

    (b)  may direct that a designation of a station previously made shall cease to operate.

(4)  In this Act 'designated police station' means a police station designated under this section.

## 36  Custody officers at police stations

(1)  One or more custody officers shall be appointed for each designated police station.

(2)  A custody officer for a police station designated under section 35(1) above shall be appointed—

    (a)  by the chief officer of police for the area in which the designated police station is situated; or

    (b)  by such other police officer as the chief officer of police for that area may direct.

(2A) A custody officer for a police station designated under section 35(2A) above shall be appointed—

    (a) by the Chief Constable of the British Transport Police Force; or

    (b) by such other member of that Force as that Chief Constable may direct.

(3) No officer may be appointed a custody officer unless the officer is of at least the rank of sergeant.

(4) An officer of any rank may perform the functions of a custody officer at a designated police station if a custody officer is not readily available to perform them.

(5) Subject to the following provisions of this section and to section 39(2) below, none of the functions of a custody officer in relation to a person shall be performed by an officer who at the time when the function falls to be performed is involved in the investigation of an offence for which that person is in police detention at that time.

(6) Nothing in subsection (5) above is to be taken to prevent a custody officer—

    (a) performing any function assigned to custody officers—

        (i) by this Act; or

        (ii) by a code of practice issued under this Act;

    (b) carrying out the duty imposed on custody officers by section 39 below;

    (c) doing anything in connection with the identification of a suspect; or

    (d) doing anything under sections 7 and 8 of the Road Traffic Act 1988.

(7) Where an arrested person is taken to a police station which is not a designated police station, the functions in relation to him which at a designated police station would be the functions of a custody officer shall be performed—

    (a) by an officer who is not involved in the investigation of an offence for which he is in police detention, if such an officer is readily available; and

    (b) if no such officer is readily available, by the officer who took him to the station or any other officer.

(7A) Subject to subsection (7B), subsection (7) applies where a person attends a police station which is not a designated station to answer to bail granted under section 30A as it applies where a person is taken to such a station.

(7B) Where subsection (7) applies because of subsection (7A), the reference in subsection (7)(b) to the officer who took him to the station is to be read as a reference to the officer who granted him bail.

(8) References to a custody officer in section 34 above or in the following provisions of this Act include references to a person other than a custody officer who is performing the functions of a custody officer by virtue of subsection (4) or (7) above.

(9) Where by virtue of subsection (7) above an officer of a force maintained by a local policing body who took an arrested person to a police station is to perform the functions of a custody officer in relation to him, the officer shall inform an officer who—

    (a) is attached to a designated police station; and

    (b) is of at least the rank of inspector,

that he is to do so.

(10) The duty imposed by subsection (9) above shall be performed as soon as it is practicable to perform it.

## 37    Duties of custody officer before charge*

(1) Where—

    (a) a person is arrested for an offence—

        (i) without a warrant; or

        (ii) under a warrant not endorsed for bail,

---

* **Editor's Note:** Section 37 has effect, in relation to a person arrested following a criminal investigation by the Revenue and Customs, as if references to the Director of Public Prosecutions were a reference to the Director of Revenue and Customs Prosecutions. See Commissioner for Revenue and Customs Act 2005 Schedule 4 paragraph 30.

the custody officer at each police station where he is detained after his arrest shall determine whether he has before him sufficient evidence to charge that person with the offence for which he was arrested and may detain him at the police station for such period as is necessary to enable him to do so.

(2) If the custody officer determines that he does not have such evidence before him, the person arrested shall be released.

(a) without bail unless the pre-conditions for bail are satisfied, or

(b) on bail if those pre-conditions are satisfied,

(subject to subsection (3)).

(3) If the custody officer has reasonable grounds for believing that the person's detention without being charged is necessary to secure or preserve evidence relating to an offence for which the person is under arrest or to obtain such evidence by questioning the person he may authorise the person arrested to be kept in police detention.

(4) Where a custody officer authorises a person who has not been charged to be kept in police detention, he shall, as soon as is practicable, make a written record of the grounds for the detention.

(5) Subject to subsection (6) below, the written record shall be made in the presence of the person arrested who shall at that time be informed by the custody officer of the grounds for his detention.

(6) Subsection (5) above shall not apply where the person arrested is, at the time when the written record is made—

(a) incapable of understanding what is said to him;

(b) violent or likely to become violent; or

(c) in urgent need of medical attention.

(7) Subject to section 41(7) below, if the custody officer determines that he has before him sufficient evidence to charge the person arrested with the offence for which he was arrested, the person arrested—

(a) shall be

(i) released without charge and on bail, or

(ii) kept in police detention

for the purpose of enabling the Director of Public Prosecutions to make a decision under section 37B below, or

(b) shall be released without charge and without bail unless the pre-conditions for bail are satisfied,

(c) shall be released without charge and on bail if those pre-conditions are satisfied but not for the purpose mentioned in paragraph (a),

(d) shall be charged.

(7A) The decision as to how a person is to be dealt with under subsection (7) above shall be that of the custody officer.

(7B) Where a person is dealt with under subsection (7)(a) above, it shall be the duty of the custody officer to inform him that he is being released, or (as the case may be) detained, to enable the Director of Public Prosecutions to make a decision under section 37B below.

(8) Where—

(a) a person is dealt with under subsection (7)(b) or (c) above; and

(b) at the time of his release a decision whether he should be prosecuted for the offence for which he was arrested has not been taken,

it shall be the duty of the custody officer so to inform him.

(8A) Subsection (8B) applies if the offence for which the person is arrested is one in relation to which a sample could be taken under section 63B below and the custody officer—

(a) is required in pursuance of subsection (2) above to release the person arrested and decides to release him on bail, or

(b) decides in pursuance of subsection (7)(a) or (b) above to release the person without charge and on bail.

(8B)  The detention of the person may be continued to enable a sample to be taken under section 63B, but this subsection does not permit a person to be detained for a period of more than 24 hours after the relevant time.

(9)  If the person arrested is not in a fit state to be dealt with under subsection (7) above, he may be kept in police detention until he is.

(10)  The duty imposed on the custody officer under subsection (1) above shall be carried out by him as soon as practicable after the person arrested arrives at the police station or, in the case of a person arrested at the police station, as soon as practicable after the arrest.

(15)  In this Part of this Act—

'arrested juvenile' means a person arrested with or without a warrant who appears to be under the age of 18;

'endorsed for bail' means endorsed with a direction for bail in accordance with section 117(2) of the Magistrates' Courts Act 1980.

### 37A   Guidance*

(1)  The Director of Public Prosecutions may issue guidance—
   (a)  for the purpose of enabling custody officers to decide how persons should be dealt with under section 37(7) above or 37C(2) or 37CA(2) below, and
   (b)  as to the information to be sent to the Director of Public Prosecutions under section 37B(1) below.

(2)  The Director of Public Prosecutions may from time to time revise guidance issued under this section.

(3)  Custody officers are to have regard to guidance under this section in deciding how persons should be dealt with under section 37(7) above or 37C(2) or 37CA(2) below.

(4)  A report under section 9 of the Prosecution of Offences Act 1985 (report by DPP to Attorney General) must set out the provisions of any guidance issued, and any revisions to guidance made, in the year to which the report relates.

(5)  The Director of Public Prosecutions must publish in such manner as he thinks fit—
   (a)  any guidance issued under this section, and
   (b)  any revisions made to such guidance.

(6)  Guidance under this section may make different provision for different cases, circumstances or areas.

### 37B   Consultation with the Director of Public Prosecutions**

(1)  Where a person is dealt with under section 37(7)(a) above, an officer involved in the investigation of the offence shall, as soon as is practicable, send to the Director of Public Prosecutions such information as may be specified in guidance under section 37A above.

(2)  The Director of Public Prosecutions shall decide whether there is sufficient evidence to charge the person with an offence.

(3)  If he decides that there is sufficient evidence to charge the person with an offence, he shall decide—
   (a)  whether or not the person should be charged and, if so, the offence with which he should be charged, and
   (b)  whether or not the person should be given a caution and, if so, the offence in respect of which he should be given a caution.

(4)  The Director of Public Prosecutions shall give notice of his decision to an officer involved in the investigation of the offence.

---

\* **Editor's Note:** Section 37A has effect, in relation to a person arrested following a criminal investigation by the Revenue and Customs, as if a reference to the Director of Public Prosecutions were references to the Director of Revenue and Customs Prosecutions. See Commissioner for Revenue and Customs Act 2005 Schedule 4 paragraph 30.

\*\* **Editor's Note:** Section 37B has effect, in relation to a person arrested following a criminal investigation by the Revenue and Customs, as if a reference to the Director of Public Prosecutions were references to the Director of Revenue and Customs Prosecutions. See Commissioner for Revenue and Customs Act 2005 Schedule 4 paragraph 30

(4A)  Notice under subsection (4) above shall be in writing, but in the case of a person kept in police detention under section 37(7)(a) above it may be given orally in the first instance and confirmed in writing subsequently.

(5)  If his decision is—

    (a)  that there is not sufficient evidence to charge the person with an offence, or

    (b)  that there is sufficient evidence to charge the person with an offence but that the person should not be charged with an offence or given a caution in respect of an offence,

a custody officer shall give the person notice in writing that he is not to be prosecuted.

(5A)  Subsection (5) does not prevent the prosecution of the person for an offence if new evidence comes to light after the notice was given.

(6)  If the decision of the Director of Public Prosecutions is that the person should be charged with an offence, or given a caution in respect of an offence, the person shall be charged or cautioned accordingly.

(7)  But if his decision is that the person should be given a caution in respect of the offence and it proves not to be possible to give the person such a caution, he shall instead be charged with the offence.

(8)  For the purposes of this section, a person is to be charged with an offence either—

    (a)  when he is in police detention at a police station (whether because he has returned to answer bail, because he is detained under section 37(7)(a) above or for some other reason), or

    (b)  in accordance with section 29 of the Criminal Justice Act 2003.

### 37C  Breach of bail following release under section 37(7)(a)

(1)  This section applies where—

    (a)  a person released on bail under section 37(7)(a) above or subsection (2)(b) below is arrested under section 46A below in respect of that bail, and

    (b)  at the time of his detention following that arrest at the police station mentioned in section 46A(2) below, notice under section 37B(4) above has not been given.

(2)  The person arrested—

    (a)  shall be charged, or

    (b)  shall be released without charge, either on bail or without bail.

(3)  The decision as to how a person is to be dealt with under subsection (2) above shall be that of a custody officer.

(4)  A person released on bail under subsection (2)(b) above shall be released on bail subject to the same conditions (if any) which applied immediately before his arrest.

### 37CA  Breach of bail following release under section 37(7)(c)

(1)  This section applies where a person released on bail under section 37(7)(c) above or subsection (2)(b) below—

    (a)  is arrested under section 46A below in respect of that bail, and

    (b)  is being detained following that arrest at the police station mentioned in section 46A(2) below.

(2)  The person arrested—

    (a)  shall be charged, or

    (b)  shall be released without charge—

        (i)  without bail unless the pre-conditions for bail are satisfied, or

        (ii)  on bail if those pre-conditions are satisfied.

(3)  The decision as to how a person is to be dealt with under subsection (2) above shall be that of a custody officer.

(4)  A person released on bail under subsection (2)(b) above shall be released on bail subject to the same conditions (if any) which applied immediately before his arrest (and the reference in section 50A to any conditions of bail which would be imposed is to be read accordingly).

(5) Subsection (6) applies where—.

   (a) a person is released under subsection (2), and

   (b) a custody officer determines that—

      (i) there is not sufficient evidence to charge the person with an offence, or

      (ii) there is sufficient evidence to charge the person with an offence but the person should not be charged with an offence or given a caution in respect of an offence.

(6) The custody officer must give the person notice in writing that the person is not to be prosecuted.

(7) Subsection (6) does not prevent the prosecution of the person for an offence if new evidence comes to light after the notice was given.

### 37D  Release under section 37(7): further provision

(4) Where a person released on bail under section 37(7)(a) or 37C(2)(b) above returns to a police station to answer bail or is otherwise in police detention at a police station, he may be kept in police detention to enable him to be dealt with in accordance with section 37B or 37C above or to enable the power under section 47(4A) above to be exercised.

(4A) Where a person released on bail under section 37(7)(c) or 37CA(2)(b) above returns to a police station to answer bail or is otherwise in police detention at a police station, he may be kept in police detention to enable him to be dealt with in accordance with section 37CA above or to enable the power under section 47(4A) above to be exercised.

(5) If the person mentioned in subsection (4) or (4A) above is not in a fit state to enable him to be so dealt with as mentioned in that subsection or to enable the power under section 47(4A) above to be exercised, he may be kept in police detention until he is.

(6) Where a person is kept in police detention by virtue of subsection (4), (4A) or (5) above, section 37(1) to (3) and (7) above (and section 40(8) below so far as it relates to section 37(1) to (3)) shall not apply to the offence in connection with which he was released on bail under section 37(7), 37C(2)(b) or 37CA(2)(b) above.

### 38  Duties of custody officer after charge

(1) Where a person arrested for an offence otherwise than under a warrant endorsed for bail is charged with an offence, the custody officer shall, subject to section 25 of the Criminal Justice and Public Order Act 1994, order his release from police detention, either on bail or without bail, unless—

   (a) if the person arrested is not an arrested juvenile—

      (i) his name or address cannot be ascertained or the custody officer has reasonable grounds for doubting whether a name or address furnished by him as his name or address is his real name or address;

      (ii) the custody officer has reasonable grounds for believing that the person arrested will fail to appear in court to answer to bail;

      (iii) in the case of a person arrested for an imprisonable offence, the custody officer has reasonable grounds for believing that the detention of the person arrested is necessary to prevent him from committing an offence;

      (iiia) in a case where a sample may be taken from the person under section 63B below, the custody officer has reasonable grounds for believing that the detention of the person is necessary to enable the sample to be taken from him;

      (iv) in the case of a person arrested for an offence which is not an imprisonable offence, the custody officer has reasonable grounds for believing that the detention of the person arrested is necessary to prevent him from causing physical injury to any other person or from causing loss of or damage to property;

      (v) the custody officer has reasonable grounds for believing that the detention of the person arrested is necessary to prevent him from interfering with the administration of justice or with the investigation of offences or of a particular offence; or

(vi)  the custody officer has reasonable grounds for believing that the detention of the person arrested is necessary for his own protection;

(b)  if he is an arrested juvenile—

(i)  any of the requirements of paragraph (a) above is satisfied (but, in the case of paragraph (a)(iiia) above, only if the arrested juvenile has attained the minimum age); or

(ii)  the custody officer has reasonable grounds for believing that he ought to be detained in his own interests.

(c)  the offence with which the person is charged is murder.

(2)  If the release of a person arrested is not required by subsection (1) above, the custody officer may authorise him to be kept in police detention but may not authorise a person to be kept in police detention by virtue of subsection (1)(a)(iiia) after the end of the period of six hours beginning with when he was charged with the offence.

(2A)  The custody officer, in taking the decisions required by subsection (1)(a) and (b) above (except (a)(i) and (vi) and (b)(ii), shall have regard to the same considerations as those which a court is required to have regard to in taking the corresponding decisions under paragraph 2 of Part I of Schedule 1 to the Bail Act 1976 disregarding paragraphs 1A and 2(2) of that Part.

(3)  Where a custody officer authorises a person who has been charged to be kept in police detention, he shall, as soon as practicable, make a written record of the grounds for the detention.

(4)  Subject to subsection (5) below, the written record shall be made in the presence of the person charged who shall at that time be informed by the custody officer of the grounds for his detention.

(5)  Subsection (4) above shall not apply where the person charged is, at the time when the written record is made—

(a)  incapable of understanding what is said to him;

(b)  violent or likely to become violent; or

(c)  in urgent need of medical attention.

(6)  Where a custody officer authorises an arrested juvenile to be kept in police detention under subsection (1) above, the custody officer shall, unless he certifies—

(a)  that, by reason of such circumstances as are specified in the certificate, it is impracticable for him to do so; or

(b)  in the case of an arrested juvenile who has attained the age of 12 years, that no secure accommodation is available and that keeping him in other local authority accommodation would not be adequate to protect the public from serious harm from him,

secure that the arrested juvenile is moved to local authority accommodation.

(6A)  In this section, 'local authority accommodation' means accommodation provided by or on behalf of a local authority (within the meaning of the Children Act 1989);

'minimum age' means the age specified in section 63B(3)(b) below;

'secure accommodation' means accommodation provided for the purpose of restricting liberty;

'sexual offence' means an offence specified in Part 2 of Schedule 15 to the Criminal Justice Act 2003;

'violent offence' means murder or an offence specified in Part 1 of that Schedule;

and any reference, in relation to an arrested juvenile charged with a violent or sexual offence, to protecting the public from serious harm from him shall be construed as a reference to protecting members of the public from death or serious injury, whether physical or psychological, occasioned by further such offences committed by him.

(6B)  Where an arrested juvenile is moved to local authority accommodation under subsection (6) above, it shall be lawful for any person acting on behalf of the authority to detain him.

(7)  A certificate made under subsection (6) above in respect of an arrested juvenile shall be produced to the court before which he is first brought thereafter.

(7A)  In this section 'imprisonable offence' has the same meaning as in Schedule 1 to the Bail Act 1976.

(8)  In this Part of this Act 'local authority' has the same meaning as in the Children Act 1989.

### 39   Responsibilities in relation to persons detained

(1)  Subject to subsections (2) and (4) below, it shall be the duty of the custody officer at a police station to ensure—

(a)  that all persons in police detention at that station are treated in accordance with this Act and any code of practice issued under it and relating to the treatment of persons in police detention; and

(b)  that all matters relating to such persons which are required by this Act or by such codes of practice to be recorded are recorded in the custody records relating to such persons.

(2)  If the custody officer, in accordance with any code of practice issued under this Act, transfers or permits the transfer of a person in police detention—

(a)  to the custody of another police officer at the police station where the person is in police detention, for the purpose of an interview that is part of the investigation of an offence for which the person is in police detention or otherwise in connection with the investigation of such an offence; or

(b)  to the custody of an officer who has charge of that person outside the police station,

the custody officer shall cease in relation to that person to be subject to the duty imposed on him by subsection (1)(a) above; and it shall be the duty of the officer to whom the transfer is made to ensure that he is treated in accordance with the provisions of this Act and of any such codes of practice as are mentioned in subsection (1) above.

(3)  If the person detained is subsequently returned to the custody of the custody officer, it shall be the duty of the officer investigating the offence to report to the custody officer as to the manner in which this section and the codes of practice have been complied with while that person was in his custody.

(3A)  Subsections (3B) and (3C) apply if the custody officer, in accordance with any code of practice issued under this Act, transfers or permits the transfer of a person in police detention to an officer mentioned in subsection (2)(a) for the purpose of an interview that is to be conducted to any extent by means of a live link by another police officer who is investigating the offence but is not at the police station where the person in police detention is held at the time of the interview.

(3B)  The officer who is not at the police station has the same duty as the officer mentioned in subsection (2)(a) to ensure that the person is treated in accordance with the provisions of this Act and of any such codes of practice as are mentioned in subsection (1).

(3C)  If the person detained is subsequently returned to the custody of the custody officer, the officer who is not at the police station also has the same duty under subsection (3) as the officer mentioned in subsection (2)(a).

(3D)  For the purpose of subsection (3C), subsection (3) applies as if the reference to 'in his custody' were a reference to 'being interviewed'.

(3E)  In subsection (3A), 'live link' means an arrangement by which the officer who is not at the police station is able to see and hear, and to be seen and heard by, the person in police detention, any legal representative of that person and the officer who has custody of that person at the police station (and for this purpose any impairment of eyesight or hearing is to be disregarded).

(4)  If an arrested juvenile is moved to local authority accommodation under section 38(6) above, the custody officer shall cease in relation to that person to be subject to the duty imposed on him by subsection (1) above.

(6)  Where—

(a)  an officer of higher rank than the custody officer gives directions relating to a person in police detention; and

(b)  the directions are at variance—

(i)   with any decision made or action taken by the custody officer in the performance of a duty imposed on him under this Part of this Act; or

(ii)  with any decision or action which would but for the directions have been made or taken by him in the performance of such a duty,

the custody officer shall refer the matter at once to an officer of the rank of superintendent or above who is responsible for the police station for which the custody officer is acting as custody officer.

## 40   Review of police detention

(1) Reviews of the detention of each person in police detention in connection with the investigation of an offence shall be carried out periodically in accordance with the following provisions of this section—

(a) in the case of a person who has been arrested and charged, by the custody officer; and

(b) in the case of a person who has been arrested but not charged, by an officer of at least the rank of inspector who has not been directly involved in the investigation.

(2) The officer to whom it falls to carry out a review is referred to in this section as a 'review officer'.

(3) Subject to subsection (4) below—

(a) the first review shall be not later than six hours after the detention was first authorised;

(b) the second review shall be not later than nine hours after the first;

(c) subsequent reviews shall be at intervals of not more than nine hours.

(4) A review may be postponed—

(a) if, having regard to all the circumstances prevailing at the latest time for it specified in subsection (3) above, it is not practicable to carry out the review at that time;

(b) without prejudice to the generality of paragraph (a) above—

(i) if at that time the person in detention is being questioned by a police officer and the review officer is satisfied that an interruption of the questioning for the purpose of carrying out the review would prejudice the investigation in connection with which he is being questioned; or

(ii) if at that time no review officer is readily available.

(5) If a review is postponed under subsection (4) above it shall be carried out as soon as practicable after the latest time specified for it in subsection (3) above.

(6) If a review is carried out after postponement under subsection (4) above, the fact that it was so carried out shall not affect any requirement of this section as to the time at which any subsequent review is to be carried out.

(7) The review officer shall record the reasons for any postponement of a review in the custody record.

(8) Subject to subsection (9) below, where the person whose detention is under review has not been charged before the time of the review, section 37(1) to (6) above shall have effect in relation to him, but with the modifications specified in subsection (8A).

(8A) The modifications are—

(a) the substitution of references to the person whose detention is under review for references to the person arrested;

(b) the substitution of references to the review officer for references to the custody officer; and

(c) in subsection (6), the insertion of the following paragraph after paragraph (a)—

'(aa) 'asleep;'.'

(9) Where a person has been kept in police detention by virtue of section 37(9) or 37D(5) above, section 37(1) to (6) shall not have effect in relation to him but it shall be the duty of the review officer to determine whether he is yet in a fit state.

(10) Where the person whose detention is under review has been charged before the time of the review, section 38(1) to (6B) above shall have effect in relation to him, but with the modifications specified in subsection (10A).

(10A) The modifications are—

(a) the substitution of a reference to the person whose detention is under review for any reference to the person arrested or to the person charged; and

(b) in subsection (5), the insertion of the following paragraph after paragraph (a)—

'(aa) 'asleep;'.'

(11) Where—

(a) an officer of higher rank than the review officer gives directions relating to a person in police detention; and

(b) the directions are at variance—

    (i) with any decision made or action taken by the review officer in the performance of a duty imposed on him under this Part of this Act; or

    (ii) with any decision or action which would but for the directions have been made or taken by him in the performance of such a duty,

the review officer shall refer the matter at once to an officer of the rank of superintendent or above who is responsible for the police station for which the review officer is acting as review officer in connection with the detention.

(12) Before determining whether to authorise a person's continued detention the review officer shall give—

    (a) that person (unless he is asleep); or

    (b) any solicitor representing him who is available at the time of the review,

an opportunity to make representations to him about the detention.

(13) Subject to subsection (14) below, the person whose detention is under review or his solicitor may make representations under subsection (12) above either orally or in writing.

(14) The review officer may refuse to hear oral representations from the person whose detention is under review if he considers that he is unfit to make such representations by reason of his condition or behaviour.

### 40A   Use of telephone for review under s. 40

(1) A review under section 40(1)(b) may be carried out by means of a discussion, conducted by telephone, with one or more persons at the police station where the arrested person is held.

(2) But subsection (1) does not apply if—

    (a) the review is of a kind authorised by regulations under section 45A to be carried out using a live link; and

    (b) it is reasonably practicable to carry it out in accordance with those regulations.

(3) Where any review is carried out under this section by an officer who is not present at the station where the arrested person is held—

    (a) any obligation of that officer to make a record in connection with the carrying out of the review shall have effect as an obligation to cause another officer to make the record;

    (b) any requirement for the record to be made in the presence of the arrested person shall apply to the making of that record by that other officer; and

    (c) the requirements under section 40(12) and (13) above for—

        (i) the arrested person, or

        (ii) solicitor representing him,

to be given any opportunity to make representations (whether in writing or orally to that officer shall have effect as a requirement for that person, or such a solicitor, to be given an opportunity to make representations in a manner authorised by subsection (4) below.

(4) Representations are made in a manner authorised by this subsection—

    (a) in a case where facilities exist for the immediate transmission of written representations to the officer carrying out the review, if they are made either—

        (i) orally by telephone to that officer; or

        (ii) in writing to that officer by means of those facilities;

    and

    (b) in any other case, if they are made orally by telephone to that officer.

(5) In this section 'a live link' has the same meaning as in section 45A below.

### 41   Limits on period of detention without charge

(1) Subject to the following provisions of this section and to sections 42 and 43 below, a person shall not be kept in police detention for more than 24 hours without being charged.

(2) The time from which the period of detention of a person is to be calculated (in this Act referred to as 'the relevant time')—

    (a) in the case of a person to whom this paragraph applies, shall be—
       (i) the time at which that person arrives at the relevant police station; or
      (ii) the time 24 hours after the time of that person's arrest,
      whichever is the earlier;
    (b) in the case of a person arrested outside England and Wales, shall be—
       (i) the time at which that person arrives at the first police station to which he is taken in the police area in England or Wales in which the offence for which he was arrested is being investigated; or
      (ii) the time 24 hours after the time of that person's entry into England and Wales, whichever is the earlier;
    (c) in the case of a person who—
       (i) attends voluntarily at a police station; or
      (ii) accompanies a constable to a police station without having been arrested, and is arrested at the police station,
      the time of his arrest;
   (ca) in the case of a person who attends a police station to answer to bail granted under section 30A, the time when he arrives at the police station;
    (d) in any other case, except where subsection (5) below applies, shall be the time at which the person arrested arrives at the first police station to which he is taken after his arrest.
  (3) Subsection (2)(a) above applies to a person if—
    (a) his arrest is sought in one police area in England and Wales;
    (b) he is arrested in another police area; and
    (c) he is not questioned in the area in which he is arrested in order to obtain evidence in relation to an offence for which he is arrested;
and in sub-paragraph (i) of that paragraph 'the relevant police station' means the first police station to which he is taken in the police area in which his arrest was sought.
  (4) Subsection (2) above shall have effect in relation to a person arrested under section 31 above as if every reference in it to his arrest or his being arrested were a reference to his arrest or his being arrested for the offence for which he was originally arrested.
  (5) If—
    (a) a person is in police detention in a police area in England and Wales ('the first area'); and
    (b) his arrest for an offence is sought in some other police area in England and Wales ('the second area'); and
    (c) he is taken to the second area for the purposes of investigating that offence, without being questioned in the first area in order to obtain evidence in relation to it,
the relevant time shall be—
       (i) the time 24 hours after he leaves the place where he is detained in the first area; or
      (ii) the time at which he arrives at the first police station to which he is taken in the second area,
whichever is the earlier.
  (6) When a person who is in police detention at a police station is removed to hospital because he is in need of medical treatment, any time during which he is being questioned in hospital or on the way there or back by a police officer for the purpose of obtaining evidence relating to an offence shall be included in any period which falls to be calculated for the purposes of this Part of this Act, but any other time while he is in hospital or on his way there or back shall not be so included.
  (7) Subject to subsection (8) below, a person who at the expiry of 24 hours after the relevant time is in police detention and has not been charged shall be released at that time
    (a) without bail unless the pre-conditions for bail are satisfied, or
    (b) on bail if those pre-conditions are satisfied.
  (8) Subsection (7) above does not apply to a person whose detention for more than 24 hours after the relevant time has been authorised or is otherwise permitted in accordance with section 42 or 43 below.

(9)  A person released under subsection (7) above shall not be re-arrested without a warrant for the offence for which he was previously arrested unless new evidence justifying a further arrest has come to light since his release; but this subsection does not prevent an arrest under section 46A below.

(10)  Subsection (11) applies where—

    (a)  a person is released under subsection (7), and

    (b)  a custody officer determines that—

        (i)    there is not sufficient evidence to charge the person with an offence, or

        (ii)   there is sufficient evidence to charge the person with an offence but the person should not be charged with an offence or given a caution in respect of an offence.

(11)  The custody officer must give the person notice in writing that the person is not to be prosecuted.

(12)  Subsection (11) does not prevent the prosecution of the person for an offence if new evidence comes to light after the notice was given.

## 42  Authorisation of continued detention

(1)  Where a police officer of the rank of superintendent or above who has not been directly involved in the investigation has reasonable grounds for believing that—

    (a)  the detention of that person without charge is necessary to secure or preserve evidence relating to an offence for which he is under arrest or to obtain such evidence by questioning him;

    (b)  an offence for which he is under arrest is an indictable offence; and

    (c)  the investigation is being conducted diligently and expeditiously,

he may authorise the keeping of that person in police detention for a period expiring at or before 36 hours after the relevant time.

(2)  Where an officer such as is mentioned in subsection (1) above has authorised the keeping of a person in police detention for a period expiring less than 36 hours after the relevant time, such an officer may authorise the keeping of that person in police detention for a further period expiring not more than 36 hours after that time if the conditions specified in subsection (1) above are still satisfied when he gives the authorisation.

(3)  If it is proposed to transfer a person in police detention to another police area, the officer determining whether or not to authorise keeping him in detention under subsection (1) above shall have regard to the distance and the time the journey would take.

(4)  No authorisation under subsection (1) above shall be given in respect of any person—

    (a)  more than 24 hours after the relevant time; or

    (b)  before the second review of his detention under section 40 above has been carried out.

(5)  Where an officer authorises the keeping of a person in police detention under subsection (1) above, it shall be his duty—

    (a)  to inform that person of the grounds for his continued detention; and

    (b)  to record the grounds in that person's custody record.

(6)  Before determining whether to authorise the keeping of a person in detention under subsection (1) or (2) above, an officer shall give—

    (a)  that person; or

    (b)  any solicitor representing him who is available at the time when it falls to the officer to determine whether to give the authorisation,

an opportunity to make representations to him about the detention.

(7)  Subject to subsection (8) below, the person in detention or his solicitor may make representations under subsection (6) above either orally or in writing.

(8)  The officer to whom it falls to determine whether to give the authorisation may refuse to hear oral representations from the person in detention if he considers that he is unfit to make such representations by reason of his condition or behaviour.

(9)  Where—

    (a)  an officer authorises the keeping of a person in detention under subsection (1) above; and

    (b) at the time of the authorisation he has not yet exercised a right conferred on him by section 56 or 58 below,

the officer—

    (i) shall inform him of that right;

    (ii) shall decide whether he should be permitted to exercise it;

    (iii) shall record the decision in his custody record; and

    (iv) if the decision is to refuse to permit the exercise of the right, shall also record the grounds for the decision in that record.

(10) Where an officer has authorised the keeping of a person who has not been charged in detention under subsection (1) or (2) above, he shall be released from detention not later than 36 hours after the relevant time—

    (a) without bail unless the pre-conditions for bail are satisfied, or

    (b) on bail if those pre-conditions are satisfied,

(subject to subsection (10A)).

(10A) Subsection (10) does not apply if—

    (a) the person has been charged with an offence, or

    (b) the person's continued detention is authorised or otherwise permitted in accordance with section 43.

(11) A person released under subsection (10) above shall not be re-arrested without a warrant for the offence for which he was previously arrested unless since the person's release, new evidence has come to light or an examination or analysis of existing evidence has been made which could not reasonably have been made before his release but this subsection does not prevent an arrest under section 46A below.

(12) Subsection (13) applies where—

    (a) a person is released under subsection (10), and

    (b) a custody officer determines that—

    (i) there is not sufficient evidence to charge the person with an offence, or

    (ii) there is sufficient evidence to charge the person with an offence but the person should not be charged with an offence or given a caution in respect of an offence.

(13) The custody officer must give the person notice in writing that the person is not to be prosecuted.

(14) Subsection (13) does not prevent the prosecution of the person for an offence if new evidence comes to light after the notice was given.

## 43   Warrants of further detention

(1) Where, on an application on oath made by a constable and supported by an information, a magistrates' court is satisfied that there are reasonable grounds for believing that the further detention of the person to whom the application relates is justified, it may issue a warrant of further detention authorising the keeping of that person in police detention.

(2) A court may not hear an application for a warrant of further detention unless the person to whom the application relates—

    (a) has been furnished with a copy of the information; and

    (b) has been brought before the court for the hearing.

(3) The person to whom the application relates shall be entitled to be legally represented at the hearing and, if he is not so represented but wishes to be so represented—

    (a) the court shall adjourn the hearing to enable him to obtain representation; and

    (b) he may be kept in police detention during the adjournment.

(4) A person's further detention is only justified for the purposes of this section or section 44 below if—

    (a) his detention without charge is necessary to secure or preserve evidence relating to an offence for which he is under arrest or to obtain such evidence by questioning him;

    (b) an offence for which he is under arrest is an indictable offence; and

    (c) the investigation is being conducted diligently and expeditiously.

(5) Subject to subsection (7) below, an application for a warrant of further detention may be made—

    (a) at any time before the expiry of 36 hours after the relevant time; or

    (b) in a case where—

        (i) it is not practicable for the magistrates' court to which the application will be made to sit at the expiry of 36 hours after the relevant time; but

        (ii) the court will sit during the 6 hours following the end of that period, at any time before the expiry of the said 6 hours.

(6) In a case to which subsection (5)(b) above applies—

    (a) the person to whom the application relates may be kept in police detention until the application is heard; and

    (b) the custody officer shall make a note in that person's custody record—

        (i) of the fact that he was kept in police detention for more than 36 hours after the relevant time; and

        (ii) of the reason why he was so kept.

(7) If—

    (a) an application for a warrant of further detention is made after the expiry of 36 hours after the relevant time; and

    (b) it appears to the magistrates' court that it would have been reasonable for the police to make it before the expiry of that period,

the court shall dismiss the application.

(8) Where on an application such as is mentioned in subsection (1) above a magistrates' court is not satisfied that there are reasonable grounds for believing that the further detention of the person to whom the application relates is justified, it shall be its duty—

    (a) to refuse the application; or

    (b) to adjourn the hearing of it until a time not later than 36 hours after the relevant time.

(9) The person to whom the application relates may be kept in police detention during the adjournment.

(10) A warrant of further detention shall—

    (a) state the time at which it is issued;

    (b) authorise the keeping in police detention of the person to whom it relates for the period stated in it.

(11) Subject to subsection (12) below, the period stated in a warrant of further detention shall be such period as the magistrates' court thinks fit, having regard to the evidence before it.

(12) The period shall not be longer than 36 hours.

(13) If it is proposed to transfer a person in police detention to a police area other than that in which he is detained when the application for a warrant of further detention is made, the court hearing the application shall have regard to the distance and the time the journey would take.

(14) Any information submitted in support of an application under this section shall state—

    (a) the nature of the offence for which the person to whom the application relates has been arrested;

    (b) the general nature of the evidence on which that person was arrested;

    (c) what inquiries relating to the offence have been made by the police and what further inquiries are proposed by them;

    (d) the reasons for believing the continued detention of that person to be necessary for the purposes of such further inquiries.

(15) Where an application under this section is refused, the person to whom the application relates shall forthwith be charged or, subject to subsection (16) below, released—

    (a) without bail unless the pre-conditions for bail are satisfied, or

    (b) on bail if those pre-conditions are satisfied.

(16) A person need not be released under subsection (15) above—

    (a) before the expiry of 24 hours after the relevant time; or

(b) before the expiry of any longer period for which his continued detention is or has been authorised under section 42 above.

(17) Where an application under this section is refused, no further application shall be made under this section in respect of the person to whom the refusal relates, unless supported by evidence which has come to light since the refusal.

(18) Where a warrant of further detention is issued, the person to whom it relates unless the person is charged, be released from police detention upon or before the expiry of the warrant—

(a) without bail unless the pre-conditions for bail are satisfied, or

(b) on bail if those pre-conditions are satisfied.

(19) A person released under subsection (18) above shall not be re-arrested without a warrant for the offence for which he was previously arrested unless since the person's release, new evidence has come to light or an examination or analysis of existing evidence has been made which could not reasonably have been made before his release; but this subsection does not prevent an arrest under section 46A below.

(20) Subsection (21) applies where—

(a) a person is released under subsection (15) or (18), and

(b) a custody officer determines that—

    (i) there is not sufficient evidence to charge the person with an offence, or

    (ii) there is sufficient evidence to charge the person with an offence but the person should not be charged with an offence or given a caution in respect of an offence.

(21) The custody officer must give the person notice in writing that the person is not to be prosecuted.

(22) Subsection (21) does not prevent the prosecution of the person for an offence if new evidence comes to light after the notice was given.

## 44  Extension of warrants of further detention

(1) On an application made by a constable and supported by an information a magistrates' court may extend a warrant of further detention issued under section 43 above if it is satisfied that there are reasonable grounds for believing that the further detention of the person to whom the application relates is justified.

(2) Subject to subsection (3) below, the period for which a warrant of further detention may be extended shall be such period as the court thinks fit, having regard to the evidence before it.

(3) The period shall not—

(a) be longer than 36 hours; or

(b) end later than 96 hours after the relevant time.

(4) Where a warrant of further detention has been extended under subsection (1) above, or further extended under this subsection, for a period ending before 96 hours after the relevant time, on an application such as is mentioned in that subsection a magistrates' court may further extend the warrant if it is satisfied as there mentioned; and subsections (2) and (3) above apply to such further extensions as they apply to extensions under subsection (1) above.

(5) A warrant of further detention shall, if extended under this section, be endorsed with a note of the period of the extension.

(6) Subsections (2), (3) and (14) of section 43 above shall apply to an application made under this section as they apply to an application made under that section.

(7) Where an application under this section is refused, the person to whom the application relates shall forthwith be charged or, subject to subsection (8) below, released—

(a) without bail unless the pre-conditions for bail are satisfied, or

(b) on bail if those pre-conditions are satisfied.

(8) A person need not be released under subsection (7) above before the expiry of any period for which a warrant of further detention issued in relation to him has been extended or further extended on an earlier application made under this section.

(9) Subsection (10) applies where—
    (a) a person is released under subsection (7), and
    (b) a custody officer determines that—
        (i)   there is not sufficient evidence to charge the person with an offence, or
        (ii)  there is sufficient evidence to charge the person with an offence but the person
             should not be charged with an offence or given a caution in respect of an offence.

(10) The custody officer must give the person notice in writing that the person is not to be prosecuted.

(11) Subsection (10) does not prevent the prosecution of the person for an offence if new evidence comes to light after the notice was given.

## 45   Detention before charge—supplementary

(1) In sections 43, 44 and 45ZB of this Act 'magistrates' court' means a court consisting of two or more justices of the peace sitting otherwise than in open court.

(2) Any reference in this Part of this Act to a period of time or a time of day is to be treated as approximate only.

## 45ZA   Functions of extending detention: use of live links

(1) The functions of a police officer under section 42(1) or (2) may be performed, in relation to an arrested person who is held at a police station, by an officer who is not present at the police station but has access to the use of a live link if—
    (a) a custody officer considers that the use of the live link is appropriate,
    (b) the arrested person has had advice from a solicitor on the use of the live link, and
    (c) the appropriate consent to the use of the live link has been given.

(2) In subsection (1)(c), 'the appropriate consent' means—
    (a) in relation to a person who has attained the age of 18, the consent of that person;
    (b) in relation to a person who has not attained that age but has attained the age of 14, the consent of that person and of his or her parent or guardian;
    (c) in relation to a person who has not attained the age of 14, the consent of his or her parent or guardian.

(3) The consent of a person who has not attained the age of 18 (but has attained the age of 14), or who is a vulnerable adult, may only be given in the presence of an appropriate adult.

(4) Section 42 applies with the modifications set out in subsections (5) to (7) below in any case where the functions of a police officer under that section are, by virtue of subsection (1), performed by an officer who is not at the police station where the arrested person is held.

(5) Subsections (5)(b) and (9)(iii) and (iv) of that section are each to be read as if, instead of requiring the officer to make a record, they required the officer to cause another police officer to make a record.

(6) Subsection (6) of that section is to be read as if it required the officer to give the persons mentioned in that subsection an opportunity to make representations—
    (a) if facilities exist for the immediate transmission of written representations to the officer, either in writing by means of those facilities or orally by means of the live link, or
    (b) in any other case, orally by means of the live link.

(7) Subsection (9) of that section is to be read as if the reference in paragraph (b) to the right conferred by section 58 were omitted.

(8) In this section—
'live link' means an arrangement by which an officer who is not present at the police station where an arrested person is held is able to see and hear, and to be seen and heard by, the arrested person and the arrested person's solicitor (and for this purpose any impairment of eyesight or hearing is to be disregarded);
'vulnerable adult' means a person aged 18 or over who may have difficulty understanding the purpose of an authorisation under section 42(1) or (2) or anything that occurs in connection with a

decision whether to give such an authorisation (whether because of a mental disorder or for any other reason);

'appropriate adult', in relation to a person who has not attained the age of 18, means—

(a) the person's parent or guardian or, if the person is in the care of a local authority or voluntary organisation, a person representing that authority or organisation,

(b) a social worker of a local authority, or

(c) if no person falling within paragraph (a) or (b) is available, any responsible person aged 18 or over who is not a police officer or a person employed for, or engaged on, police purposes;

'appropriate adult', in relation to a vulnerable adult, means—

(a) a relative, guardian or other person responsible for the vulnerable adult's care,

(b) a person who is experienced in dealing with vulnerable adults but who is not a police officer or a person employed for, or engaged on, police purposes, or

(c) if no person falling within paragraph (a) or (b) is available, any responsible person aged 18 or over who is not a police officer or a person employed for, or engaged on, police purposes.

(9) In subsection (8), in both definitions of 'appropriate adult', 'police purposes' has the meaning given by section 101(2) of the Police Act 1996.

### 45ZB   Warrants for further detention: use of live links

(1) A magistrates' court may give a live link direction for the purpose of the hearing of an application under section 43 for a warrant authorising further detention of a person, or the hearing of an application under section 44 for an extension of such a warrant, if—

(a) a custody officer considers that the use of a live link for that purpose is appropriate,

(b) the person to whom the application relates has had legal advice on the use of the live link,

(c) the appropriate consent to the use of the live link has been given, and

(d) it is not contrary to the interests of justice to give the direction.

(2) In subsection (1)(c), 'the appropriate consent' means—

(a) in relation to a person who has attained the age of 18, the consent of that person;

(b) in relation to a person who has not attained that age but has attained the age of 14, the consent of that person and of his or her parent or guardian;

(c) in relation to a person who has not attained the age of 14, the consent of his or her parent or guardian.

(3) Where a live link direction is given, the requirement under section 43(2)(b) for the person to whom the application relates to be brought before the court for the hearing does not apply.

(4) In this section—

'live link direction' means a direction that a live link be used for the purposes of the hearing;

'live link' means an arrangement by which a person (when not in the place where the hearing is being held) is able to see and hear, and to be seen and heard by, the court during a hearing (and for this purpose any impairment of eyesight or hearing is to be disregarded);

'vulnerable adult' means a person aged 18 or over who may have difficulty understanding the purpose of the hearing or what occurs at it (whether because of a mental disorder or for any other reason);

'appropriate adult', in relation to a person aged under 18, means—

(a) the person's parent or guardian or, if the person is in the care of a local authority or voluntary organisation, a person representing that authority or organisation,

(b) a social worker of a local authority, or

(c) if no person falling within paragraph (a) or (b) is available, any responsible person aged 18 or over who is not a police officer or a person employed for, or engaged on, police purposes;

'appropriate adult', in relation to a vulnerable adult, means—

(a) a relative, guardian or other person responsible for the appropriate adult's care,

(b) a person who is experienced in dealing with vulnerable adults but who is not a police officer or a person employed for, or engaged on, police purposes, or

(c) if no person falling within paragraph (a) or (b) is available, any responsible person aged 18 or over who is not a police officer or a person employed for, or engaged on, police purposes.

(5) In subsection (4), in both definitions of 'appropriate adult', 'police purposes' has the meaning given by section 101(2) of the Police Act 1996.

### 45A    Use of live links for other decisions about detention

(1) Subject to the following provisions of this section, the Secretary of State may by regulations provide that, in the case of an arrested person who is held in a police station, some or all of the functions mentioned in subsection (2) may be performed (notwithstanding anything in the preceding provisions of this Part) by an officer who—

(a) is not present in that police station; but

(b) has access to the use of a live link.

(2) Those functions are—

(a) the functions in relation to an arrested person taken to, or answering to bail at, a police station that is not a designated police station which, in the case of an arrested person taken to a station that is a designated police station, are functions of a custody officer under section 37, 38 or 40 above; and

(b) the function of carrying out a review under section 40(1)(b) above (review, by an officer of at least the rank of inspector, of the detention of person arrested but not charged).

(3) Regulations under this section shall specify the use to be made in the performance of the functions mentioned in subsection (2) above of a live link.

(4) Regulations under this section shall not authorise the performance of any of the functions mentioned in subsection (2)(a) above by such an officer as is mentioned in subsection (1) above unless he is a custody officer for a designated police station.

(5) Where any functions mentioned in subsection (2) above are performed in a manner authorised by regulations under this section—

(a) any obligation of the officer performing those functions to make a record in connection with the performance of those functions shall have effect as an obligation to cause another officer to make the record; and

(b) any requirement for the record to be made in the presence of the arrested person shall apply to the making of that record by that other officer.

(6) Where the functions mentioned in subsection (2)(b) are performed in a manner authorised by regulations under this section, the requirements under section 40(12) and (13) above for—

(a) the arrested person, or

(b) a solicitor representing him,

to be given any opportunity to make representations (whether in writing or orally) to the person performing those functions shall have effect as a requirement for that person, or such a solicitor, to be given an opportunity to make representations in a manner authorised by subsection (7) below.

(7) Representations are made in a manner authorised by this subsection—

(a) in a case where facilities exist for the immediate transmission of written representations to the officer performing the functions, if they are made either—

(i) orally to that officer by means of the live link used by him for performing those functions; or

(ii) in writing to that officer by means of the facilities available for the immediate transmission of the representations; and

(b) in any other case if they are made orally to that officer by means of the live link used by him for performing the functions.

(8) Regulations under this section may make different provision for different cases and may be made so as to have effect in relation only to the police stations specified or described in the regulations.

(9) Regulations under this section shall be made by statutory instrument and shall be subject to annulment in pursuance of a resolution of either House of Parliament.

(10) In this section, 'live link', in relation to any functions, means an arrangement by which the functions may be performed by an officer who is not present at the police station where an arrested person is held but who is able (for the purpose of the functions) to see and hear, and to be seen and heard by, the arrested person and any legal representative of that person (and for this purpose any impairment of eyesight or hearing is to be disregarded).

*Detention—miscellaneous*

## 46   Detention after charge

(1) Where a person—
> (a) is charged with an offence; and
> (b) after being charged—
>> (i) is kept in police detention; or
>> (ii) is detained by a local authority in pursuance of arrangements made under section 38(6) above,

he shall be brought before a magistrates' court in accordance with the provisions of this section.

(2) If he is to be brought before a magistrates' court in the local justice area in which the police station at which he was charged is situated, he shall be brought before such a court as soon as is practicable and in any event not later than the first sitting after he is charged with the offence.

(3) If no magistrates' court in that area is due to sit either on the day on which he is charged or on the next day, the custody officer for the police station at which he was charged shall inform the designated officer for the area that there is a person in the area to whom subsection (2) above applies.

(4) If the person charged is to be brought before a magistrates' court in a local justice area other than that in which the police station at which he was charged is situated, he shall be removed to that area as soon as is practicable and brought before such a court as soon as is practicable after his arrival in the area and in any event not later than the first sitting of a magistrates' court in that area after his arrival in the area.

(5) If no magistrates' court in that area is due to sit either on the day on which he arrives in the area or on the next day—
> (a) he shall be taken to a police station in the area; and
> (b) the custody officer at that station shall inform the designated officer for the area that there is a person in the area to whom subsection (4) applies.

(6) Subject to subsection (8) below, where the designated officer for a local justice area has been informed—
> (a) under subsection (3) above that there is a person in the area to whom subsection (2) above applies; or
> (b) under subsection (5) above that there is a person in the area to whom subsection (4) above applies,

the designated officer shall arrange for a magistrates' court to sit not later than the day next following the relevant day.

(7) In this section 'the relevant day'—
> (a) in relation to a person who is to be brought before a magistrates' court in the local justice area in which the police station at which he was charged is situated, means the day on which he was charged; and
> (b) in relation to a person who is to be brought before a magistrates' court in any other local justice area, means the day on which he arrives in the area.

(8) Where the day next following the relevant day is Christmas Day, Good Friday or a Sunday, the duty of the designated officer under subsection (6) above is a duty to arrange for a magistrates' court to sit not later than the first day after the relevant day which is not one of those days.

(9) Nothing in this section requires a person who is in hospital to be brought before a court if he is not well enough.

### 46ZA  Persons granted live link bail

(1) This section applies in relation to bail granted under this Part subject to the duty mentioned in section 47(3)(b) ('live link bail').

(2) An accused person who attends a police station to answer to live link bail is not to be treated as in police detention for the purposes of this Act.

(3) Subsection (2) does not apply in relation to an accused person if—

> (b) at any time before the beginning of proceedings in relation to a live link direction under section 57C of the Crime and Disorder Act 1998 in relation to the accused person, a constable informs him that a live link will not be available for his use for the purposes of that section; or

> (d) the court determines for any reason not to give such a direction.

(4) If paragraph (b) or (d) of subsection (3) applies in relation to a person, he is to be treated for the purposes of this Part—

> (a) as if he had been arrested for and charged with the offence in connection with which he was granted bail, and

> (b) as if he had been so charged at the time when that paragraph first applied in relation to him.

(5) An accused person who is arrested under section 46A for failing to attend at a police station to answer to live link bail, and who is brought to a police station in accordance with that section, is to be treated for the purposes of this Part—

> (a) as if he had been arrested for and charged with the offence in connection with which he was granted bail, and

> (b) as if he had been so charged at the time when he is brought to the station.

(6) Nothing in subsection (4) or (5) affects the operation of section 47(6).

### 46A  Power of arrest for failure to answer to police bail

(1) A constable may arrest without a warrant any person who, having been released on bail under this Part of this Act subject to a duty to attend at a police station, fails to attend at that police station at the time appointed for him to do so.

(1ZA) The reference in subsection (1) to a person who fails to attend at a police station at the time appointed for him to do so includes a reference to a person who—

> (a) attends at a police station to answer to bail granted subject to the duty mentioned in section 47(3)(b), but

> (b) leaves the police station at any time before the beginning of proceedings in relation to a live link direction under section 57C of the Crime and Disorder Act 1998 in relation to him.

(1ZB) The reference in subsection (1) to a person who fails to attend at a police station at the time appointed for the person to do so includes a reference to a person who—

> (a) attends at a police station to answer to bail granted subject to the duty mentioned in section 47(3)(b), but

> (b) refuses to be searched under section 54B.

(1A) A person who has been released on bail under this Part may be arrested without warrant by a constable if the constable has reasonable grounds for suspecting that the person has broken any of the conditions of bail.

(2) A person who is arrested under this section shall be taken to the police station appointed as the place at which he is to surrender to custody as soon as practicable after the arrest.

(3) For the purposes of—

> (a) section 30 above (subject to the obligation in subsection (2) above), and

> (b) section 31 above,

an arrest under this section shall be treated as an arrest for an offence.

## 47   Bail after arrest

(1)  Subject to the following provisions of this section, a release on bail of a person under this Part of this Act shall be a release on bail granted in accordance with sections 3, 3A, 5 and 5A of the Bail Act 1976 as they apply to bail granted by a constable.

(1A)  The normal powers to impose conditions of bail shall be available to him where a custody officer releases a person on bail under this Part.

In this subsection, 'the normal powers to impose conditions of bail' has the meaning given in section 3(6) of the Bail Act 1976.

(1B)  No application may be made under section 5B of the Bail Act 1976 if a person is released on bail under section 37C(2)(b) or 37CA(2)(b) above.

(1C)  Subsections (1D) to (1F) below apply where a person released on bail under section 37C(2) (b) or 37CA(2)(b) above is on bail subject to conditions.

(1D)  The person shall not be entitled to make an application under section 43B of the Magistrates' Courts Act 1980.

(1E)  A magistrates' court may, on an application by or on behalf of the person, vary the conditions of bail; and in this subsection 'vary' has the same meaning as in the Bail Act 1976.

(1F)  Where a magistrates' court varies the conditions of bail under subsection (1E) above, that bail shall not lapse but shall continue subject to the conditions as so varied.

(2)  Nothing in the Bail Act 1976 shall prevent the re-arrest without warrant of a person released on bail subject to a duty to attend at a police station if, since the person's release, new evidence has come to light or an examination or analysis of existing evidence has been made which could not reasonably have been made before the person's release.

(3)  Subject to subsections (3A) and (4) below, in this Part of this Act references to 'bail' are references to bail subject to a duty—

(a)  to appear before a magistrates' court at such time and such place as the custody officer may appoint;

(b)  to attend at such police station as the custody officer may appoint at such time as he may appoint for the purposes of—

(i)   proceedings in relation to a live link direction under section 57C of the Crime and Disorder Act 1998 (use of live link direction at preliminary hearings where accused is at police station); and

(ii)  any preliminary hearing in relation to which such a direction is given; or

(c)  to attend at such police station as the custody officer may appoint at such time as he may appoint for purposes other than those mentioned in paragraph (b) (subject to section 47ZA)

(3A)  Where a custody officer grants bail to a person subject to a duty to appear before a magistrates' court, he shall appoint for the appearance—

(a)  a date which is not later than the first sitting of the court after the person is charged with the offence; or

(b)  where he is informed by the designated officer for the relevant local justice area that the appearance cannot be accommodated until a later date, that later date.

(4)  Where a custody officer has granted bail to a person subject to a duty to appear at a police station, the custody officer may give notice in writing to that person that his attendance at the police station is not required.

(4A)  Where a person has been granted bail under this Part subject to a duty to attend at a police station, a custody officer may subsequently appoint a different time, or an additional time, at which the person is to attend at the police station to answer bail.

(4B)  The custody officer must give the person notice in writing of the exercise of the power under subsection (4A).

(4C)  The exercise of the power under subsection (4A) does not affect the conditions of bail (if any).

(4D) A custody officer may not appoint a time for a person's attendance under subsection (4A) which is after the end of the applicable bail period in relation to the person.

(4E) Subsection (4D) is subject to section 47ZL.

(6) Where a person who has been granted bail under this Part and has either attended at the police station in accordance with the grant of bail or has been arrested under section 46A above is detained at a police station, any time during which he was in police detention prior to being granted bail shall be included as part of any period which falls to be calculated under this Part of this Act and any time during which he was on bail shall not be so included.

(7) Where a person who was released on bail under this Part subject to a duty to attend at a police station is re-arrested, the provisions of this Part of this Act shall apply to him as they apply to a person arrested for the first time, but this subsection does not apply to a person who is arrested under section 46A above or has attended a police station in accordance with the grant of bail (and who accordingly is deemed by section 34(7) above to have been arrested for an offence) or to a person to whom section 46ZA(4) or (5) applies.

(8) …*

### 47ZA  Limits on period of bail without charge

(1) This section applies in relation to the power conferred on a custody officer, when releasing a person on bail under this Part, to appoint a time for the person to attend at a police station in accordance with section 47(3)(c).

(2) The power must be exercised so as to appoint a time on the day on which the applicable bail period in relation to the person ends, unless subsection (3) or (4) applies.

(3) This subsection applies where—
> (a) at the time of the exercise of the power the person is on bail under this Part in relation to one or more offences other than the relevant offence, and
> (b) the custody officer believes that it is appropriate to align the person's attendance in relation to the relevant offence with the person's attendance in relation to the one or more other offences.

(4) This subsection applies where the custody officer believes that a decision as to whether to charge the person with the relevant offence would be made before the end of the applicable bail period in relation to the person.

(5) Where subsection (3) or (4) applies, the power may be exercised so as to appoint a time on a day falling before the end of the applicable bail period in relation to the person.

(6) This section is subject to section 47ZL.

(7) In this section references to attendance are to attendance at a police station in accordance with section 47(3)(c).

(8) In this Part the 'relevant offence', in relation to a person, means the offence in respect of which the power mentioned in subsection (1) is exercised in relation to the person.

### 47ZB  Applicable bail period: initial limit

(1) In this Part the 'applicable bail period', in relation to a person, means—
> (a) in an SFO case, the period of 3 months beginning with the person's bail start date, or
> (b) in an FCA case or any other case, the period of 28 days beginning with the person's bail start date.

(2) The applicable bail period in relation to a person may be extended under sections 47ZD to 47ZG or treated as extended under section 47ZJ(3).

(3) Subsection (1) and sections 47ZD to 47ZG are subject to sections 47ZL and 47ZM.

(4) For the purposes of this Part—
> (a) a person's bail start date is the day after the day on which the person was arrested for the relevant offence,

---

\* **Editor's Note:** Makes changes to the Magistrates' Courts Act 1980 sections 43 and 117(3).

(b) an 'FCA case' is a case in which—
  (i)  the relevant offence in relation to the person is being investigated by the Financial Conduct Authority, and
  (ii) a senior officer confirms that sub-paragraph (i) applies,
(c) an 'SFO case' is a case in which—
  (i)  the relevant offence in relation to the person is being investigated by the Director of the Serious Fraud Office, and
  (ii) a senior officer confirms that sub-paragraph (i) applies, and
(d) 'senior officer' means a police officer of the rank of superintendent or above.

### 47ZC  Applicable bail period: conditions A to D in sections 47ZD to 47ZG

(1) This section applies for the purposes of sections 47ZD to 47ZG.

(2) Condition A is that the decision-maker has reasonable grounds for suspecting the person in question to be guilty of the relevant offence.

(3) Condition B is that the decision-maker has reasonable grounds for believing—
  (a) in a case where the person in question is or is to be released on bail under section 37(7)(c) or 37CA(2)(b), that further time is needed for making a decision as to whether to charge the person with the relevant offence, or
  (b) otherwise, that further investigation is needed of any matter in connection with the relevant offence.

(4) Condition C is that the decision-maker has reasonable grounds for believing—
  (a) in a case where the person in question is or is to be released on bail under section 37(7)(c) or 37CA(2)(b), that the decision as to whether to charge the person with the relevant offence is being made diligently and expeditiously, or
  (b) otherwise, that the investigation is being conducted diligently and expeditiously.

(5) Condition D is that the decision-maker has reasonable grounds for believing that the release on bail of the person in question is necessary and proportionate in all the circumstances (having regard, in particular, to any conditions of bail which are, or are to be, imposed).

(6) In this section 'decision-maker' means—
  (a) in relation to a condition which falls to be considered by virtue of section 47ZD, the senior officer in question;
  (b) in relation to a condition which falls to be considered by virtue of section 47ZE, the appropriate decision-maker in question;
  (c) in relation to a condition which falls to be considered by virtue of section 47ZF or 47ZG, the court in question.

### 47ZD  Applicable bail period: extension of initial limit in standard cases

(1) This section applies in relation to a person if—
  (a) the applicable bail period in relation to the person is the period mentioned in section 47ZB(1)(b),
  (b) that period has not ended, and
  (c) a senior officer is satisfied that conditions A to D are met in relation to the person.

(2) The senior officer may authorise the applicable bail period in relation to the person to be extended so that it ends at the end of the period of 3 months beginning with the person's bail start date.

(3) Before determining whether to give an authorisation under subsection (2) in relation to a person, the senior officer must arrange for the person or the person's legal representative to be informed that a determination is to be made.

(4) In determining whether to give an authorisation under subsection (2) in relation to a person, the senior officer must consider any representations made by the person or the person's legal representative.

(5) The senior officer must arrange for the person or the person's legal representative to be informed whether an authorisation under subsection (2) has been given in relation to the person.

**47ZE Applicable bail period: extension of limit in designated cases**

(1) This section applies in relation to a person if—

(a) the person's case is an SFO case, or

(b) a senior officer has authorised an extension of the applicable bail period in relation to the person under section 47ZD.

(2) A qualifying prosecutor may designate the person's case as being an exceptionally complex case (a 'designated case').

(3) If an appropriate decision-maker is satisfied that conditions A to D are met in relation to the person in a designated case, the decision-maker may authorise the applicable bail period in relation to the person to be extended so that it ends at the end of the period of 6 months beginning with the person's bail start date.

(4) An appropriate decision-maker is—

(a) a member of staff of the Financial Conduct Authority who is of the description designated for the purposes of this paragraph by the Chief Executive of the Authority (in an FCA case),

(b) a member of the Serious Fraud Office who is of the Senior Civil Service (in an SFO case), or

(c) a qualifying police officer (in any other case).

(5) Before determining whether to give an authorisation under subsection (3) in relation to a person—

(a) the appropriate decision-maker must arrange for the person or the person's legal representative to be informed that a determination is to be made, and

(b) if the appropriate decision-maker is a qualifying police officer, the officer must consult a qualifying prosecutor.

(6) In determining whether to give an authorisation under subsection (3) in relation to a person, the appropriate decision-maker must consider any representations made by the person or the person's legal representative.

(7) The appropriate decision-maker must arrange for the person or the person's legal representative to be informed whether an authorisation under subsection (3) has been given in relation to the person.

(8) Any designation under subsection (2) must be made, and any authorisation under subsection (3) must be given, before the applicable bail period in relation to the person has ended.

(9) In this section—

'qualifying police officer' means a police officer of the rank of commander or assistant chief constable or above, and

'qualifying prosecutor' means a prosecutor of the description designated for the purposes of this section by the Chief Executive of the Financial Conduct Authority, the Director of the Serious Fraud Office or the Director of Public Prosecutions.

**47ZF Applicable bail period: first extension of limit by court**

(1) This section applies in relation to a person if—

(a) the person's case is an SFO case,

(b) a senior officer has authorised an extension of the applicable bail period in relation to the person under section 47ZD, or

(c) an appropriate decision-maker has authorised an extension of the applicable bail period in relation to the person under section 47ZE.

(2) Before the applicable bail period in relation to the person ends a qualifying applicant may apply to a magistrates' court for it to authorise an extension of the applicable bail period in relation to the person under this section.

(3) If the court is satisfied that—

(a) conditions B to D are met in relation to the person, and

(b) the case does not fall within subsection (7),

it may authorise the applicable bail period to be extended as specified in subsection (4).

(4) The applicable bail period is to end—

(a) in a case falling within subsection (1)(a) or (b), at the end of the period of 6 months beginning with the person's bail start date;

(b) in a case falling within subsection (1)(c), at the end of the period of 9 months beginning with the person's bail start date.

(5) If the court is satisfied that—

(a) conditions B to D are met in relation to the person, and

(b) the case falls within subsection (7),

it may authorise the applicable bail period to be extended as specified in subsection (6).

(6) The applicable bail period is to end—

(a) in a case falling within subsection (1)(a) or (b), at the end of the period of 9 months beginning with the person's bail start date;

(b) in a case falling within subsection (1)(c), at the end of the period of 12 months beginning with the person's bail start date.

(7) A case falls within this subsection if the nature of the decision or further investigations mentioned in condition B means that that decision is unlikely to be made or those investigations completed if the applicable bail period in relation to the person is not extended as specified in subsection (6).

(8) In this section 'qualifying applicant' means—

(a) a constable,

(b) a member of staff of the Financial Conduct Authority who is of the description designated for the purposes of this subsection by the Chief Executive of the Authority,

(c) a member of the Serious Fraud Office, or

(d) a Crown Prosecutor.

### 47ZG   Applicable bail period: subsequent extensions of limit by court

(1) Subsections (2) to (6) apply where a court has authorised an extension of the applicable bail period in relation to a person under section 47ZF.

(2) Before the applicable bail period in relation to the person ends a qualifying applicant may apply to a magistrates' court for it to authorise an extension of the applicable bail period in relation to the person under this section.

(3) If the court is satisfied that—

(a) conditions B to D are met in relation to the person, and

(b) the case does not fall within subsection (8),

it may authorise the applicable bail period to be extended as specified in subsection (4).

(4) The applicable bail period is to end at the end of the period of 3 months beginning with the end of the current applicable bail period in relation to the person.

(5) If the court is satisfied that—

(a) conditions B to D are met in relation to the person, and

(b) the case falls within subsection (8),

it may authorise the applicable bail period to be extended as specified in subsection (6).

(6) The applicable bail period is to end at the end of the period of 6 months beginning with the end of the current applicable bail period in relation to the person.

(7) Where a court has authorised an extension of the applicable bail period in relation to a person under subsection (3) or (5), a qualifying applicant may make further applications under subsection (2) (and subsections (3) to (6) apply accordingly).

(8) A case falls within this subsection if the nature of the decision or further investigations mentioned in condition B means that that decision is unlikely to be made or those investigations completed if the current applicable bail period in relation to the person is not extended as specified in subsection (6).

(9) For the purposes of this section—

(a) references to the current applicable bail period in relation to a person are to the applicable bail period applying to the person when the application under this section is made (subject to section 47ZJ(3)), and

(b) 'qualifying applicant' has the same meaning as in section 47ZF.

**47ZH  Sections 47ZF and 47ZG: withholding sensitive information**

(1)  This section applies where a qualifying applicant makes an application to a magistrates' court under section 47ZF or 47ZG in relation to a person.

(2)  The qualifying applicant may apply to the court for it to authorise the specified information to be withheld from the person and any legal representative of the person.

(3)  The court may grant an application under subsection (2) only if satisfied that there are reasonable grounds for believing that the specified information is sensitive information.

(4)  For the purposes of this section information is sensitive information if its disclosure would have one or more of the following results—

    (a)  evidence connected with an indictable offence would be interfered with or harmed;

    (b)  a person would be interfered with or physically injured;

    (c)  a person suspected of having committed an indictable offence but not yet arrested for the offence would be alerted;

    (d)  the recovery of property obtained as a result of an indictable offence would be hindered.

(5)  In this section 'specified information' means the information specified in the application under subsection (2).

**47ZI  Sections 47ZF to 47ZH: proceedings in magistrates' court**

(1)  An application made to a magistrates' court under section 47ZF or 47ZG in relation to a person is to be determined by a single justice of the peace on written evidence unless subsection (2) or (3) applies.

(2)  This subsection applies if—

    (a)  the effect of the application would be to extend the applicable bail period in relation to the person so that it ends at or before the end of the period of 12 months beginning with the person's bail start date, and

    (b)  a single justice of the peace considers that the interests of justice require an oral hearing.

(3)  This subsection applies if—

    (a)  the effect of the application would be to extend the applicable bail period in relation to the person so that it ends after the end of the period of 12 months beginning with the person's bail start date, and

    (b)  the person, or the person who made the application, requests an oral hearing.

(4)  If subsection (2) or (3) applies, the application is to be determined by two or more justices of the peace sitting otherwise than in open court.

(5)  Where an application under section 47ZF or 47ZG in relation to a person is to be determined as mentioned in subsection (4), the justices may direct that the person and any legal representative of the person be excluded from any part of the hearing.

(6)  The justices may give a direction under subsection (5) only if satisfied that there are reasonable grounds for believing that sensitive information would be disclosed at the part of the hearing in question.

(7)  An application under section 47ZH is to be determined by a single justice of the peace on written evidence unless the justice determines that the interests of justice require an oral hearing.

(8)  If the justice makes a determination under subsection (7)—

    (a)  the application is to be determined by two or more justices of the peace sitting otherwise than in open court, and

    (b)  the justices hearing the application must direct that the person to whom the application relates and any legal representative of the person be excluded from the hearing.

(9)  In this section 'sensitive information' has the meaning given in section 47ZH(4).

**47ZJ  Sections 47ZF and 47ZG: late applications to magistrates' court**

(1)  This section applies where—

    (a)  an application under section 47ZF or 47ZG is made to a magistrates' court before the end of the applicable bail period in relation to a person, but

    (b)  it is not practicable for the court to determine the application before the end of that period.

(2) The court must determine the application as soon as is practicable.

(3) The applicable bail period in relation to the person is to be treated as extended until the application is determined.

(4) If it appears to the court that it would have been reasonable for the application to have been made in time for it to have been determined by the court before the end of the applicable bail period in relation to the person, it may refuse the application.

### 47ZK  Rules

Criminal Procedure Rules may make provision in connection with applications under sections 47ZF, 47ZG and 47ZH and the proceedings for determining such applications.

### 47ZL  Applicable bail period and bail return date: special case of release on bail under section 37(7)(a) or 37C(2)(b)

(1) This section applies where a person is released on bail under section 37(7)(a) or 37C(2)(b).

(2) The running of the applicable bail period in relation to the person—
  (a) does not begin (in the case of a first release on bail), or
  (b) is suspended (in any other case),
(subject to subsection (6)).

(3) Accordingly section 47ZA does not apply to the exercise of the power mentioned in section 47ZA(1) when releasing the person on bail.

(4) Subsections (5) and (6) apply if a DPP request is made in relation to the person.

(5) A custody officer must exercise the power mentioned in section 47(4A) to appoint a different time for the person to attend at the police station (and section 47(4B) to (4D) applies accordingly).

(6) The applicable bail period in relation to the person—
  (a) begins to run on the day on which the DPP request is made (in the case of a first release on bail), or
  (b) resumes running on that day (in any other case).

(7) Subsection (8) applies where—
  (a) a DPP request has been made in relation to the person, and
  (b) the applicable bail period in relation to the person would end before the end of the period of 7 days beginning with the day on which the DPP request was made.

(8) The running of the applicable bail period in relation to the person is suspended for the number of days necessary to secure that the applicable bail period ends at the end of the period of 7 days beginning with the day on which the DPP request was made.

(9) Subsections (10) and (11) apply if the DPP request made in relation to the person is met.

(10) The running of the applicable bail period in relation to the person is suspended.

(11) Accordingly section 47(4D) does not apply to any exercise of the power under section 47(4A).

(12) For the purposes of this section—
  (a) a 'DPP request', in relation to a person, means a request by the Director of Public Prosecutions for the further information specified in the request to be provided before the Director decides under section 37B(2) whether there is sufficient evidence to charge the person with the relevant offence,
  (b) a DPP request is met when the further information specified in the request is provided, and
  (c) references to the case of a first release on bail are to a case where the person has not been released on bail in relation to the relevant offence under any other provision of this Part or under section 30A.

### 47ZM  Applicable bail period: special cases of release on bail under section 30A and periods in hospital

(1) Subsections (2) and (3) apply where a person was released on bail under section 30A.

(2) The period of 28 days mentioned in section 30B(8) in relation to the person is to be treated as being the period of 28 days mentioned in section 47ZB(1)(b) in relation to the person.

(3)  Any reference to the relevant offence, in relation to the person, is to be read as a reference to the offence in respect of which the power in section 30A(1) was exercised.

(4)  Subsection (5) applies if, at any time on the day on which the applicable bail period in relation to a person would end, the person is in hospital as an in-patient.

(5)  The running of the applicable bail period in relation to the person is to be treated as having been suspended for any day on which the patient was in hospital as an in-patient.

### 47A    Early administrative hearings conducted by justices' clerk

Where a person has been charged with an offence at a police station, any requirement imposed under this Part for the person to appear or be brought before a magistrates' court shall be taken to be satisfied if the person appears or is brought before a justices' clerk in order for the clerk to conduct a hearing under section 50 of the Crime and Disorder Act 1998 (early administrative hearings).

### 48    Remands to police detention

...*

### 49    Police detention to count towards custodial sentence

...**

### 50    Records of detention

(1)  Each police force shall keep written records showing on an annual basis—
- (a)  the number of persons kept in police detention for more than 24 hours and subsequently released without charge;
- (b)  the number of applications for warrants of further detention and the results of the applications; and
- (c)  in relation to each warrant of further detention—
  - (i)    the period of further detention authorised by it;
  - (ii)   the period which the person named in it spent in police detention on its authority; and
  - (iii)  whether he was charged or released without charge.

(2)  Every annual report—
- (a)  under section 22 of the Police Act 1996; or
- (b)  made by the Commissioner of Police of the Metropolis,

shall contain information about the matters mentioned in subsection (1) above in respect of the period to which the report relates.

### 50A    Interpretation of references to pre-conditions for bail

For the purposes of this Part the following are the pre-conditions for bail in relation to the release of a person by a custody officer—
- (a)  that the custody officer is satisfied that releasing the person on bail is necessary and proportionate in all the circumstances (having regard, in particular, to any conditions of bail which would be imposed), and
- (b)  that an officer of the rank of inspector or above authorises the release on bail (having considered any representations made by the person or the person's legal representative).

### 51    Savings

Nothing in this Part of this Act shall affect—
- (a)  the powers conferred on immigration officers by section 4 of and Schedule 2 to the Immigration Act 1971 (administrative provisions as to control on entry etc.);
- (b)  the powers conferred by or by virtue of section 41 of, or Schedule 7 to, the Terrorism Act 2000 (Power of arrest and detention);
- (d)  any right of a person in police detention to apply for a writ of habeas corpus or other prerogative remedy.

---

* **Editor's Note:** Makes changes to the Magistrates' Court Act 1980 section 128.
** **Editor's Note:** Makes changes to the Criminal Justice Act 1967 section 67.

# PART V  QUESTIONING AND TREATMENT OF PERSONS BY POLICE

### 53  Abolition of certain powers of constables to search persons

(1) Subject to subsection (2) below, there shall cease to have effect any Act (including a local Act) passed before this Act in so far as it authorises—

    (a) any search by a constable of a person in police detention at a police station; or

    (b) an intimate search of a person by a constable;

and any rule of common law which authorises a search such as is mentioned in paragraph (a) or (b) above is abolished.

### 54  Searches of detained persons

(1) The custody officer at a police station shall ascertain everything which a person has with him when he is—

    (a) brought to the station after being arrested elsewhere or after being committed to custody by an order or sentence of a court; or

    (b) arrested at the station or detained there, as a person falling within section 34(7), under section 37 above or as a person to whom section 46ZA(4) or (5) applies.

(2) The custody officer may record or cause to be recorded all or any of the things which he ascertains under subsection (1).

(2A) In the case of an arrested person, any such record may be made as part of his custody record.

(3) Subject to subsection (4) below, a custody officer may seize and retain any such thing or cause any such thing to be seized and retained.

(4) Clothes and personal effects may only be seized if the custody officer—

    (a) believes that the person from whom they are seized may use them—

        (i) to cause physical injury to himself or any other person;

        (ii) to damage property;

        (iii) to interfere with evidence; or

        (iv) to assist him to escape; or

    (b) has reasonable grounds for believing that they may be evidence relating to an offence.

(5) Where anything is seized, the person from whom it is seized shall be told the reason for the seizure unless he is—

    (a) violent or likely to become violent; or

    (b) incapable of understanding what is said to him.

(6) Subject to subsection (7) below, a person may be searched if the custody officer considers it necessary to enable him to carry out his duty under subsection (1) above and to the extent that the custody officer considers necessary for that purpose.

(6A) A person who is in custody at a police station or is in police detention otherwise than at a police station may at any time be searched in order to ascertain whether he has with him anything which he could use for any of the purposes specified in subsection 4(a) above.

(6B) Subject to subsection (6C) below, a constable may seize and detain, or cause to be seized and detained, anything found in such a search.

(6C) A constable may only seize clothes and personal effects in the circumstances specified in subsection (4) above.

(7) An intimate search may not be conducted under this section.

(8) A search under this section shall be carried out by a constable.

(9) The constable carrying out a search shall be of the same sex as the person searched.

### 54A  Searches and examination to ascertain identity

(1) If an officer of at least the rank of inspector authorises it, a person who is detained in a police station may be searched or examined, or both—

    (a) for the purpose of ascertaining whether he has any mark that would tend to identify him as a person involved in the commission of an offence; or

    (b) for the purpose of facilitating the ascertainment of his identity.

(2) An officer may only give an authorisation under subsection (1) for the purpose mentioned in paragraph (a) of that subsection if—

    (a) the appropriate consent to a search or examination that would reveal whether the mark in question exists has been withheld; or

    (b) it is not practicable to obtain such consent.

(3) An officer may only give an authorisation under subsection (1) in a case in which subsection (2) does not apply if—

    (a) the person in question has refused to identify himself; or

    (b) the officer has reasonable grounds for suspecting that that person is not who he claims to be.

(4) An officer may give an authorisation under subsection (1) orally or in writing but, if he gives it orally, he shall confirm it in writing as soon as is practicable.

(5) Any identifying mark found on a search or examination under this section may be photographed—

    (a) with the appropriate consent; or

    (b) if the appropriate consent is withheld or it is not practicable to obtain it, without it.

(6) Where a search or examination may be carried out under this section, or a photograph may be taken under this section, the only persons entitled to carry out the search or examination, or to take the photograph, are constables.

(7) A person may not under this section carry out a search or examination of a person of the opposite sex or take a photograph of any part of the body of a person of the opposite sex.

(8) An intimate search may not be carried out under this section.

(9) A photograph taken under this section—

    (a) may be used by, or disclosed to, any person for any purpose related to the prevention or detection of crime, the investigation of an offence or the conduct of a prosecution; and

    (b) after being so used or disclosed, may be retained but may not be used or disclosed except for a purpose so related.

(10) In subsection—

    (a) the reference to crime includes a reference to any conduct which—

        (i) constitutes one or more criminal offences (whether under the law of a part of the United Kingdom or of a country or territory outside the United Kingdom); or

        (ii) is, or corresponds to, any conduct which, if it all took place in any one part of the United Kingdom, would constitute one or more criminal offences;

    and

    (b) the references to an investigation and to a prosecution include references, respectively, to any investigation outside the United Kingdom of any crime or suspected crime and to a prosecution brought in respect of any crime in a country or territory outside the United Kingdom.

(11) In this section—

    (a) references to ascertaining a person's identity include references to showing that he is not a particular person; and

    (b) references to taking a photograph include references to using any process by means of which a visual image may be produced, and references to photographing a person shall be construed accordingly.

(12) In this section 'mark' includes features and injuries; and a mark is an identifying mark for the purposes of this section if its existence in any person's case facilitates the ascertainment of his identity or his identification as a person involved in the commission of an offence.

(13) Nothing in this section applies to a person arrested under an extradition arrest power.

### 54B  Searches of persons answering to live link bail

(1) A constable may search at any time—

    (a) any person who is at a police station to answer to live link bail; and

    (b) any article in the possession of such a person.

(2) If the constable reasonably believes a thing in the possession of the person ought to be seized on any of the grounds mentioned in subsection (3), the constable may seize and retain it or cause it to be seized and retained.

(3) The grounds are that the thing—

(a) may jeopardise the maintenance of order in the police station;

(b) may put the safety of any person in the police station at risk; or

(c) may be evidence of, or in relation to, an offence.

(4) The constable may record or cause to be recorded all or any of the things seized and retained pursuant to subsection (2).

(5) An intimate search may not be carried out under this section.

(6) The constable carrying out a search under subsection (1) must be of the same sex as the person being searched.

(7) In this section 'live link bail' means bail granted under Part 4 of this Act subject to the duty mentioned in section 47(3)(b).

## 54C  Power to retain articles seized

(1) Except as provided by subsections (2) and (3), a constable may retain a thing seized under section 54B until the time when the person from whom it was seized leaves the police station.

(2) A constable may retain a thing seized under section 54B in order to establish its lawful owner, where there are reasonable grounds for believing that it has been obtained in consequence of the commission of an offence.

(3) If a thing seized under section 54B may be evidence of, or in relation to, an offence, a constable may retain it—

(a) for use as evidence at a trial for an offence; or

(b) for forensic examination or for investigation in connection with an offence.

(4) Nothing may be retained for either of the purposes mentioned in subsection (3) if a photograph or copy would be sufficient for that purpose.

(5) Nothing in this section affects any power of a court to make an order under section 1 of the Police (Property) Act 1897.

(6) The references in this section to anything seized under section 54B include anything seized by a person to whom paragraph 27A of Schedule 4 to the Police Reform Act 2002 applies.

## 55  Intimate searches

(1) Subject to the following provisions of this section, if an officer of at least the rank of inspector has reasonable grounds for believing—

(a) that a person who has been arrested and is in police detention may have concealed on him anything which—

(i) he could use to cause physical injury to himself or others; and

(ii) he might so use while he is in police detention or in the custody of a court;

or

(b) that such a person—

(i) may have a Class A drug concealed on him; and

(ii) was in possession of it with the appropriate criminal intent before his arrest,

he may authorise an intimate search of that person.

(2) An officer may not authorise an intimate search of a person for anything unless he has reasonable grounds for believing that it cannot be found without his being intimately searched.

(3) An officer may give an authorisation under subsection (1) above orally or in writing but, if he gives it orally, he shall confirm it in writing as soon as is practicable.

(3A) A drug offence search shall not be carried out unless the appropriate consent has been given in writing.

(3B) Where it is proposed that a drug offence search be carried out, an appropriate officer shall inform the person who is to be subject to it—

(a) of the giving of the authorisation for it; and

(b) of the grounds for giving the authorisation.

(4) An intimate search which is only a drug offence search shall be by way of examination by a suitably qualified person.

(5) Except as provided by subsection (4) above, an intimate search shall be by way of examination by a suitably qualified person unless an officer of at least the rank of inspector considers that this is not practicable.

(6) An intimate search which is not carried out as mentioned in subsection (5) above shall be carried out by a constable.

(7) A constable may not carry out an intimate search of a person of the opposite sex.

(8) No intimate search may be carried out except—

(a) at a police station;

(b) at a hospital;

(c) at a registered medical practitioner's surgery; or

(d) at some other place used for medical purposes.

(9) An intimate search which is only a drug offence search may not be carried out at a police station.

(10) If an intimate search of a person is carried out, the custody record relating to him shall state—

(a) which parts of his body were searched; and

(b) why they were searched.

(10A) If the intimate search is a drug offence search, the custody record relating to that person shall also state—

(a) the authorisation by virtue of which the search was carried out;

(b) the grounds for giving the authorisation; and

(c) the fact that the appropriate consent was given

(11) The information required to be recorded by subsections (10) and (10A) above shall be recorded as soon as practicable after the completion of the search.

(12) The custody officer at a police station may seize and retain anything which is found on an intimate search of a person, or cause any such thing to be seized and retained—

(a) if he believes that the person from whom it is seized may use it—

(i) to cause physical injury to himself or any other person;

(ii) to damage property;

(iii) to interfere with evidence; or

(iv) to assist him to escape; or

(b) if he has reasonable grounds for believing that it may be evidence relating to an offence.

(13) Where anything is seized under this section, the person from whom it is seized shall be told the reason for the seizure unless he is—

(a) violent or likely to become violent; or

(b) incapable of understanding what is said to him.

(13A) Where the appropriate consent to a drug offence search of any person was refused without good cause, in any proceedings against that person for an offence—

(a) the court, in determining whether there is a case to answer;

(b) a judge, in deciding whether to grant an application made by the accused under paragraph 2 of Schedule 3 to the Crime and Disorder Act 1998 (applications for dismissal); and

(c) the court or jury, in determining whether that person is guilty of the offence charged,

may draw such inferences from the refusal as appear proper.

(14)–(16) …*

(17) In this section—

'the appropriate criminal intent' means an intent to commit an offence under—

(a) section 5(3) of the Misuse of Drugs Act 1971 (possession of controlled drug with intent to supply to another); or

(b) section 68(2) of the Customs and Excise Management Act 1979 (exportation etc., with intent to evade a prohibition or restriction);

---

* **Editor's Note:** Information to be contained in annual reports.

'appropriate officer' means—

(a) a constable,

'Class A drug' has the meaning assigned to it by section 2(1)(b) of the Misuse of Drugs Act 1971;

'drug offence search' means an intimate search for a Class A drug which an officer has authorised by virtue of subsection (1)(b) above; and

'suitably qualified person' means—

(a) a registered medical practitioner; or

(b) a registered nurse.

## 55A  X-rays and ultrasound scans

(1) If an officer of at least the rank of inspector has reasonable grounds for believing that a person who has been arrested for an offence and is in police detention—

(a) may have swallowed a Class A drug, and

(b) was in possession of it with the appropriate criminal intent before his arrest,

the officer may authorise that an x-ray is taken of the person or an ultrasound scan is carried out on the person (or both).

(2) An x-ray must not be taken of a person and an ultrasound scan must not be carried out on him unless the appropriate consent has been given in writing.

(3) If it is proposed that an x-ray is taken or an ultrasound scan is carried out, an appropriate officer must inform the person who is to be subject to it—

(a) of the giving of the authorisation for it, and

(b) of the grounds for giving the authorisation.

(4) An x-ray may be taken or an ultrasound scan carried out only by a suitably qualified person and only at—

(a) a hospital,

(b) a registered medical practitioner's surgery, or

(c) some other place used for medical purposes.

(5) The custody record of the person must also state—

(a) the authorisation by virtue of which the x-ray was taken or the ultrasound scan was carried out,

(b) the grounds for giving the authorisation, and

(c) the fact that the appropriate consent was given.

(6) The information required to be recorded by subsection (5) must be recorded as soon as practicable after the x-ray has been taken or ultrasound scan carried out (as the case may be).

(7), (8) ...*

(9) If the appropriate consent to an x-ray or ultrasound scan of any person is refused without good cause, in any proceedings against that person for an offence—

(a) the court, in determining whether there is a case to answer,

(b) a judge, in deciding whether to grant an application made by the accused under paragraph 2 of Schedule 3 to the Crime and Disorder Act 1998 (applications for dismissal), and

(c) the court or jury, in determining whether that person is guilty of the offence charged,

may draw such inferences from the refusal as appear proper.

(10) In this section 'the appropriate criminal intent', 'appropriate officer', 'Class A drug' and 'suitably qualified person' have the same meanings as in section 55 above.

## 56  Right to have someone informed when arrested

(1) Where a person has been arrested and is being held in custody in a police station or other premises, he shall be entitled, if he so requests, to have one friend or relative or other person who is known to him or who is likely to take an interest in his welfare told, as soon as is practicable except to the extent that delay is permitted by this section, that he has been arrested and is being detained there.

* **Editor's Note:** Annual reports.

(2) Delay is only permitted—

(a) in the case of a person who is in police detention for an indictable offence; and

(b) if an officer of at least the rank of inspector authorises it.

(3) In any case the person in custody must be permitted to exercise the right conferred by subsection (1) above within 36 hours from the relevant time, as defined in section 41(2) above.

(4) An officer may give an authorisation under subsection (2) above orally or in writing but, if he gives it orally, he shall confirm it in writing as soon as is practicable.

(5) Subject to subsection (5A) below an officer may only authorise delay where he has reasonable grounds for believing that telling the named person of the arrest—

(a) will lead to interference with or harm to evidence connected with an indictable offence or interference with or physical injury to other persons; or

(b) will lead to the alerting of other persons suspected of having committed such an offence but not yet arrested for it; or

(c) will hinder the recovery of any property obtained as a result of such an offence.

(5A) An officer may also authorise delay where he has reasonable grounds for believing that—

(a) the person detained for the indictable offence has benefited from his criminal conduct, and

(b) the recovery of the value of the property constituting the benefit will be hindered by telling the named person of the arrest.

(5B) For the purposes of subsection (5A) above the question whether a person has benefited from his criminal conduct is to be decided in accordance with Part 2 of the Proceeds of Crime Act 2002.

(6) If a delay is authorised—

(a) the detained person shall be told the reason for it, and

(b) the reason shall be noted on his custody record.

(7) The duties imposed by subsection (6) above shall be performed as soon as is practicable.

(8) The rights conferred by this section on a person detained at a police station or other premises are exercisable whenever he is transferred from one place to another; and this section applies to each subsequent occasion on which they are exercisable as it applies to the first such occasion.

(9) There may be no further delay in permitting the exercise of the right conferred by subsection (1) above once the reason for authorising delay ceases to subsist.

(10) Nothing in this section applies to a person arrested or detained under the terrorism provisions.

## 57    Additional rights of children and young persons

...*

## 58    Access to legal advice

(1) A person arrested and held in custody in a police station or other premises shall be entitled, if he so requests, to consult a solicitor privately at any time.

(2) Subject to subsection (3) below, a request under subsection (1) above and the time at which it was made shall be recorded in the custody record.

(3) Such a request need not be recorded in the custody record of a person who makes it at a time while he is at a court after being charged with an offence.

(4) If a person makes such a request, he must be permitted to consult a solicitor as soon as is practicable except to the extent that delay is permitted by this section.

(5) In any case he must be permitted to consult a solicitor within 36 hours from the relevant time, as defined in section 41(2) above.

(6) Delay in compliance with a request is only permitted—

(a) in the case of a person who is in police detention for an indictable offence; and

(b) if an officer of at least the rank of superintendent authorises it.

---

* **Editor's Note:** Amends the Children and Young Persons Act 1933 section 34(2).

(7) An officer may give an authorisation under subsection (6) above orally or in writing but, if he gives it orally, he shall confirm it in writing as soon as is practicable.

(8) Subject to subsection (8A) below an officer may only authorise delay where he has reasonable grounds for believing that the exercise of the right conferred by subsection (1) above at the time when the person detained desires to exercise it—

    (a) will lead to interference with or harm to evidence connected with an indictable offence or interference with or physical injury to other persons; or

    (b) will lead to the alerting of other persons suspected of having committed such an offence but not yet arrested for it; or

    (c) will hinder the recovery of any property obtained as a result of such an offence.

(8A) An officer may also authorise delay where he has reasonable grounds for believing that—

    (a) the person detained for the indictable offence has benefited from his criminal conduct, and

    (b) the recovery of the value of the property constituting the benefit will be hindered by the exercise of the right conferred by subsection (1) above.

(8B) For the purposes of subsection (8A) above the question whether a person has benefited from his criminal conduct is to be decided in accordance with Part 2 of the Proceeds of Crime Act 2002.

(9) If delay is authorised—

    (a) the detained person shall be told the reason for it; and

    (b) the reason shall be noted on his custody record.

(10) The duties imposed by subsection (9) above shall be performed as soon as is practicable.

(11) There may be no further delay in permitting the exercise of the right conferred by subsection (1) above once the reason for authorising delay ceases to subsist.

(12) Nothing in this section applies to a person arrested or detained under the terrorism provisions.

## 60  Audio recording of interviews

(1) It shall be the duty of the Secretary of State—

    (a) to issue a code of practice in connection with the audio recording of interviews of persons suspected of the commission of criminal offences which are held by police officers at police stations; and

    (b) to make an order requiring the audio recording of interviews of persons suspected of the commission of criminal offences, or of such descriptions of criminal offences as may be specified in the order, which are so held, in accordance with the code as it has effect for the time being.

(2) An order under subsection (1) above shall be made by statutory instrument and shall be subject to annulment in pursuance of a resolution of either House of Parliament.

## 60A  Visual recording of interviews

(1) The Secretary of State shall have power—

    (a) to issue a code of practice for the visual recording of interviews held by police officers at police stations; and

    (b) to make an order requiring the visual recording of interviews so held, and requiring the visual recording to be in accordance with the code for the time being in force under this section.

(2) A requirement imposed by an order under this section may be imposed in relation to such cases or police stations in such areas, or both, as may be specified or described in the order.

(3) An order under subsection (1) above shall be made by statutory instrument and shall be subject to annulment in pursuance of a resolution of either House of Parliament.

(4) In this section—

    (a) references to any interview are references to an interview of a person suspected of a criminal offence; and

    (b) references to a visual recording include references to a visual recording in which an audio recording is comprised.

### 60B    Notification of decision not to prosecute person interviewed

(1)  This section applies where—

(a)  a person suspected of the commission of a criminal offence is interviewed by a police officer but is not arrested for the offence, and

(b)  the police officer in charge of investigating the offence determines that—

(i)    there is not sufficient evidence to charge the person with an offence, or

(ii)   there is sufficient evidence to charge the person with an offence but the person should not be charged with an offence or given a caution in respect of an offence.

(2)  A police officer must give the person notice in writing that the person is not to be prosecuted.

(3)  Subsection (2) does not prevent the prosecution of the person for an offence if new evidence comes to light after the notice was given.

(4)  In this section 'caution' includes—

(a)  a conditional caution within the meaning of Part 3 of the Criminal Justice Act 2003;

(b)  a youth conditional caution within the meaning of Chapter 1 of Part 4 of the Crime and Disorder Act 1998;

(c)  a youth caution under section 66ZA of that Act.

## 61    Finger-printing

(1)  Except as provided by this section no person's fingerprints may be taken without the appropriate consent.

(2)  Consent to the taking of a person's fingerprints must be in writing if it is given at a time when he is at a police station.

(3)  The fingerprints of a person detained at a police station may be taken without the appropriate consent if—

(a)  he is detained in consequence of his arrest for a recordable offence; and

(b)  he has not had his fingerprints taken in the course of the investigation of the offence by the police.

(3A)  Where a person mentioned in paragraph (a) of subsection (3) or (4) has already had his fingerprints taken in the course of the investigation of the offence by the police, that fact shall be disregarded for the purposes of that subsection if—

(a)  the fingerprints taken on the previous occasion do not constitute a complete set of his fingerprints; or

(b)  some or all of the fingerprints taken on the previous occasion are not of sufficient quality to allow satisfactory analysis, comparison or matching (whether in the case in question or generally).

(4)  The fingerprints of a person detained at a police station may be taken without the appropriate consent if—

(a)  he has been charged with a recordable offence or informed that he will be reported for such an offence; and

(b)  he has not had his fingerprints taken in the course of the investigation of the offence by the police.

(4A)  The fingerprints of a person who has answered to bail at a court or police station may be taken without the appropriate consent at the court or station if—

(a)  the court, or

(b)  an officer of at least the rank of inspector,

authorises them to be taken.

(4B)  A court or officer may only give an authorisation under subsection (4A) if—

(a)  the person who has answered to bail has answered to it for a person whose fingerprints were taken on a previous occasion and there are reasonable grounds for believing that he is not the same person; or

(b)  the person who has answered to bail claims to be a different person from a person whose fingerprints were taken on a previous occasion.

(5) An officer may give an authorisation under subsection (4A) above orally or in writing but, if he gives it orally, he shall confirm it in writing as soon as is practicable.

(5A) The fingerprints of a person may be taken without the appropriate consent if (before or after the coming into force of this subsection) he has been arrested for a recordable offence and released and—

> (a) ... he has not had his fingerprints taken in the course of the investigation of the offence by the police; or
>
> (b) ... he has had his fingerprints taken in the course of that investigation but
>
>> (i)    subsection (3A)(a) or (b) above applies, or
>>
>> (ii)   subsection (5C) below applies.

(5B) The fingerprints of a person not detained at a police station may be taken without the appropriate consent if (before or after the coming into force of this subsection) he has been charged with a recordable offence or informed that he will be reported for such an offence and—

> (a) he has not had his fingerprints taken in the course of the investigation of the offence by the police; or
>
> (b) he has had his fingerprints taken in the course of that investigation but
>
>> (i)    subsection (3A)(a) or (b) above applies, or
>>
>> (ii)   subsection (5C) below applies.

(5C) This subsection applies where—

> (a) the investigation was discontinued but subsequently resumed, and
>
> (b) before the resumption of the investigation the fingerprints were destroyed pursuant to section 63D(3) below.

(6) Subject to this section, the fingerprints of a person may be taken without the appropriate consent if (before or after the coming into force of this subsection)—

> (a) he has been convicted of a recordable offence, or
>
> (b) he has been given a caution in respect of a recordable offence which, at the time of the caution, he has admitted, and

either of the conditions mentioned in subsection (6ZA) below is met.

(6ZA) The conditions referred to in subsection (6) above are—

> (a) the person has not had his fingerprints taken since he was cautioned;
>
> (b) he has had his fingerprints taken since then but subsection (3A)(a) or (b) above applies.

(6ZB) Fingerprints may only be taken as specified in subsection (6) above with the authorisation of an officer of at least the rank of inspector.

(6ZC) An officer may only give an authorisation under subsection (6ZB) above if the officer is satisfied that taking the fingerprints is necessary to assist in the prevention or detection of crime.

(6A) A constable may take a person's fingerprints without the appropriate consent if—

> (a) the constable reasonably suspects that the person is committing or attempting to commit an offence, or has committed or attempted to commit an offence; and
>
> (b) either of the two conditions mentioned in subsection (6B) is met.

(6B) The conditions are that—

> (a) the name of the person is unknown to, and cannot be readily ascertained by, the constable;
>
> (b) the constable has reasonable grounds for doubting whether a name furnished by the person as his name is his real name.

(6C) The taking of fingerprints by virtue of subsection (6A) or (6BA) does not count for any of the purposes of this Act as taking them in the course of the investigation of an offence by the police.

(6D) Subject to this section, the fingerprints of a person may be taken without the appropriate consent if—

> (a) under the law in force in a country or territory outside England and Wales the person has been convicted of an offence under that law (whether before or after the coming into force of this subsection and whether or not he has been punished for it);
>
> (b) the act constituting the offence would constitute a qualifying offence if done in England and Wales (whether or not it constituted such an offence when the person was convicted); and

(c) either of the conditions mentioned in subsection (6E) below is met.

(6E) The conditions referred to in subsection (6D)(c) above are—

(a) the person has not had his fingerprints taken on a previous occasion under subsection (6D) above;

(b) he has had his fingerprints taken on a previous occasion under that subsection but subsection (3A)(a) or (b) above applies.

(6F) Fingerprints may only be taken as specified in subsection (6D) above with the authorisation of an officer of at least the rank of inspector.

(6G) An officer may only give an authorisation under subsection (6F) above if the officer is satisfied that taking the fingerprints is necessary to assist in the prevention or detection of crime.

(7) Where a person's fingerprints are taken without the appropriate consent by virtue of any power conferred by this section—

(a) before the fingerprints are taken, the person shall be informed of—

(i) the reason for taking the fingerprints;

(ii) the power by virtue of which they are taken; and

(iii) in a case where the authorisation of the court or an officer is required for the exercise of the power, the fact that the authorisation has been given; and

(b) those matters shall be recorded as soon as practicable after the fingerprints are taken.

(7A) If a person's fingerprints are taken at a police station or by virtue of subsection (4A), (6A) at a place other than a police station, whether with or without the appropriate consent—

(a) before the fingerprints are taken, an officer (or, where by virtue of subsection (4A), (6A) or (6BA) the fingerprints are taken at a place other than a police station, the constable taking the fingerprints) shall inform him that they may be the subject of a speculative search; and

(b) the fact that the person has been informed of this possibility shall be recorded as soon as is practicable after the fingerprints have been taken.

(8) If he is detained at a police station when the fingerprints are taken, the matters referred to in subsection (7)(a)(i) to (iii) above and, in the case falling within subsection (7A) above, the fact referred to in paragraph (b) of that subsection shall be recorded on his custody record.

(8B) Any power under this section to take the fingerprints of a person without the appropriate consent, if not otherwise specified to be exercisable by a constable, shall be exercisable by a constable.

(9) Nothing in this section—

(a) affects any power conferred by paragraph 18(2) of Schedule 2 to the Immigration Act 1971; or

(b) applies to a person arrested or detained under the terrorism provisions.

(10) Nothing in this section applies to a person arrested under an extradition arrest power.

### 61A Impressions of footwear

(1) Except as provided by this section, no impression of a person's footwear may be taken without the appropriate consent.

(2) Consent to the taking of an impression of a person's footwear must be in writing if it is given at a time when he is at a police station.

(3) Where a person is detained at a police station, an impression of his footwear may be taken without the appropriate consent if—

(a) he is detained in consequence of his arrest for a recordable offence, or has been charged with a recordable offence, or informed that he will be reported for a recordable offence; and

(b) he has not had an impression taken of his footwear in the course of the investigation of the offence by the police.

(4) Where a person mentioned in paragraph (a) of subsection (3) above has already had an impression taken of his footwear in the course of the investigation of the offence by the police, that fact shall be disregarded for the purposes of that subsection if the impression of his footwear taken previously is—

(a) incomplete; or

(b) is not of sufficient quality to allow satisfactory analysis, comparison or matching (whether in the case in question or generally).

(5) If an impression of a person's footwear is taken at a police station, whether with or without the appropriate consent—

(a) before it is taken, an officer shall inform him that it may be the subject of a speculative search; and

(b) the fact that the person has been informed of this possibility shall be recorded as soon as is practicable after the impression has been taken, and if he is detained at a police station, the record shall be made on his custody record.

(6) In a case where, by virtue of subsection (3) above, an impression of a person's footwear is taken without the appropriate consent—

(a) he shall be told the reason before it is taken; and

(b) the reason shall be recorded on his custody record as soon as is practicable after the impression is taken.

(7) The power to take an impression of the footwear of a person detained at a police station without the appropriate consent shall be exercisable by any constable.

(8) Nothing in this section applies to any person—

(a) arrested or detained under the terrorism provisions;

(b) arrested under an extradition arrest power.

## 62   Intimate samples

(1) Subject to section 63B below an intimate sample may be taken from a person in police detention only—

(a) if a police officer of at least the rank of inspector authorises it to be taken; and

(b) if the appropriate consent is given.

(1A) An intimate sample may be taken from a person who is not in police detention but from whom, in the course of the investigation of an offence, two or more non-intimate samples suitable for the same means of analysis have been taken which have proved insufficient—

(a) if a police officer of at least the rank of inspector authorises it to be taken; and

(b) if the appropriate consent is given.

(2) An officer may only give an authorisation under subsection (1) or (1A) above if he has reasonable grounds—

(a) for suspecting the involvement of the person from whom the sample is to be taken in a recordable offence; and

(b) for believing that the sample will tend to confirm or disprove his involvement.

(2A)  An intimate sample may be taken from a person where—

(a) two or more non-intimate samples suitable for the same means of analysis have been taken from the person under section 63(3E) below (persons convicted of offences outside England and Wales etc.) but have proved insufficient;

(b) a police officer of at least the rank of inspector authorises it to be taken; and

(c) the appropriate consent is given.

(2B) An officer may only give an authorisation under subsection (2A) above if the officer is satisfied that taking the sample is necessary to assist in the prevention or detection of crime.

(3) An officer may give an authorisation under subsection (1) or (1A) or (2A) above orally or in writing but, if he gives it orally, he shall confirm it in writing as soon as is practicable.

(4) The appropriate consent must be given in writing.

(5) Before an intimate sample is taken from a person, an officer shall inform him of the following—

(a) the reason for taking the sample;

(b) the fact that authorisation has been given and the provision of this section under which it has been given; and

(c) if the sample was taken at a police station, the fact that the sample may be the subject of a speculative search.

(6) The reason referred to in subsection (5)(a) above must include, except in a case where the sample is taken under subsection (2A) above, a statement of the nature of the offence in which it is suspected that the person has been involved.

(7) After an intimate sample has been taken from a person, the following shall be recorded as soon as practicable—

(a) the matters referred to in subsection (5)(a) and (b) above;

(b) if the sample was taken at a police station, the fact that the person has been informed as specified in subsection (5)(c) above; and

(c) the fact that the appropriate consent was given.

(8) If an intimate sample is taken from a person detained at a police station, the matters required to be recorded by subsection (7) above shall be recorded in his custody record.

(9) In the case of an intimate sample which is a dental impression, the sample may be taken from a person only by a registered dentist.

(9A) In the case of any other form of intimate sample, except in the case of a sample of urine, the sample may be taken from a person only by—

(a) a registered medical practitioner; or

(b) a registered health care professional.

(10) Where the appropriate consent to the taking of an intimate sample from a person was refused without good cause, in any proceedings against that person for an offence—

(a) the court, in determining—

(ii) whether there is a case to answer; and

(aa) a judge, in deciding whether to grant an application made by the accused under—

(i) paragraph 2 of Schedule 3 to the Crime and Disorder Act 1998 (applications for dismissal); and

(b) the court or jury, in determining whether that person is guilty of the offence charged, may draw such inferences from the refusal as appear proper.

(11) Nothing in this section applies to the taking of a specimen for the purposes of any of the provisions of sections 4 to 11 of the Road Traffic Act 1988 or of sections 26 to 38 of the Transport and Works Act 1992.

(12) Nothing in this section applies to a person arrested or detained under the terrorism provisions; and subsection (1A) shall not apply where the non-intimate samples mentioned in that subsection were taken under paragraph 10 of Schedule 8 to the Terrorism Act 2000.

### 63   Other samples

(1) Except as provided by this section, a non-intimate sample may not be taken from a person without the appropriate consent.

(2) Consent to the taking of a non-intimate sample must be given in writing.

(2A) A non-intimate sample may be taken from a person without the appropriate consent if two conditions are satisfied.

(2B) The first is that the person is in police detention in consequence of his arrest for a recordable offence.

(2C) The second is that—

(a) he has not had a non-intimate sample of the same type and from the same part of the body taken in the course of the investigation of the offence by the police, or

(b) he has had such a sample taken but it proved insufficient.

(3) A non-intimate sample may be taken from a person without the appropriate consent if—

(a) he is being held in custody by the police on the authority of a court; and

(b) an officer of at least the rank of inspector authorises it to be taken without the appropriate consent.

(3ZA)  A non-intimate sample may be taken from a person without the appropriate consent if (before or after the coming into force of this subsection) he has been arrested for a recordable offence and released and—

    (a)  he has not had a non-intimate sample of the same type and from the same part of the body taken from him in the course of the investigation of the offence by the police; or

    (b)  he has had a non-intimate sample taken from him in the course of that investigation but—

        (i)  it was not suitable for the same means of analysis, or

        (ii)  it proved insufficient, or

        (iii)  subsection (3AA) below applies.

(3A)  A non-intimate sample may be taken from a person (whether or not he is in police detention or held in custody by the police on the authority of a court) without the appropriate consent if he has been charged with a recordable offence or informed that he will be reported for such an offence and—

    (a)  he has not had a non-intimate sample taken from him in the course of the investigation of the offence by the police; or

    (b)  he has had a non-intimate sample taken from him in the course of that investigation but—

        (i)  it was not suitable for the same means of analysis, or

        (ii)  it proved insufficient, or

        (iii)  subsection (3AA) below applies; or

    (c)  he has had a non-intimate sample taken from him in the course of that investigation and—

        (i)  the sample has been destroyed pursuant to section 63R below or any other enactment, and

        (ii)  it is disputed, in relation to any proceedings relating to the offence, whether a DNA profile relevant to the proceedings is derived from the sample.

(3AA)  This subsection applies where the investigation was discontinued but subsequently resumed, and before the resumption of the investigation—

    (a)  any DNA profile derived from the sample was destroyed pursuant to section 63D(3) below, and

    (b)  the sample itself was destroyed pursuant to section 63R(4), (5) or (12) below.

(3B)  Subject to this section, a non-intimate sample may be taken from a person without the appropriate consent if (before or after the coming into force of this subsection)—

    (a)  he has been convicted of a recordable offence,

    (b)  he has been given a caution in respect of a recordable offence which, at the time of the caution, he has admitted

and

either of the conditions mentioned in subsection (3BA) below is met.

(3BA)  The conditions referred to in subsection (3B) above are—

    (a)  a non-intimate sample has not been taken from the person since he was convicted, cautioned or warned or reprimanded;

    (b)  such a sample has been taken from him since then but—

        (i)  it was not suitable for the same means of analysis, or

        (ii)  it proved insufficient.

(3BB)  A non-intimate sample may only be taken as specified in subsection (3B) above with the authorisation of an officer of at least the rank of inspector.

(3BC)  An officer may only give an authorisation under subsection (3BB) above if the officer is satisfied that taking the sample is necessary to assist in the prevention or detection of crime.

(3C)  A non-intimate sample may also be taken from a person without the appropriate consent if he is a person to whom section 2 of the Criminal Evidence (Amendment) Act 1997 applies (persons detained following acquittal on grounds of insanity or finding of unfitness to plead).

(3E)  Subject to this section, a non-intimate sample may be taken without the appropriate consent from a person if—

(a) under the law in force in a country or territory outside England and Wales the person has been convicted of an offence under that law (whether before or after the coming into force of this subsection and whether or not he has been punished for it);

(b) the act constituting the offence would constitute a qualifying offence if done in England and Wales (whether or not it constituted such an offence when the person was convicted); and

(c) either of the conditions mentioned in subsection (3F) below is met.

(3F)  The conditions referred to in subsection (3E)(c) above are—

(a) the person has not had a non-intimate sample taken from him on a previous occasion under subsection (3E) above;

(b) he has had such a sample taken from him on a previous occasion under that subsection but—

   (i)   the sample was not suitable for the same means of analysis, or

   (ii)  it proved insufficient.

(3G)  A non-intimate sample may only be taken as specified in subsection (3E) above with the authorisation of an officer of at least the rank of inspector.

(3H)  An officer may only give an authorisation under subsection (3G) above if the officer is satisfied that taking the sample is necessary to assist in the prevention or detection of crime.

(4)  An officer may only give an authorisation under subsection (3) above if he has reasonable grounds—

(a) for suspecting the involvement of the person from whom the sample is to be taken in a recordable offence; and

(b) for believing that the sample will tend to confirm or disprove his involvement.

(5)  An officer may give an authorisation under subsection (3) above orally or in writing but, if he gives it orally, he shall confirm it in writing as soon as is practicable.

(5A)  An officer shall not give an authorisation under subsection (3) above for the taking from any person of a non-intimate sample consisting of a skin impression if—

(a) a skin impression of the same part of the body has already been taken from that person in the course of the investigation of the offence; and

(b) the impression previously taken is not one that has proved insufficient.

(6)  Where a non-intimate sample is taken from a person without the appropriate consent by virtue of any power conferred by this section—

(a) before the sample is taken, an officer shall inform him of—

   (i)   the reason for taking the sample;

   (ii)  the power by virtue of which it is taken; and

   (iii) in a case where the authorisation of an officer is required for the exercise of the power, the fact that the authorisation has been given; and

(b) those matters shall be recorded as soon as practicable after the sample is taken.

(7)  The reason referred to in subsection (6)(a)(i) above must include, except in a case where the non-intimate sample is taken under subsection (3B) or (3E) above, a statement of the nature of the offence in which it is suspected that the person has been involved.

(8B)  If a non-intimate sample is taken from a person at a police station, whether with or without the appropriate consent—

(a) before the sample is taken, an officer shall inform him that it may be the subject of a speculative search; and

(b) the fact that the person has been informed of this possibility shall be recorded as soon as practicable after the sample has been taken.

(9)  If a non-intimate sample is taken from a person detained at a police station, the matters required to be recorded by subsection (6) or (8B) above shall be recorded in his custody record.

(9ZA)  The power to take a non-intimate sample from a person without the appropriate consent shall be exercisable by any constable.

(9A)  Subsection (3B) above shall not apply to

(a) any person convicted before 10 April 1995 unless he is a person to whom section 1 of the Criminal Evidence (Amendment) Act 1997 applies (persons imprisoned or detained by virtue of pre-existing conviction for sexual offence etc.); or

(b) a person given a caution after 10 April 1995.

(10) Nothing in this section applies to a person arrested or detained under the terrorism provisions.

(11) Nothing in this section applies to a person arrested under an extradition arrest power.

## 63A    Fingerprints and samples: supplementary provisions

(1) Where a person has been arrested on suspicion of being involved in a recordable offence or has been charged with such an offence or has been informed that he will be reported for such an offence, fingerprints, impressions of footwear or samples or the information derived from samples taken under any power conferred by this Part of this Act from the person may be checked against—

(a) other fingerprints impressions of footwear or samples to which the person seeking to check has access and which are held by or on behalf of any one or more relevant law-enforcement authorities or which are held in connection with or as a result of an investigation of an offence;

(b) information derived from other samples if the information is contained in records to which the person seeking to check has access and which are held as mentioned in paragraph (a) above.

(1ZA) Fingerprints taken by virtue of section 61(6A) above may be checked against other fingerprints to which the person seeking to check has access and which are held by or on behalf of any one or more relevant law-enforcement authorities or which are held in connection with or as a result of an investigation of an offence.

(1A) In subsection (1) and (1ZA) above 'relevant law-enforcement authority' means—

(a) a police force;

(b) the National Crime Agency;

(d) a public authority (not falling within paragraphs (a) to (c)) with functions in any part of the British Islands which consist of or include the investigation of crimes or the charging of offenders;

(e) any person with functions in any country or territory outside the United Kingdom which—

(i) correspond to those of a police force; or

(ii) otherwise consist of or include the investigation of conduct contrary to the law of that country or territory, or the apprehension of persons guilty of such conduct;

(f) any person with functions under any international agreement which consist of or include the investigation of conduct which is—

(i) unlawful under the law of one or more places,

(ii) prohibited by such an agreement, or

(iii) contrary to international law,

or the apprehension of persons guilty of such conduct.

(1B) The reference in subsection (1A) above to a police force is a reference to any of the following—

(a) any police force maintained under section 2 of the Police Act 1996 (police forces in England and Wales outside London);

(b) the metropolitan police force;

(c) the City of London police force;

(d)–(o) …*

---

* **Editor's Note:** Applies to other forces.

(1C) Where—

  (a) fingerprints, impressions of footwear or samples have been taken from any person in connection with the investigation of an offence but otherwise than in circumstances to which subsection (1) above applies, and

  (b) that person has given his consent in writing to the use in a speculative search of the fingerprints, of the impressions of footwear or of the samples and of information derived from them,

the fingerprints or impressions of footwear or, as the case may be, those samples and that information may be checked against any of the fingerprints, impressions of footwear, samples or information mentioned in paragraph (a) or (b) of that subsection.

(1D) A consent given for the purposes of subsection (1C) above shall not be capable of being withdrawn.

(1E) Where fingerprints or samples have been taken from any person under section 61(6) or 63(3B) above (persons convicted etc.), the fingerprints or samples, or information derived from the samples, may be checked against any of the fingerprints, samples or information mentioned in subsection (1)(a) or (b) above.

(1F) Where fingerprints or samples have been taken from any person under section 61(6D), 62(2A) or 63(3E) above (offences outside England and Wales etc.), the fingerprints or samples, or information derived from the samples, may be checked against any of the fingerprints, samples or information mentioned in subsection (1)(a) or (b) above.

(2) Where a sample of hair other than pubic hair is to be taken the sample may be taken either by cutting hairs or by plucking hairs with their roots so long as no more are plucked than the person taking the sample reasonably considers to be necessary for a sufficient sample.

(3) Where any power to take a sample is exercisable in relation to a person the sample may be taken in a prison or other institution to which the Prison Act 1952 applies.

(3A) Where—

  (a) the power to take a non-intimate sample under section 63(3B) above is exercisable in relation to any person who is detained under Part III of the Mental Health Act 1983 in pursuance of—

    (i) a hospital order or interim hospital order made following his conviction for the recordable offence in question, or

    (ii) a transfer direction given at a time when he was detained in pursuance of any sentence or order imposed following that conviction, or

  (b) the power to take a non-intimate sample under section 63(3C) above is exercisable in relation to any person,

the sample may be taken in the hospital in which he is detained under that Part of that Act.

Expressions used in this subsection and in the Mental Health Act 1983 have the same meaning as in that Act.

(3B) Where the power to take a non-intimate sample under section 63(3B) above is exercisable in relation to a person detained in pursuance of directions of the Secretary of State under section 92 of the Powers of Criminal Courts (Sentencing) Act 2000 the sample may be taken at the place where he is so detained.

(4) Schedule 2A (fingerprinting and samples: power to require attendance at police station) shall have effect.

### 63AA   Inclusion of DNA profiles on National DNA Database

(1) This section applies to a DNA profile which is derived from a DNA sample and which is retained under any power conferred by any of sections 63E to 63L (including those sections as applied by section 63P).

(2) A DNA profile to which this section applies must be recorded on the National DNA Database.

### 63AB    National DNA Database Strategy Board

(1) The Secretary of State must make arrangements for a National DNA Database Strategy Board to oversee the operation of the National DNA Database.

(2) The National DNA Database Strategy Board must issue guidance about the destruction of DNA profiles which are, or may be, retained under this Part of this Act.

(3) A chief officer of a police force in England and Wales must act in accordance with guidance issued under subsection (2).

(4) The National DNA Database Strategy Board may issue guidance about the circumstances in which applications may be made to the Commissioner for the Retention and Use of Biometric Material under section 63G.

(5) Before issuing any such guidance, the National DNA Database Strategy Board must consult the Commissioner for the Retention and Use of Biometric Material.

(6) The Secretary of State must publish the governance rules of the National DNA Database Strategy Board and lay a copy of the rules before Parliament.

(7) The National DNA Database Strategy Board must make an annual report to the Secretary of State about the exercise of its functions.

(8) The Secretary of State must publish the report and lay a copy of the published report before Parliament.

(9) The Secretary of State may exclude from publication any part of the report if, in the opinion of the Secretary of State, the publication of that part would be contrary to the public interest or prejudicial to national security.

### 63B    Testing for presence of Class A drugs

(1) A sample of urine or a non-intimate sample may be taken from a person in police detention for the purpose of ascertaining whether he has any specified Class A drug in his body if—

    (a) either the arrest condition or the charge condition is met;

    (b) both the age condition and the request condition are met; and

    (c) the notification condition is met in relation to the arrest condition, the charge condition or the age condition (as the case may be).

(1A) The arrest condition is that the person concerned has been arrested for an offence but has not been charged with that offence and either—

    (a) the offence is a trigger offence; or

    (b) a police officer of at least the rank of inspector has reasonable grounds for suspecting that the misuse by that person of a specified Class A drug caused or contributed to the offence and has authorised the sample to be taken.

(2) The charge condition is either—

    (a) that the person concerned has been charged with a trigger offence; or

    (b) that the person concerned has been charged with an offence and a police officer of at least the rank of inspector, who has reasonable grounds for suspecting that the misuse by that person of any specified Class A drug caused or contributed to the offence, has authorised the sample to be taken.

(3) The age condition is—

    (a) if the arrest condition is met, that the person concerned has attained the age of 18;

    (b) if the charge condition is met, that he has attained the age of 14.

(4) The request condition is that a police officer has requested the person concerned to give the sample.

(4A) The notification condition is that—

    (a) the relevant chief officer has been notified by the Secretary of State that appropriate arrangements have been made for the police area as a whole, or for the particular police station, in which the person is in police detention, and

    (b) the notice has not been withdrawn.

(4B) For the purposes of subsection (4A) above, appropriate arrangements are arrangements for the taking of samples under this section from whichever of the following is specified in the notification—

(a) persons in respect of whom the arrest condition is met;

(b) persons in respect of whom the charge condition is met;

(c) persons who have not attained the age of 18.

(5) Before requesting the person concerned to give a sample, an officer must—

(a) warn him that if, when so requested, he fails without good cause to do so he may be liable to prosecution, and

(b) in a case within subsection (1A)(b) or (2)(b) above, inform him of the giving of the authorisation and of the grounds in question.

(5A) In the case of a person who has not attained the age of 18—

(a) the making of the request under subsection (4) above;

(b) the giving of the warning and (where applicable) the information under subsection (5) above; and

(c) the taking of the sample,

may not take place except in the presence of an appropriate adult.

(5B) If a sample is taken under this section from a person in respect of whom the arrest condition is met no other sample may be taken from him under this section during the same continuous period of detention but—

(a) if the charge condition is also met in respect of him at any time during that period, the sample must be treated as a sample taken by virtue of the fact that the charge condition is met;

(b) the fact that the sample is to be so treated must be recorded in the person's custody record.

(5C) Despite subsection (1)(a) above, a sample may be taken from a person under this section if—

(a) he was arrested for an offence (the first offence),

(b) the arrest condition is met but the charge condition is not met,

(c) before a sample is taken by virtue of subsection (1) above he would (but for his arrest as mentioned in paragraph (d) below) be required to be released from police detention,

(d) he continues to be in police detention by virtue of his having been arrested for an offence not falling within subsection (1A) above, and

(e) the sample is taken before the end of the period of 24 hours starting with the time when his detention by virtue of his arrest for the first offence began.

(5D) A sample must not be taken from a person under this section if he is detained in a police station unless he has been brought before the custody officer.

(6) A sample may be taken under this section only by a person prescribed by regulations made by the Secretary of State by statutory instrument.

No regulations shall be made under this subsection unless a draft has been laid before, and approved by resolution of, each House of Parliament.

(6A) The Secretary of State may by order made by statutory instrument amend—

(a) paragraph (a) of subsection (3) above, by substituting for the age for the time being specified a different age specified in the order, or different ages so specified for different police areas so specified;

(b) paragraph (b) of that subsection, by substituting for the age for the time being specified a different age specified in the order.

(6B) A statutory instrument containing an order under subsection (6A) above shall not be made unless a draft of the instrument has been laid before, and approved by a resolution of, each House of Parliament.

(7) Information obtained from a sample taken under this section may be disclosed—

(a) for the purpose of informing any decision about granting bail in criminal proceedings (within the meaning of the Bail Act 1976) to the person concerned;

(aa) for the purpose of informing any decision about the giving of a conditional caution under Part 3 of the Criminal Justice Act 2003 or a youth conditional caution under Chapter 1 of Part 4 of the Crime and Disorder Act 1998 to the person concerned;

(b) where the person concerned is in police detention or is remanded in or committed to custody by an order of a court or has been granted such bail, for the purpose of informing any decision about his supervision;

(c) where the person concerned is convicted of an offence, for the purpose of informing any decision about the appropriate sentence to be passed by a court and any decision about his supervision or release;

(ca) for the purpose of an assessment which the person concerned is required to attend by virtue of section 9(2) or 10(2) of the Drugs Act 2005;

(cb) for the purpose of proceedings against the person concerned for an offence under section 12(3) or 14(3) of that Act;

(d) for the purpose of ensuring that appropriate advice and treatment is made available to the person concerned.

(8) A person who fails without good cause to give any sample which may be taken from him under this section shall be guilty of an offence.

(10) In this section—

'appropriate adult', in relation to a person who has not attained the age of 18, means—

(a) his parent or guardian or, if he is in the care of a local authority or voluntary organisation, a person representing that authority or organisation; or

(b) a social worker of a local authority; or

(c) if no person falling within paragraph (a) or (b) is available, any responsible person aged 18 or over who is not a police officer or a person employed by the police;

'relevant chief officer' means—

(a) in relation to a police area, the chief officer of police of the police force for that police area; or

(b) in relation to a police station, the chief officer of police of the police force for the police area in which the police station is situated.

### 63C   Testing for presence of Class A drugs: supplementary

(1) A person guilty of an offence under section 63B above shall be liable on summary conviction to imprisonment for a term not exceeding three months, or to a fine not exceeding level 4 on the standard scale, or to both.

(2) A police officer may give an authorisation under section 63B above orally or in writing but, if he gives it orally, he shall confirm it in writing as soon as is practicable.

(3) If a sample is taken under section 63B above by virtue of an authorisation, the authorisation and the grounds for the suspicion shall be recorded as soon as is practicable after the sample is taken.

(4) If the sample is taken from a person detained at a police station, the matters required to be recorded by subsection (3) above shall be recorded in his custody record.

(5) Subsections (11) and (12) of section 62 above apply for the purposes of section 63B above as they do for the purposes of that section; and section 63B above does not prejudice the generality of sections 62 and 63 above.

(6) In section 63B above—

'Class A drug' and 'misuse' have the same meanings as in the Misuse of Drugs Act 1971;

'specified' (in relation to a Class A drug) and 'trigger offence' have the same meanings as in Part III of the Criminal Justice and Court Services Act 2000.

### 63D   Destruction of fingerprints and DNA profiles

(1) This section applies to—

(a) fingerprints—

(i) taken from a person under any power conferred by this Part of this Act, or

(ii) taken by the police, with the consent of the person from whom they were taken, in connection with the investigation of an offence by the police, and

(b) a DNA profile derived from a DNA sample taken as mentioned in paragraph (a)(i) or (ii).

(2) Fingerprints and DNA profiles to which this section applies ('section 63D material') must be destroyed if it appears to the responsible chief officer of police that—

(a) the taking of the fingerprint or, in the case of a DNA profile, the taking of the sample from which the DNA profile was derived, was unlawful, or

(b) the fingerprint was taken, or, in the case of a DNA profile, was derived from a sample taken, from a person in connection with that person's arrest and the arrest was unlawful or based on mistaken identity.

(3) In any other case, section 63D material must be destroyed unless it is retained under any power conferred by sections 63E to 63O (including those sections as applied by section 63P).

(4) Section 63D material which ceases to be retained under a power mentioned in subsection (3) may continue to be retained under any other such power which applies to it.

(5) Nothing in this section prevents a speculative search, in relation to section 63D material, from being carried out within such time as may reasonably be required for the search if the responsible chief officer of police considers the search to be desirable.

### 63E    Retention of section 63D material pending investigation or proceedings

(1) This section applies to section 63D material taken (or, in the case of a DNA profile, derived from a sample taken) in connection with the investigation of an offence in which it is suspected that the person to whom the material relates has been involved.

(2) The material may be retained until the conclusion of the investigation of the offence or, where the investigation gives rise to proceedings against the person for the offence, until the conclusion of those proceedings.

### 63F    Retention of section 63D material: persons arrested for or charged with a qualifying offence

(1) This section applies to section 63D material which—

(a) relates to a person who is arrested for, or charged with, a qualifying offence but is not convicted of that offence, and

(b) was taken (or, in the case of a DNA profile, derived from a sample taken) in connection with the investigation of the offence.

(2) If the person has previously been convicted of a recordable offence which is not an excluded offence, or is so convicted before the material is required to be destroyed by virtue of this section, the material may be retained indefinitely.

(2A) In subsection (2), references to a recordable offence include an offence under the law of a country or territory outside England and Wales where the act constituting the offence would constitute a recordable offence if done in England and Wales (and, in the application of subsection (2) where a person has previously been convicted, this applies whether or not the act constituted such an offence when the person was convicted).

(3) Otherwise, material falling within subsection (4) or (5) may be retained until the end of the retention period specified in subsection (6).

(4) Material falls within this subsection if it—

(a) relates to a person who is charged with a qualifying offence but is not convicted of that offence, and

(b) was taken (or, in the case of a DNA profile, derived from a sample taken) in connection with the investigation of the offence.

(5) Material falls within this subsection if—

(a) it relates to a person who is arrested for a qualifying offence but is not charged with that offence,

(b) it was taken (or, in the case of a DNA profile, derived from a sample taken) in connection with the investigation of the offence, and

(c) the Commissioner for the Retention and Use of Biometric Material has consented under section 63G to the retention of the material.

(6) The retention period is—

    (a) in the case of fingerprints, the period of 3 years beginning with the date on which the fingerprints were taken, and

    (b) in the case of a DNA profile, the period of 3 years beginning with the date on which the DNA sample from which the profile was derived was taken (or, if the profile was derived from more than one DNA sample, the date on which the first of those samples was taken).

(7) The responsible chief officer of police or a specified chief officer of police may apply to a District Judge (Magistrates' Courts) for an order extending the retention period.

(8) An application for an order under subsection (7) must be made within the period of 3 months ending on the last day of the retention period.

(9) An order under subsection (7) may extend the retention period by a period which—

    (a) begins with the end of the retention period, and

    (b) ends with the end of the period of 2 years beginning with the end of the retention period.

(10) The following persons may appeal to the Crown Court against an order under subsection (7), or a refusal to make such an order—

    (a) the responsible chief officer of police;

    (b) a specified chief officer of police;

    (c) the person from whom the material was taken.

(11) In this section—

'excluded offence', in relation to a person, means a recordable offence—

    (a) which—

        (i)   is not a qualifying offence,

        (ii)   is the only recordable offence of which the person has been convicted, and

        (iii)   was committed when the person was aged under 18, and

    (b) for which the person was not given a relevant custodial sentence of 5 years or more,

'relevant custodial sentence' has the meaning given by section 63K(6),

'a specified chief officer of police' means—

    (a) the chief officer of the police force of the area in which the person from whom the material was taken resides, or

    (b) a chief officer of police who believes that the person is in, or is intending to come to, the chief officer's police area.

(12) For the purposes of the definition of 'excluded offence' in subsection (11)—

    (a) references to a recordable offence or a qualifying offence include an offence under the law of a country or territory outside England and Wales where the act constituting the offence would constitute a recordable offence or (as the case may be) a qualifying offence if done in England and Wales (whether or not it constituted such an offence when the person was convicted), and

    (b) in the application of paragraph (b) of that definition in relation to an offence under the law of a country or territory outside England and Wales, the reference to a relevant custodial sentence of 5 years or more is to be read as a reference to a sentence of imprisonment or other form of detention of 5 years or more.

### 63G Retention of section 63D material by virtue of section 63F(5): consent of Commissioner

(1) The responsible chief officer of police may apply under subsection (2) or (3) to the Commissioner for the Retention and Use of Biometric Material for consent to the retention of section 63D material which falls within section 63F(5)(a) and (b).

(2) The responsible chief officer of police may make an application under this subsection if the responsible chief officer of police considers that the material was taken (or, in the case of a DNA profile, derived from a sample taken) in connection with the investigation of an offence where any alleged victim of the offence was, at the time of the offence—

    (a) under the age of 18,

(b) a vulnerable adult, or

(c) associated with the person to whom the material relates.

(3) The responsible chief officer of police may make an application under this subsection if the responsible chief officer of police considers that—

(a) the material is not material to which subsection (2) relates, but

(b) the retention of the material is necessary to assist in the prevention or detection of crime.

(4) The Commissioner may, on an application under this section, consent to the retention of material to which the application relates if the Commissioner considers that it is appropriate to retain the material.

(5) But where notice is given under subsection (6) in relation to the application, the Commissioner must, before deciding whether or not to give consent, consider any representations by the person to whom the material relates which are made within the period of 28 days beginning with the day on which the notice is given.

(6) The responsible chief officer of police must give to the person to whom the material relates notice of—

(a) an application under this section, and

(b) the right to make representations.

(7) A notice under subsection (6) may, in particular, be given to a person by—

(a) leaving it at the person's usual or last known address (whether residential or otherwise),

(b) sending it to the person by post at that address, or

(c) sending it to the person by email or other electronic means.

(8) The requirement in subsection (6) does not apply if the whereabouts of the person to whom the material relates is not known and cannot, after reasonable inquiry, be ascertained by the responsible chief officer of police.

(9) An application or notice under this section must be in writing.

(10) In this section—

'victim' includes intended victim,

'vulnerable adult' means a person aged 18 or over whose ability to protect himself or herself from violence, abuse or neglect is significantly impaired through physical or mental disability or illness, through old age or otherwise,

and the reference in subsection (2)(c) to a person being associated with another person is to be read in accordance with section 62(3) to (7) of the Family Law Act 1996.

### 63H   Retention of section 63D material: persons arrested for or charged with a minor offence

(1) This section applies to section 63D material which—

(a) relates to a person who—

    (i) is arrested for or charged with a recordable offence other than a qualifying offence,

    (ii) if arrested for or charged with more than one offence arising out of a single course of action, is not also arrested for or charged with a qualifying offence, and

    (iii) is not convicted of the offence or offences in respect of which the person is arrested or charged, and

(b) was taken (or, in the case of a DNA profile, derived from a sample taken) in connection with the investigation of the offence or offences in respect of which the person is arrested or charged.

(2) If the person has previously been convicted of a recordable offence which is not an excluded offence, the material may be retained indefinitely.

(2A) In subsection (2), the reference to a recordable offence includes an offence under the law of a country or territory outside England and Wales where the act constituting the offence would constitute a recordable offence if done in England and Wales (whether or not it constituted such an offence when the person was convicted).

(3) In this section 'excluded offence' has the meaning given by section 63F(11).

**63I   Retention of material: persons convicted of a recordable offence**

(1) This section applies, subject to subsection (3), to—

    (a) section 63D material which—

        (i) relates to a person who is convicted of a recordable offence, and

        (ii) was taken (or, in the case of a DNA profile, derived from a sample taken) in connection with the investigation of the offence, or

    (b) material taken under section 61(6) or 63(3B) which relates to a person who is convicted of a recordable offence.

(2) The material may be retained indefinitely.

(3) This section does not apply to section 63D material to which section 63K applies.

**63IA   Retention of material: persons convicted of an offence outside England and Wales after taking of section 63D material**

(1) This section applies where—

    (a) section 63D material is taken (or, in the case of a DNA profile, derived from a sample taken) in connection with the investigation of an offence,

    (b) at any time before the material is required to be destroyed by virtue of this Part of this Act, the person is convicted of an offence under the law of a country or territory outside England and Wales, and

    (c) the act constituting the offence mentioned in paragraph (b) would constitute a recordable offence if done in England and Wales.

(2) The material may be retained indefinitely.

(3) This section does not apply where section 63KA applies

**63J   Retention of material: persons convicted of an offence outside England and Wales: other cases**

(1) This section applies to material falling within subsection (2) relating to a person who is convicted of an offence under the law of any country or territory outside England and Wales.

(2) Material falls within this subsection if it is—

    (a) fingerprints taken from the person under section 61(6D) (power to take fingerprints without consent in relation to offences outside England and Wales), or

    (b) a DNA profile derived from a DNA sample taken from the person under section 62(2A) or 63(3E) (powers to take intimate and non-intimate samples in relation to offences outside England and Wales).

(3) The material may be retained indefinitely.

**63K   Retention of section 63D material: exception for persons under 18 convicted of first minor offence**

(1) This section applies to section 63D material which—

    (a) relates to a person who—

        (i) is convicted of a recordable offence other than a qualifying offence,

        (ii) has not previously been convicted of a recordable offence, and

        (iii) is aged under 18 at the time of the offence, and

    (b) was taken (or, in the case of a DNA profile, derived from a sample taken) in connection with the investigation of the offence.

In subsection (1)(a)(ii), the reference to a recordable offence includes an offence under the law of a country or territory outside England and Wales where the act constituting the offence would constitute a recordable offence if done in England and Wales (whether or not it constituted such an offence when the person was convicted).

(2) Where the person is given a relevant custodial sentence of less than 5 years in respect of the offence, the material may be retained until the end of the period consisting of the term of the sentence plus 5 years.

(3) Where the person is given a relevant custodial sentence of 5 years or more in respect of the offence, the material may be retained indefinitely.

(4) Where the person is given a sentence other than a relevant custodial sentence in respect of the offence, the material may be retained until—

(a) in the case of fingerprints, the end of the period of 5 years beginning with the date on which the fingerprints were taken, and

(b) in the case of a DNA profile, the end of the period of 5 years beginning with—

(i) the date on which the DNA sample from which the profile was derived was taken, or

(ii) if the profile was derived from more than one DNA sample, the date on which the first of those samples was taken.

(5) But if, before the end of the period within which material may be retained by virtue of this section, the person is again convicted of a recordable offence, the material may be retained indefinitely.

(5A) In subsection (5), the reference to a recordable offence includes an offence under the law of a country or territory outside England and Wales where the act constituting the offence would constitute a recordable offence if done in England and Wales.

(6) In this section, 'relevant custodial sentence' means any of the following—

(a) a custodial sentence within the meaning of section 76 of the Powers of Criminal Courts (Sentencing) Act 2000;

(b) a sentence of a period of detention and training (excluding any period of supervision) which a person is liable to serve under an order under section 211 of the Armed Forces Act 2006 or a secure training order.

### 63KA   Retention of section 63D material under section 63IA: exception for persons under 18 convicted of first minor offence outside England and Wales

(1) This section applies where—

(a) section 63D material is taken (or, in the case of a DNA profile, derived from a sample taken) in connection with the investigation of an offence,

(b) at any time before the material is required to be destroyed by virtue of this Part of this Act, the person is convicted of an offence under the law of a country or territory outside England and Wales,

(c) the act constituting the offence mentioned in paragraph (b) would constitute a recordable offence if done in England and Wales but would not constitute a qualifying offence,

(d) the person is aged under 18 at the time of the offence mentioned in paragraph (b), and

(e) the person has not previously been convicted of a recordable offence.

(2) In subsection (1)(e), the reference to a recordable offence includes an offence under the law of a country or territory outside England and Wales where the act constituting the offence would constitute a recordable offence if done in England and Wales (whether or not it constituted such an offence when the person was convicted).

(3) Where the person is sentenced to imprisonment or another form of detention for less than 5 years in respect of the offence mentioned in subsection (1)(b), the section 63D material may be retained until the end of the period consisting of the term of the sentence plus 5 years.

(4) Where the person is sentenced to imprisonment or another form of detention for 5 years or more in respect of the offence mentioned in subsection (1)(b), the material may be retained indefinitely.

(5) Where the person is given a sentence other than a sentence of imprisonment or other form of detention in respect of the offence mentioned in subsection (1)(b), the material may be retained until the end of the period of 5 years beginning with the date on which the person was arrested for the offence (or, if the person was not arrested for the offence, the date on which the person was charged with it).

(6) But if, before the end of the period within which material may be retained by virtue of this section, the person is again convicted of a recordable offence, the material may be retained indefinitely.

(7) In subsection (6), the reference to a recordable offence includes an offence under the law of a country or territory outside England and Wales where the act constituting the offence would constitute a recordable offence if done in England and Wales.

**63L    Retention of section 63D material: persons given a penalty notice**

(1)  This section applies to section 63D material which—

(a)  relates to a person who is given a penalty notice under section 2 of the Criminal Justice and Police Act 2001 and in respect of whom no proceedings are brought for the offence to which the notice relates, and

(b)  was taken (or, in the case of a DNA profile, derived from a sample taken) from the person in connection with the investigation of the offence to which the notice relates.

(2)  The material may be retained—

(a)  in the case of fingerprints, for a period of 2 years beginning with the date on which the fingerprints were taken,

(b)  in the case of a DNA profile, for a period of 2 years beginning with—

(i)   the date on which the DNA sample from which the profile was derived was taken, or

(ii)  if the profile was derived from more than one DNA sample, the date on which the first of those samples was taken.

**63M    Retention of section 63D material for purposes of national security**

(1)  Section 63D material may be retained for as long as a national security determination made by the responsible chief officer of police has effect in relation to it.

(2)  A national security determination is made if the responsible chief officer of police determines that it is necessary for any section 63D material to be retained for the purposes of national security.

(3)  A national security determination—

(a)  must be made in writing,

(b)  has effect for a maximum of 2 years beginning with the date on which it is made, and

(c)  may be renewed.

**63N    Retention of section 63D material given voluntarily**

(1)  This section applies to the following section 63D material—

(a)  fingerprints taken with the consent of the person from whom they were taken, and

(b)  a DNA profile derived from a DNA sample taken with the consent of the person from whom the sample was taken.

(2)  Material to which this section applies may be retained until it has fulfilled the purpose for which it was taken or derived.

(3)  Material to which this section applies which relates to—

(a)  a person who is convicted of a recordable offence, or

(b)  a person who has previously been convicted of a recordable offence (other than a person who has only one exempt conviction),

may be retained indefinitely.

(4)  For the purposes of subsection (3)(b), a conviction is exempt if it is in respect of a recordable offence, other than a qualifying offence, committed when the person is aged under 18.

(5)  The reference to a recordable offence in subsection (3)(a) includes an offence under the law of a country or territory outside England and Wales where the act constituting the offence would constitute a recordable offence if done in England and Wales.

(6)  The reference to a recordable offence in subsections (3)(b) and (4), and the reference to a qualifying offence in subsection (4), includes an offence under the law of a country or territory outside England and Wales where the act constituting the offence would constitute a recordable offence or (as the case may be) a qualifying offence if done in England and Wales (whether or not it constituted such an offence when the person was convicted).

**63O    Retention of section 63D material with consent**

(1)  This section applies to the following material—

(a)  fingerprints (other than fingerprints taken under section 61(6A)) to which section 63D applies, and

(b)  a DNA profile to which section 63D applies.

(2) If the person to whom the material relates consents to material to which this section applies being retained, the material may be retained for as long as that person consents to it being retained.

(3) Consent given under this section—

(a) must be in writing, and

(b) can be withdrawn at any time.

### 63P    Retention of 63D material in connection with different offence

(1) Subsection (2) applies if—

(a) section 63D material is taken (or, in the case of a DNA profile, derived from a sample taken) from a person in connection with the investigation of an offence, and

(b) the person is subsequently arrested for or charged with a different offence, or convicted of or given a penalty notice for a different offence.

(2) Sections 63E to 63O and sections 63Q and 63T have effect in relation to the material as if the material were also taken (or, in the case of a DNA profile, derived from a sample taken)—

(a) in connection with the investigation of the offence mentioned in subsection (1)(b),

(b) on the date on which the person was arrested for that offence (or charged with it or given a penalty notice for it, if the person was not arrested).

### 63Q    Destruction of copies of section 63D material

(1) If fingerprints are required by section 63D to be destroyed, any copies of the fingerprints held by the police must also be destroyed.

(2)   If a DNA profile is required by that section to be destroyed, no copy may be retained by the police except in a form which does not include information which identifies the person to whom the DNA profile relates.

### 63R    Destruction of samples

(1) This section applies to samples—

(a) taken from a person under any power conferred by this Part of this Act, or

(b) taken by the police, with the consent of the person from whom they were taken, in connection with the investigation of an offence by the police.

(2) Samples to which this section applies must be destroyed if it appears to the responsible chief officer of police that—

(a) the taking of the samples was unlawful, or

(b) the samples were taken from a person in connection with that person's arrest and the arrest was unlawful or based on mistaken identity.

(3) Subject to this, the rule in subsection (4) or (as the case may be) (5) applies.

(4) A DNA sample to which this section applies must be destroyed—

(a) as soon as a DNA profile has been derived from the sample, or

(b) if sooner, before the end of the period of 6 months beginning with the date on which the sample was taken.

(5) Any other sample to which this section applies must be destroyed before the end of the period of 6 months beginning with the date on which it was taken.

(6) The responsible chief officer of police may apply to a District Judge (Magistrates' Courts) for an order to retain a sample to which this section applies beyond the date on which the sample would otherwise be required to be destroyed by virtue of subsection (4) or (5) if—

(a) the sample was taken from a person in connection with the investigation of a qualifying offence, and

(b) the responsible chief officer of police considers that the condition in subsection (7) is met.

(7) The condition is that, having regard to the nature and complexity of other material that is evidence in relation to the offence, the sample is likely to be needed in any proceedings for the offence for the purposes of—

(a) disclosure to, or use by, a defendant, or

(b) responding to any challenge by a defendant in respect of the admissibility of material that is evidence on which the prosecution proposes to rely.

(8) An application under subsection (6) must be made before the date on which the sample would otherwise be required to be destroyed by virtue of subsection (4) or (5).

(9) If, on an application made by the responsible chief officer of police under subsection (6), the District Judge (Magistrates' Courts) is satisfied that the condition in subsection (7) is met, the District Judge may make an order under this subsection which—

(a) allows the sample to be retained for a period of 12 months beginning with the date on which the sample would otherwise be required to be destroyed by virtue of subsection (4) or (5), and

(b) may be renewed (on one or more occasions) for a further period of not more than 12 months from the end of the period when the order would otherwise cease to have effect.

(10) An application for an order under subsection (9) (other than an application for renewal)—

(a) may be made without notice of the application having been given to the person from whom the sample was taken, and

(b) may be heard and determined in private in the absence of that person.

(11) A sample retained by virtue of an order under subsection (9) must not be used other than for the purposes of any proceedings for the offence in connection with which the sample was taken.

(12) A sample that ceases to be retained by virtue of an order under subsection (9) must be destroyed.

(13) Nothing in this section prevents a speculative search, in relation to samples to which this section applies, from being carried out within such time as may reasonably be required for the search if the responsible chief officer of police considers the search to be desirable.

### 63S   Destruction of impressions of footwear

(1) This section applies to impressions of footwear—

(a) taken from a person under any power conferred by this Part of this Act, or

(b) taken by the police, with the consent of the person from whom they were taken, in connection with the investigation of an offence by the police.

(2) Impressions of footwear to which this section applies must be destroyed unless they are retained under subsection (3).

(3) Impressions of footwear may be retained for as long as is necessary for purposes related to the prevention or detection of crime, the investigation of an offence or the conduct of a prosecution.

### 63T   Use of retained material

(1) Any material to which section 63D, 63R or 63S applies must not be used other than—

(a) in the interests of national security,

(b) for the purposes of a terrorist investigation,

(c) for purposes related to the prevention or detection of crime, the investigation of an offence or the conduct of a prosecution, or

(d) for purposes related to the identification of a deceased person or of the person to whom the material relates.

(2) Material which is required by section 63D, 63R or 63S to be destroyed must not at any time after it is required to be destroyed be used—

(a) in evidence against the person to whom the material relates, or

(b) for the purposes of the investigation of any offence.

(3) In this section—

(a) the reference to using material includes a reference to allowing any check to be made against it and to disclosing it to any person,

(b) the reference to crime includes a reference to any conduct which—

(i) constitutes one or more criminal offences (whether under the law of England and Wales or of any country or territory outside England and Wales), or

(ii) is, or corresponds to, any conduct which, if it all took place in England and Wales, would constitute one or more criminal offences, and

(c) the references to an investigation and to a prosecution include references, respectively, to any investigation outside England and Wales of any crime or suspected crime and to a prosecution brought in respect of any crime in a country or territory outside England and Wales.

### 63U Exclusions for certain regimes

(1) Sections 63D to 63T do not apply to material to which paragraphs 20A to 20J of Schedule 8 to the Terrorism Act 2000 (destruction, retention and use of material taken from terrorist suspects) apply.

(2) Any reference in those sections to a person being arrested for, or charged with, an offence does not include a reference to a person—

(a) being arrested under section 41 of the Terrorism Act 2000, or

(b) being charged with an offence following an arrest under that section.

(3) Sections 63D to 63T do not apply to material to which paragraph 8 of Schedule 4 to the International Criminal Court Act 2001 (requirement to destroy material) applies.

(4) Sections 63D to 63T do not apply to material to which paragraph 6 of Schedule 6 to the Terrorism Prevention and Investigation Measures Act 2011 (requirement to destroy material) applies.

(5) Sections 63D to 63T do not apply to material which is, or may become, disclosable under—

(a) the Criminal Procedure and Investigations Act 1996, or

(b) a code of practice prepared under section 23 of that Act and in operation by virtue of an order under section 25 of that Act.

(5A) A sample that—

(a) falls within subsection (5), and

(b) but for that subsection would be required to be destroyed under section 63R,

must not be used other than for the purposes of any proceedings for the offence in connection with which the sample was taken.

(5B) A sample that once fell within subsection (5) but no longer does, and so becomes a sample to which section 63R applies, must be destroyed immediately if the time specified for its destruction under that section has already passed.

(6) Sections 63D to 63T do not apply to material which—

(a) is taken from a person, but

(b) relates to another person.

(7) Nothing in sections 63D to 63T affects any power conferred by—

(a) paragraph 18(2) of Schedule 2 to the Immigration Act 1971 (power to take reasonable steps to identify a person detained), or

(b) section 20 of the Immigration and Asylum Act 1999 (disclosure of police information to the Secretary of State for use for immigration purposes).

### 64A Photographing of suspects etc.

(1) A person who is detained at a police station may be photographed—

(a) with the appropriate consent; or

(b) if the appropriate consent is withheld or it is not practicable to obtain it, without it.

(1A) A person falling within subsection (1B) below may, on the occasion of the relevant event referred to in subsection (1B), be photographed elsewhere than at a police station—

(a) with the appropriate consent; or

(b) if the appropriate consent is withheld or it is not practicable to obtain it, without it.

(1B) A person falls within this subsection if he has been—

(a) arrested by a constable for an offence;

(b) taken into custody by a constable after being arrested for an offence by a person other than a constable;

(c) made subject to a requirement to wait with a community support officer or a community support volunteer under paragraph 7 of Schedule 3B to the Police Reform Act 2002 ('the 2002 Act').

(ca) given a direction by a constable under section 35 of the Anti-social Behaviour, Crime and Policing Act 2014;

(d) given a penalty notice by a constable in uniform under Chapter 1 of Part 1 of the Criminal Justice and Police Act 2001, a penalty notice by a constable under section 444A of the Education Act 1996, or a fixed penalty notice by a constable in uniform under section 54 of the Road Traffic Offenders Act 1988;

(e) given a fixed penalty notice by a community support officer or community support volunteer who is authorised to give the notice by virtue of his or her designation under section 38 of the Police Reform Act 2002;

(f) given a notice in relation to a relevant fixed penalty offence (within the meaning of paragraph 1 of Schedule 5 to the 2002 Act) by an accredited person by virtue of accreditation specifying that that paragraph applies to him; or

(g) given a notice in relation to a relevant fixed penalty offence (within the meaning of Schedule 5A to the 2002 Act) by an accredited inspector by virtue of accreditation specifying that paragraph 1 of Schedule 5A to the 2002 Act applies to him.

(2) A person proposing to take a photograph of any person under this section—

(a) may, for the purpose of doing so, require the removal of any item or substance worn on or over the whole or any part of the head or face of the person to be photographed; and

(b) if the requirement is not complied with, may remove the item or substance himself.

(3) Where a photograph may be taken under this section, the only persons entitled to take the photograph are constables.

(4) A photograph taken under this section—

(a) may be used by, or disclosed to, any person for any purpose related to the prevention or detection of crime, the investigation of an offence or the conduct of a prosecution or to the enforcement of a sentence; and

(b) after being so used or disclosed, may be retained but may not be used or disclosed except for a purpose so related.

(5) In subsection (4)—

(a) the reference to crime includes a reference to any conduct which—

   (i) constitutes one or more criminal offences (whether under the law of a part of the United Kingdom or of a country or territory outside the United Kingdom); or

   (ii) is, or corresponds to, any conduct which, if it all took place in any one part of the United Kingdom, would constitute one or more criminal offences;

   and

(b) the references to an investigation and to a prosecution include references, respectively, to any investigation outside the United Kingdom of any crime or suspected crime and to a prosecution brought in respect of any crime in a country or territory outside the United Kingdom; and

(c) 'sentence' includes any order made by a court in England and Wales when dealing with an offender in respect of his offence.

(6) References in this section to taking a photograph include references to using any process by means of which a visual image may be produced; and references to photographing a person shall be construed accordingly.

(6A) In this section, a 'photograph' includes a moving image, and corresponding expressions shall be construed accordingly.

(7) Nothing in this section applies to a person arrested under an extradition arrest power.

## 65    Part V—supplementary

(1) In this Part of this Act—

'analysis', in relation to a skin impression, includes comparison and matching;

'appropriate consent' means—

(a) in relation to a person who has attained the age of 18 years, the consent of that person;

(b) in relation to a person who has not attained that age but has attained the age of 14 years, the consent of that person and his parent or guardian; and

(c) in relation to a person who has not attained the age of 14 years, the consent of his parent or guardian;

'DNA profile' means any information derived from a DNA sample;

'DNA sample' means any material that has come from a human body and consists of or includes human cells;

'extradition arrest power' means any of the following—

(a) a Part 1 warrant (within the meaning given by the Extradition Act 2003) in respect of which a certificate under section 2 of that Act has been issued;

(b) section 5 of that Act;

(c) a warrant issued under section 71 of that Act;

(d) a provisional warrant (within the meaning given by that Act);

'fingerprints', in relation to any person, means a record (in any form and produced by any method) of the skin pattern and other physical characteristics or features of—

(a) any of that person's fingers; or

(b) either of his palms;

'intimate sample' means—

(a) a sample of blood, semen or any other tissue fluid, urine or pubic hair;

(b) a dental impression;

(c) a swab taken from any part of a person's genitals (including pubic hair) or from a person's body orifice other than the mouth;

'intimate search' means a search which consists of the physical examination of a person's body orifices other than the mouth;

'non-intimate sample' means—

(a) a sample of hair other than pubic hair;

(b) a sample taken from a nail on from under a nail;

(c) a swab taken from any part of a person's body other than a part from which a swab taken would be an intimate sample;

(d) saliva;

(e) a skin impression;

'offence', in relation to any country or territory outside England and Wales, includes an act punishable under the law of that country or territory, however it is described;

'registered dentist' has the same meaning as in the Dentists Act 1984;

'skin impression', in relation to any person, means any record (other than a fingerprint) which is a record (in any form and produced by any method) of the skin pattern and other physical characteristics or features of the whole or any part of his foot or of any other part of his body;

'registered health care professional' means a person (other than a medical practitioner) who is—

(a) a registered nurse; or

(b) a registered member of a health care profession which is designated for the purposes of this paragraph by an order made by the Secretary of State;

'the responsible chief officer of police', in relation to material to which section 63D or 63R applies, means the chief officer of police for the police area—

(a) in which the material concerned was taken, or

(b) in the case of a DNA profile, in which the sample from which the DNA profile was derived was taken;

'section 63D material' means fingerprints or DNA profiles to which section 63D applies;

'speculative search', in relation to a person's fingerprints or samples, means such a check against other fingerprints or samples or against information derived from other samples as is referred to in section 63A(1) above;

'sufficient' and 'insufficient', in relation to a sample, means (subject to subsection (2) below) sufficient or insufficient (in point of quantity or quality) for the purpose of enabling information to be produced by the means of analysis used or to be used in relation to the sample.

'the terrorism provisions' means section 41 of the Terrorism Act 2000, and any provision of Schedule 7 to that Act conferring a power of detention; and 'terrorism' has the meaning given in section 1 of that Act;

'terrorist investigation' has the meaning given by section 32 of that Act;

(1A) A health care profession is any profession mentioned in section 60(2) of the Health Act 1999 other than the profession of practising medicine and the profession of nursing.

(1B) An order under subsection (1) shall be made by statutory instrument and shall be subject to annulment in pursuance of a resolution of either House of Parliament.

(2) References in this Part of this Act to a sample's proving insufficient include references to where, as a consequence of—

(a) the loss, destruction or contamination of the whole or any part of the sample,

(b) any damage to the whole or a part of the sample, or

(c) the use of the whole or a part of the sample for an analysis which produced no results or which produced results some or all of which must be regarded, in the circumstances, as unreliable, the sample has become unavailable or insufficient for the purpose of enabling information, or information of a particular description, to be obtained by means of analysis of the sample.

(2A) In subsection (2), the reference to the destruction of a sample does not include a reference to the destruction of a sample under section 63R (requirement to destroy samples).

(2B) Any reference in sections 63F, 63H, 63P or 63U to a person being charged with an offence includes a reference to a person being informed that the person will be reported for an offence.

(3) For the purposes of this Part, a person has in particular been convicted of an offence under the law of a country or territory outside England and Wales if—

(a) a court exercising jurisdiction under the law of that country or territory has made in respect of such an offence a finding equivalent to a finding that the person is not guilty by reason of insanity; or

(b) such a court has made in respect of such an offence a finding equivalent to a finding that the person is under a disability and did the act charged against him in respect of the offence.

## 65A  Qualifying offence

(1) In this Part, 'qualifying offence' means—

(a) an offence specified in subsection (2) below, or

(b) an ancillary offence relating to such an offence.

(2) The offences referred to in subsection (1)(a) above are—

(a) murder;

(b) manslaughter;

(c) false imprisonment;

(d) kidnapping;

(da) an offence of indecent exposure;

(db) an offence under section 4 of the Vagrancy Act 1824, committed by a person by wilfully, openly, lewdly, and obscenely exposing his person with intent to insult any female;

(dc) an offence under section 28 of the Town Police Clauses Act 1847, committed by a person by wilfully and indecently exposing his person;

(e) an offence under section 4, 16, 18, 20 to 24 or 47 of the Offences Against the Person Act 1861;

(f) an offence under section 2 or 3 of the Explosive Substances Act 1883;

(fa) an offence under section 1 of the Infant Life (Preservation) Act 1929;

(g) an offence under section 1 of the Children and Young Persons Act 1933;

(ga) an offence under section 1 of the Infanticide Act 1938;

(gb) an offence under section 12 or 13 of the Sexual Offences Act 1956, other than an offence committed by a person where the other person involved in the conduct constituting the offence consented to it and was aged 16 or over;

(gc) an offence under any other section of that Act, other than sections 18 and 32;

(gd) an offence under section 128 of the Mental Health Act 1959;

(ge) an offence under section 1 of the Indecency with Children Act 1960;

(h) an offence under section 4(1) of the Criminal Law Act 1967 committed in relation to murder;

(ha) an offence under section 5 of the Sexual Offences Act 1967;

(i) an offence under sections 16 to 18 of the Firearms Act 1968;

(j) an offence under section 8, 9 or 10 of the Theft Act 1968 or an offence under section 12A of that Act involving an accident which caused a person's death;

(ja) an offence under section 1(1) of the Genocide Act 1969;

(k) an offence under section 1 of the Criminal Damage Act 1971 required to be charged as arson;

(ka) an offence under section 54 of the Criminal Law Act 1977;

(l) an offence under section 1 of the Protection of Children Act 1978;

(m) an offence under section 1 of the Aviation Security Act 1982;

(n) an offence under section 2 of the Child Abduction Act 1984;

(na) an offence under section 1 of the Prohibition of Female Circumcision Act 1985;

(nb) an offence under section 1 of the Public Order Act 1986;

(o) an offence under section 9 of the Aviation and Maritime Security Act 1990;

(oa) an offence under section 3 of the Sexual Offences (Amendment) Act 2000;

(ob) an offence under section 51 of the International Criminal Court Act 2001;

(oc) an offence under section 1, 2 or 3 of the Female Genital Mutilation Act 2003;

(p) an offence under any of sections 1 to 19, 25, 26, 30 to 41, 47 to 50, 52, 53, 57 to 59A, 61 to 67, 69 and 70 of the Sexual Offences Act 2000;

(q) an offence under section 5 of the Domestic Violence, Crime and Victims Act 2004;

(r) an offence for the time being listed in section 41(1) of the Counter-Terrorism Act 2008;

(s) an offence under section 2 of the Modern Slavery Act 2015 (human trafficking).

(3) The Secretary of State may by order made by statutory instrument amend subsection (2) above.

(4) A statutory instrument containing an order under subsection (3) above shall not be made unless a draft of the instrument has been laid before, and approved by resolution of, each House of Parliament.

(5) In subsection (1)(b) above 'ancillary offence', in relation to an offence, means—

(a) aiding, abetting, counselling or procuring the commission of the offence;

(b) an offence under Part 2 of the Serious Crime Act 2007 (encouraging or assisting crime) in relation to the offence (including, in relation to times before the commencement of that Part, an offence of incitement);

(c) attempting or conspiring to commit the offence.

## 65B  Persons convicted of an offence

(1) For the purposes of this Part, any reference to a person who is convicted of an offence includes a reference to—

(a) a person who has been given a caution in respect of the offence which, at the time of the caution, the person has admitted,

(b) a person who has been warned or reprimanded under section 65 of the Crime and Disorder Act 1998 for the offence,

(c) a person who has been found not guilty of the offence by reason of insanity, or

(d) a person who has been found to be under a disability and to have done the act charged in respect of the offence.

(2) This Part, so far as it relates to persons convicted of an offence, has effect despite anything in the Rehabilitation of Offenders Act 1974.

(3) But a person is not to be treated as having been convicted of an offence if that conviction is a disregarded conviction or caution by virtue of section 92 of the Protection of Freedoms Act 2012.

(4) If a person is convicted of more than one offence arising out of a single course of action, those convictions are to be treated as a single conviction for the purposes of calculating under sections 63F, 63H and 63N whether the person has been convicted of only one offence.

(5) …*

---

\* **Editor's Note:** Applies to countries outside England and Wales.

# PART VI  CODES OF PRACTICE—GENERAL

## 66  Codes of practice

The Secretary of State shall issue codes of practice in connection with—

    (a) the exercise by police officers of statutory powers—

        (i)   to search a person without first arresting him;

        (ii)  to search a vehicle without making an arrest; or

        (iii) to arrest a person;

    (b) the detention, treatment, questioning and identification of persons by police officers;

    (c) searches of premises by police officers; and

    (d) the seizure of property found by police officers on persons or premises.

    (2) Codes shall (in particular) include provision in connection with the exercise by police officers of powers under section 63B above.

    (3) …*

## 67  Codes of practice—supplementary

    (1) In this section, 'code' means a code of practice under section 60, 60A or 66.

    (2) The Secretary of State may at any time revise the whole or any part of a code.

    (3) A code may be made, or revised, so as to—

        (a) apply only in relation to one or more specified areas,

        (b) have effect only for a specified period,

        (c) apply only in relation to specified offences or descriptions of offender.

    (4) Before issuing a code, or any revision of a code, the Secretary of State must consult—

        (a)  such persons as appear to the Secretary of State to represent the views of police and crime commissioners,

        (aa) the Mayor's Office for Policing and Crime,

        (ab) the Common Council of the City of London,

        (b)  The National Police Chiefs' Council,

        (c)  the General Council of the Bar,

        (d)  the Law Society of England and Wales,

        (e)  the Institute of Legal Executives, and

        (f)  such other persons as he thinks fit.

    (4A) The duty to consult under subsection (4) does not apply to a revision of a code where the Secretary of State considers that—

        (a) the revision is necessary in consequence of legislation, and

        (b) the Secretary of State has no discretion as to the nature of the revision.

    (4B) Where, in consequence of subsection (4A), a revision of a code is issued without prior consultation with the persons mentioned in subsection (4), the Secretary of State must (at the same time as issuing the revision) publish a statement that, in his or her opinion, paragraphs (a) and (b) of subsection (4A) apply to the revision.

    (4C) In subsection (4A), 'legislation' means any provision of—

        (a) an Act,

        (b) subordinate legislation within the meaning of the Interpretation Act 1978.

    (5) A code, or a revision of a code, does not come into operation until the Secretary of State by order so provides.

    (6) The power conferred by subsection (5) is exercisable by statutory instrument.

    (7) An order bringing a code into operation may not be made unless a draft of the order has been laid before Parliament and approved by a resolution of each House.

    (7A) An order bringing a revision of a code into operation must be laid before Parliament if the order has been made without a draft having been so laid and approved by a resolution of each House.

---

* **Editor's Note:** Applies to terrorism.

(7B)  When an order or draft of an order is laid, the code or revision of a code to which it relates must also be laid.

(7C)  No order or draft of an order may be laid until the consultation required by subsection (4) has taken place.

(7D)  An order bringing a code, or a revision of a code, into operation may include transitional or saving provisions.

(9)  Persons other than police officers who are charged with the duty of investigating offences or charging offenders shall in the discharge of that duty have regard to any relevant provision of a code.

(9A)  Persons on whom powers are conferred by—

    (a)  any designation under section 38 or 39 of the Police Reform Act 2002 (police powers for civilian staff and volunteers), or

    (b)  any accreditation under section 41 of that Act (accreditation under community safety accreditation schemes),

shall have regard to any relevant provision of a code in the exercise or performance of the powers and duties conferred or imposed on them by that designation or accreditation.

(10)  A failure on the part—

    (a)  of a police officer to comply with any provision of a code;

    (b)  of any person other than a police officer who is charged with the duty of investigating offences or charging offenders to have regard to any relevant provision of a code in the discharge of that duty; or

    (c)  of a person designated under section 38 or 39 or accredited under section 41 of the Police Reform Act 2002 to have regard to any relevant provision of a code in the exercise or performance of the powers and duties conferred or imposed on him by that designation or accreditation,

shall not of itself render him liable to any criminal or civil proceedings.

(11)  In all criminal and civil proceedings any code shall be admissible in evidence; and if any provision of a code appears to the court or tribunal conducting the proceedings to be relevant to any question arising in the proceedings it shall be taken into account in determining that question.

(12)  In subsection (11) 'criminal proceedings' includes service proceedings.

(13)  …*

# PART VII  DOCUMENTARY EVIDENCE IN CRIMINAL PROCEEDINGS

## 71  Microfilm copies

In any proceedings the contents of a document may (whether or not the document is still in existence) be proved by the production of an enlargement of a microfilm copy of that document or of the material part of it, authenticated in such manner as the court may approve.

## 72  Part VII—supplementary

(1)  In this Part of this Act—

'copy' in relation to a document means anything onto which information recorded in the document has been copied, by whatever means and whether directly or indirectly, and 'statement' means any representation of fact however made; and

'proceedings' means criminal proceedings, including service proceedings

(1A)  …**

(2)  Nothing in this Part of this Act shall prejudice any power of a court to exclude evidence (whether by preventing questions from being put or otherwise) at its discretion.

---

  * **Editor's Note:** Applies to service proceedings.
  ** **Editor's Note:** Defines 'service proceedings'.

# PART VIII  EVIDENCE IN CRIMINAL PROCEEDINGS—GENERAL

## *Convictions and acquittals*

### 73  Proof of convictions and acquittals

(1) Where in any proceedings the fact that a person has in the United Kingdom or any other member State been convicted or acquitted of an offence otherwise than by a Service court is admissible in evidence, it may be proved by producing a certificate of conviction or, as the case may be, of acquittal relating to that offence, and proving that the person named in the certificate as having been convicted or acquitted of the offence is the person whose conviction or acquittal of the offence is to be proved.

(2) For the purposes of this section a certificate of conviction or of acquittal—

   (a) shall, as regards a conviction or acquittal on indictment, consist of a certificate, signed by the proper officer where the conviction or acquittal took place, giving the substance and effect (omitting the formal parts) of the indictment and of the conviction or acquittal; and

   (b) shall, as regards a conviction or acquittal on a summary trial, consist of a copy of the conviction or of the dismissal of the information, signed by the proper officer of the court where the conviction or acquittal took place or by the proper officer of the court, if any, to which a memorandum of the conviction or acquittal was sent; and

   (c) shall, as regards a conviction or acquittal by a court in a member State (other than the United Kingdom), consist of a certificate, signed by the proper officer of the court where the conviction or acquittal took place, giving details of the offence, of the conviction or acquittal, and of any sentence;

and a document purporting to be a duly signed certificate of conviction or acquittal under this section shall be taken to be such a certificate unless the contrary is proved.

(3) In subsection (2) above 'proper officer' means:

   (a) in relation to a magistrates' court in England and Wales, the designated officer for the court; and

   (b) in relation to any other court in the United Kingdom, the clerk of a court, his deputy and to any other person having the custody of the court record; and

   (c) in relation to any court in another member State ('the EU court'), a person who would be the proper officer of the EU court if that court were in the United Kingdom.

(4) The method of proving a conviction or acquittal authorised by this section shall be in addition to and not to the exclusion of any other authorised manner of proving a conviction or acquittal.

### 74  Conviction as evidence of commission of offence

(1) In any proceedings the fact that a person other than the accused has been convicted of an offence by or before any court in the United Kingdom or any other member State or by a Service court outside the United Kingdom shall be admissible in evidence for the purpose of proving that that person committed that offence, where evidence of his having done so is admissible, whether or not any other evidence of his having committed that offence is given.

(2) In any proceedings in which by virtue of this section a person other than the accused is proved to have been convicted of an offence by or before any court in the United Kingdom or any other member State or by a Service court outside the United Kingdom, he shall be taken to have committed that offence unless the contrary is proved.

(3) In any proceedings where evidence is admissible of that fact that the accused has committed an offence, if the accused is proved to have been convicted of the offence—

   (a) by or before any court in the United Kingdom or any other member State; or

   (b) by a Service court outside the United Kingdom,

he shall be taken to have committed that offence unless the contrary is proved.

(4) Nothing in this section shall prejudice—

  (a) the admissibility in evidence of any conviction which would be admissible apart from this section; or

  (b) the operation of any enactment whereby a conviction or a finding of fact in any proceedings is for the purposes of any other proceedings made conclusive evidence of any fact.

## 75  Provisions supplementary to section 74

(1) Where evidence that a person has been convicted of an offence is admissible by virtue of section 74 above, then without prejudice to the reception of any other admissible evidence for the purpose of identifying the facts on which the conviction was based—

  (a) the contents of any document which is admissible as evidence of the conviction; and

  (b) the contents of—

    (i) the information, complaint, indictment or charge-sheet on which the person in question was convicted, or

    (ii) in the case of a conviction of an offence by a court in a member State (other than the United Kingdom), any document produced in relation to the proceedings for that offence which fulfils a purpose similar to any document or documents specified in sub-paragraph (i),

shall be admissible in evidence for that purpose.

(2) Where in any proceedings the contents of any document are admissible in evidence by virtue of subsection (1) above, a copy of that document, or of the material part of it, purporting to be certified or otherwise authenticated by or on behalf of the court or authority having custody of that document shall be admissible in evidence and shall be taken to be a true copy of that document or part unless the contrary is shown.

(3) Nothing in any of the following—

  (a) section 14 of the Powers of Criminal Courts (Sentencing) Act 2000 (under which a conviction leading to probation or discharge is to be disregarded except as mentioned in that section);

  (aa) ...*

  (b), (c) ...**

shall affect the operation of section 74 above; ...

(4) Nothing in section 74 above shall be construed as rendering admissible in any proceedings evidence of any conviction other than a subsisting one.

*Confessions*

## 76  Confessions

(1) In any proceedings a confession made by an accused person may be given in evidence against him in so far as it is relevant to any matter in issue in the proceedings and is not excluded by the court in pursuance of this section.

(2) If, in any proceedings where the prosecution proposes to give in evidence a confession made by an accused person, it is represented to the court that the confession was or may have been obtained—

  (a) by oppression of the person who made it; or

  (b) in consequence of anything said or done which was likely, in the circumstances existing at the time, to render unreliable any confession which might be made by him in consequence thereof,

the court shall not allow the confession to be given in evidence against him except in so far as the prosecution proves to the court beyond reasonable doubt that the confession (notwithstanding that it may be true) was not obtained as aforesaid.

(3) In any proceedings where the prosecution proposes to give in evidence a confession made by an accused person, the court may of its own motion require the prosecution, as a condition of allowing it to do so, to prove that the confession was not obtained as mentioned in subsection (2) above.

---

* **Editor's Note:** Applies to service convictions.
** **Editor's Note:** Apply to Scotland and Northern Ireland only.

(4) The fact that a confession is wholly or partly excluded in pursuance of this section shall not affect the admissibility in evidence—

    (a) of any facts discovered as a result of the confession; or

    (b) where the confession is relevant as showing that the accused speaks, writes or expresses himself in a particular way, of so much of the confession as is necessary to show that he does so.

(5) Evidence that a fact to which this subsection applies was discovered as a result of a statement made by an accused person shall not be admissible unless evidence of how it was discovered is given by him or on his behalf.

(6) Subsection (5) above applies—

    (a) to any fact discovered as a result of a confession which is wholly excluded in pursuance of this section; and

    (b) to any fact discovered as a result of a confession which is partly so excluded, if the fact is discovered as a result of the excluded part of the confession.

(7) Nothing in Part VII of this Act shall prejudice the admissibility of a confession made by an accused person.

(8) In this section 'oppression' includes torture, inhuman or degrading treatment, and the use or threat of violence (whether or not amounting to torture).

## 76A    Confessions may be given in evidence for co-accused

(1) In any proceedings a confession made by an accused person may be given in evidence for another person charged in the same proceedings (a co-accused) in so far as it is relevant to any matter in issue in the proceedings and is not excluded by the court in pursuance of this section.

(2) If, in any proceedings where a co-accused proposes to give in evidence a confession made by an accused person, it is represented to the court that the confession was or may have been obtained—

    (a) by oppression of the person who made it; or

    (b) in consequence of anything said or done which was likely, in the circumstances existing at the time, to render unreliable any confession which might be made by him in consequence thereof,

the court shall not allow the confession to be given in evidence for the co-accused except in so far as it is proved to the court on the balance of probabilities that the confession (notwithstanding that it may be true) was not so obtained.

(3) Before allowing a confession made by an accused person to be given in evidence for a co-accused in any proceedings, the court may of its own motion require the fact that the confession was not obtained as mentioned in subsection (2) above to be proved in the proceedings on the balance of probabilities.

(4) The fact that a confession is wholly or partly excluded in pursuance of this section shall not affect the admissibility in evidence—

    (a) of any facts discovered as a result of the confession; or

    (b) where the confession is relevant as showing that the accused speaks, writes or expresses himself in a particular way, of so much of the confession as is necessary to show that he does so.

(5) Evidence that a fact to which this subsection applies was discovered as a result of a statement made by an accused person shall not be admissible unless evidence of how it was discovered is given by him or on his behalf.

(6) Subsection (5) above applies—

    (a) to any fact discovered as a result of a confession which is wholly excluded in pursuance of this section; and

    (b) to any fact discovered as a result of a confession which is partly so excluded, if the fact is discovered as a result of the excluded part of the confession.

(7) In this section 'oppression' includes torture, inhuman or degrading treatment, and the use or threat of violence (whether or not amounting to torture).

## 77    Confessions by mentally handicapped persons

(1) Without prejudice to the general duty of the court at a trial on indictment with a jury to direct the jury on any matter on which it appears to the court appropriate to do so, where at such a trial—

(a) the case against the accused depends wholly or substantially on a confession by him; and

(b) the court is satisfied—

(i)    that he is mentally handicapped; and

(ii)   that the confession was not made in the presence of an independent person;

the court shall warn the jury that there is special need for caution before convicting the accused in reliance on the confession, and shall explain that the need arises because of the circumstances mentioned in paragraphs (a) and (b) above.

(2) In any case where at the summary trial of a person for an offence it appears to the court that a warning under subsection (1) above would be required if the trial were on indictment with a jury, the court shall treat the case as one in which there is a special need for caution before convicting the accused on his confession.

(2A) In any case where at the trial on indictment without a jury of a person for an offence it appears to the court that a warning under subsection (1) above would be required if the trial were with a jury, the court shall treat the case as one in which there is a special need for caution before convicting the accused on his confession.

(3) In this section—

'independent person' does not include a police officer or a person employed for, or engaged on, police purposes;

'mentally handicapped', in relation to a person, means that he is in a state of arrested or incomplete development of mind which includes significant impairment of intelligence and social functioning; and

'police purposes' has the meaning assigned to it by section 101(2) of the Police Act 1996.

## 78    Exclusion of unfair evidence

(1) In any proceedings the court may refuse to allow evidence on which the prosecution proposes to rely to be given if it appears to the court that, having regard to all the circumstances, including the circumstances in which the evidence was obtained, the admission of the evidence would have such an adverse effect on the fairness of the proceedings that the court ought not to admit it.

(2) Nothing in this section shall prejudice any rule of law requiring a court to exclude evidence.

## 79    Time for taking accused's evidence

If at the trial of any person for an offence—

(a)  the defence intends to call two or more witnesses to the facts of the case; and

(b)  those witnesses include the accused,

the accused shall be called before the other witness or witnesses unless the court in its discretion otherwise directs.

## 80    Competence and compellability of accused's spouse or civil partner

(2) In any proceedings the spouse or civil partner of a person charged in the proceedings shall, subject to subsection (4) below, be compellable to give evidence on behalf of that person.

(2A) In any proceedings spouse or civil partner of a person charged in the proceedings shall, subject to subsection (4) below, be compellable—

(a)  to give evidence on behalf of any other person charged in the proceedings but only in respect of any specified offence with which that other person is charged; or

(b)  to give evidence for the prosecution but only in respect of any specified offence with which any person is charged in the proceedings.

(3) In relation to the spouse or civil partner of a person charged in any proceedings, an offence is a specified offence for the purposes of subsection (2A) above if—

    (a) it involves an assault on, or injury or a threat of injury to, the wife or husband or a person who was at the material time under the age of 16;

    (b) it is a sexual offence alleged to have been committed in respect of a person who was at the material time under that age; or

    (c) it consists of attempting or conspiring to commit, or of aiding, abetting, counselling, procuring or inciting the commission of, an offence falling within paragraph (a) or (b) above.

    (4) No person who is charged in any proceedings shall be compellable by virtue of subsection (2) or (2A) above to give evidence in the proceedings.

    (4A) References in this section to a person charged in any proceedings do not include a person who is not, or is no longer, liable to be convicted of any offence in the proceedings (whether as a result of pleading guilty or for any other reason).

    (5) In any proceedings a person who has been but is no longer married to the accused shall be compellable to give evidence as if that person and the accused had never been married.

    (5A) In any proceedings a person who has been but is no longer the civil partner of the accused shall be compellable to give evidence as if that person and the accused had never been civil partners.

    (6) Where in any proceedings the age of any person at any time is material for the purposes of subsection (3) above, his age at the material time shall for the purposes of that provision be deemed to be or to have been that which appears to the court to be or to have been his age at that time.

    (7) In subsection (3)(b) above 'sexual offence' means an offence under the Protection of Children Act 1978 or Part I of the Sexual Offences Act 2003 or an offence under section 2 of the Modern Slavery Act 2015 (human trafficking) committed with a view to exploitation that consists of or includes behaviour within section 3(3) of that Act (sexual exploitation).

    (9) Section 1(d) of the Criminal Evidence Act 1898 (communications between husband and wife) and section 43(1) of the Matrimonial Causes Act 1965 (evidence as to marital intercourse) shall cease to have effect.

### 80A   Rule where accused's spouse or civil partner not compellable

The failure of the spouse or civil partner of a person charged in any proceedings to give evidence shall not be made the subject of any comment by the prosecution.

### 81   Advance notice of expert evidence in Crown Court

    (1) Criminal Procedure Rules may make provision for—

    (a) requiring any party to proceedings before the Court to disclose to the other party or parties any expert evidence which he proposes to adduce in the proceedings; and

    (b) prohibiting a party who fails to comply in respect of any evidence with any requirement imposed by virtue of paragraph (a) above from adducing that evidence without the leave of the court.

    (2) Criminal Procedure Rules made by virtue of this section may specify the kinds of expert evidence to which they apply and may exempt facts or matters of any description specified in the rules.

# PART VIII  SUPPLEMENTARY

### 82   Part VIII—interpretation

    (1) In this Part of this Act—

'confession' includes any statement wholly or partly adverse to the person who made it, whether made to a person in authority or not and whether made in words or otherwise;

'proceedings' means criminal proceedings, including service proceedings.

'Service court' means the Court Martial or the Service Civilian Court.

    (1A) ...*

    (3) Nothing in this Part of this Act shall prejudice any power of a court to exclude evidence (whether by preventing questions from being put or otherwise) at its discretion.

---

\* **Editor's Note:** Defines 'service proceedings'.

# PART X POLICE—GENERAL

## 107 Police officers performing duties of higher rank

(1) For the purpose of any provision of this Act or any other Act under which a power in respect of the investigation of offences or the treatment of persons in police custody is exercisable only by or with the authority of a police officer of at least the rank of superintendent, an officer of the rank of chief inspector shall be treated as holding the rank of superintendent if—

(a) he has been authorised by an officer holding a rank above the rank of superintendent to exercise the power or, as the case may be, to give his authority for its exercise, or

(b) he is acting during the absence of an officer holding the rank of superintendent who has authorised him, for the duration of that absence, to exercise the power, or as the case may be, to give his authority for its exercise.

(2) For the purpose of any provision of this Act or any other Act under which such a power is exercisable only by or with the authority of an officer of at least the rank of inspector, an officer of the rank of sergeant shall be treated as holding the rank of inspector if he has been authorised by an officer of at least the rank of superintendent to exercise the power or, as the case may be, to give this authority for its exercise.

## 111 Regulations for Police Forces and Police Cadets—Scotland

. . .*

# PART XI MISCELLANEOUS AND SUPPLEMENTARY

## 117 Power of constable to use reasonable force

Where any provision of this Act—

(a) confers a power on a constable; and

(b) does not provide that the power may only be exercised with the consent of some person, other than a police officer,

the officer may use reasonable force, if necessary, in the exercise of the power.

## 118 General interpretation

(1) In this Act—

'designated police station' has the meaning assigned to it by section 35 above;

'document' has the same meaning as in Part I of the Civil Evidence Act 1968;

'item subject to legal privilege' has the meaning assigned to it by section 10 above;

'parent or guardian' means—

(a) in the case of a child or young person in the care of a local authority, that authority;

'premises' has the meaning assigned to it by section 27 above;

'recordable offence' means any offence to which regulations under section 23 above apply;

'vessel' includes any ship, boat, raft or other apparatus constructed or adapted for floating on water.

(2) Subject to subsection (2A) a person is in police detention for the purposes of this Act if—

(a) he has been taken to a police station after being arrested for an offence or after being arrested under section 41 of the Terrorism Act 2000;

(b) he is arrested at a police station after attending voluntarily at the station or accompanying a constable to it,

and is detained there or is detained elsewhere in the charge of a constable, except that a person who is at a court after being charged is not in police detention for those purposes.

(2A) Where a person is in another's lawful custody by virtue of paragraph 22, 34(1) or 35(3) of Schedule 4 to the Police Reform Act 2002, he shall be treated as in police detention.

## 122 Short title

This Act may be cited as the Police and Criminal Evidence Act 1984.

---

* **Editor's Note:** Applies to Scotland.

# SCHEDULE 2A

# FINGERPRINTING AND SAMPLES: POWER TO REQUIRE ATTENDANCE AT POLICE STATION

## PART 1  FINGERPRINTING

### Persons arrested and released

1 (1) A constable may require a person to attend a police station for the purpose of taking his fingerprints under section 61(5A).

(2) The power under sub-paragraph (1) above may not be exercised in a case falling within section 61(5A)(b)(i) (fingerprints taken on previous occasion insufficient etc.) after the end of the period of six months beginning with the day on which the appropriate officer was informed that section 61(3A)(a) or (b) applied.

(3) In sub-paragraph (2) above 'appropriate officer' means the officer investigating the offence for which the person was arrested.

(4) The power under sub-paragraph (1) above may not be exercised in a case falling within section 61(5A)(b)(ii) (fingerprints destroyed where investigation interrupted) after the end of the period of six months beginning with the day on which the investigation was resumed.

### Persons charged etc.

2 (1) A constable may require a person to attend a police station for the purpose of taking his fingerprints under section 61(5B).

(2) The power under sub-paragraph (1) above may not be exercised after the end of the period of six months beginning with—

(a) in a case falling within section 61(5B)(a) (fingerprints not taken previously), the day on which the person was charged or informed that he would be reported, or

(b) in a case falling within section 61(5B)(b)(i) (fingerprints taken on previous occasion insufficient etc.), the day on which the appropriate officer was informed that section 61(3A)(a) or (b) applied or

(c) in a case falling within section 61(5B)(b)(ii) (fingerprints destroyed where investigation interrupted), the day on which the investigation was resumed.

(3) In sub-paragraph (2)(b) above 'appropriate officer' means the officer investigating the offence for which the person was charged or informed that he would be reported.

### Persons convicted etc. of an offence in England and Wales

3 (1) A constable may require a person to attend a police station for the purpose of taking his fingerprints under section 61(6).

(2) Where the condition in section 61(6ZA)(a) is satisfied (fingerprints not taken previously), the power under sub-paragraph (1) above may not be exercised after the end of the period of two years beginning with—

(a) the day on which the person was convicted or cautioned, or

(b) if later, the day on which this Schedule comes into force.

(3) Where the condition in section 61(6ZA)(b) is satisfied (fingerprints taken on previous occasion insufficient etc.), the power under sub-paragraph (1) above may not be exercised after the end of the period of two years beginning with—

(a) the day on which an appropriate officer was informed that section 61(3A)(a) or (b) applied, or

(b) if later, the day on which this Schedule comes into force.

(4) In sub-paragraph (3)(a) above 'appropriate officer' means an officer of the police force which investigated the offence in question.

(5) Sub-paragraphs (2) and (3) above do not apply where the offence is a qualifying offence (whether or not it was such an offence at the time of the conviction, caution or warning or reprimand).

*Persons convicted etc. of an offence outside England and Wales*

5 A constable may require a person to attend a police station for the purpose of taking his fingerprints under section 61(6D).

*Multiple attendance*

6 (1)  Where a person's fingerprints have been taken under section 61 on two occasions in relation to any offence, he may not under this Schedule be required to attend a police station to have his fingerprints taken under that section in relation to that offence on a subsequent occasion without the authorisation of an officer of at least the rank of inspector.

(2)  Where an authorisation is given under sub-paragraph (1) above—

(a)  the fact of the authorisation, and

(b)  the reasons for giving it,

shall be recorded as soon as practicable after it has been given.

# PART 2  INTIMATE SAMPLES

*Persons suspected to be involved in an offence*

7 A constable may require a person to attend a police station for the purpose of taking an intimate sample from him under section 62(1A) if, in the course of the investigation of an offence, two or more non-intimate samples suitable for the same means of analysis have been taken from him but have proved insufficient.

*Persons convicted etc. of an offence outside England and Wales*

8 A constable may require a person to attend a police station for the purpose of taking a sample from him under section 62(2A) if two or more non-intimate samples suitable for the same means of analysis have been taken from him under section 63(3E) but have proved insufficient.

# PART 3  NON-INTIMATE SAMPLES

*Persons arrested and released*

9 (1)  A constable may require a person to attend a police station for the purpose of taking a non-intimate sample from him under section 63(3ZA).

(2)  The power under sub-paragraph (1) above may not be exercised in a case falling within section 63(3ZA)(b)(i) or (ii) (sample taken on a previous occasion not suitable etc.) after the end of the period of six months beginning with the day on which the appropriate officer was informed of the matters specified in section 63(3ZA)(b)(i) or (ii).

(3)  In sub-paragraph (2) above, 'appropriate officer' means the officer investigating the offence for which the person was arrested.

(4)  The power under sub-paragraph (1) above may not be exercised in a case falling within section 63(3ZA)(b)(iii) (sample, and any DNA profile, destroyed where investigation interrupted) after the end of the period of six months beginning with the day on which the investigation was resumed.

*Persons charged etc.*

10 (1)  A constable may require a person to attend a police station for the purpose of taking a non-intimate sample from him under section 63(3A).

(2)  The power under sub-paragraph (1) above may not be exercised in a case falling within section 63(3A)(a) (sample not taken previously) after the end of the period of six months beginning with the day on which he was charged or informed that he would be reported.

(3)  The power under sub-paragraph (1) above may not be exercised in a case falling within section 63(3A)(b) (sample taken on a previous occasion not suitable etc.) after the end of the period of six

months beginning with the day on which the appropriate officer was informed of the matters specified in section 63(3A)(b)(i) or (ii).

(4) In sub-paragraph (3) above 'appropriate officer' means the officer investigating the offence for which the person was charged or informed that he would be reported.

(5) The power under sub-paragraph (1) above may not be exercised in a case falling within section 63(3A)(b)(iii) (sample, and any DNA profile, destroyed where investigation interrupted) after the end of the period of six months beginning with the day on which the investigation was resumed.

### Persons convicted etc. of an offence in England and Wales

11 (1) A constable may require a person to attend a police station for the purpose of taking a non-intimate sample from him under section 63(3B).

(2) Where the condition in section 63(3BA)(a) is satisfied (sample not taken previously), the power under sub-paragraph (1) above may not be exercised after the end of the period of two years beginning with—

(a) the day on which the person was convicted, cautioned or warned or reprimanded, or

(b) if later, the day on which this Schedule comes into force.

(3) Where the condition in section 63(3BA)(b) is satisfied (sample taken on a previous occasion not suitable etc.), the power under sub-paragraph (1) above may not be exercised after the end of the period of two years beginning with—

(a) the day on which an appropriate officer was informed of the matters specified in section 63(3BA)(b)(i) or (ii), or

(b) if later, the day on which this Schedule comes into force.

(4) In sub-paragraph (3)(a) above 'appropriate officer' means an officer of the police force which investigated the offence in question.

(5) Sub-paragraphs (2) and (3) above do not apply where—

(a) the offence is a qualifying offence (whether or not it was such an offence at the time of the conviction, caution or warning or reprimand), or

(b) he was convicted before 10th April 1995 and is a person to whom section 1 of the Criminal Evidence (Amendment) Act 1997 applies.

### Persons convicted etc. of an offence outside England and Wales

13 A constable may require a person to attend a police station for the purpose of taking a non-intimate sample from him under section 63(3E).

### Multiple exercise of power

14 (1) Where a non-intimate sample has been taken from a person under section 63 on two occasions in relation to any offence, he may not under this Schedule be required to attend a police station to have another such sample taken from him under that section in relation to that offence on a subsequent occasion without the authorisation of an officer of at least the rank of inspector.

(2) Where an authorisation is given under sub-paragraph (1) above—

(a) the fact of the authorisation, and

(b) the reasons for giving it,

shall be recorded as soon as practicable after it has been given.

## PART 4 GENERAL AND SUPPLEMENTARY

### Requirement to have power to take fingerprints or sample

15 A power conferred by this Schedule to require a person to attend a police station for the purposes of taking fingerprints or a sample under any provision of this Act may be exercised only in a case where the fingerprints or sample may be taken from the person under that provision (and, in particular, if any necessary authorisation for taking the fingerprints or sample under that provision has been obtained).

*Date and time of attendance*

16 (1)  A requirement under this Schedule—

(a) shall give the person a period of at least seven days within which he must attend the police station; and

(b) may direct him so to attend at a specified time of day or between specified times of day.

(2)  In specifying a period or time or times of day for the purposes of sub-paragraph (1) above, the constable shall consider whether the fingerprints or sample could reasonably be taken at a time when the person is for any other reason required to attend the police station.

(3)  A requirement under this Schedule may specify a period shorter than seven days if—

(a) there is an urgent need for the fingerprints or sample for the purposes of the investigation of an offence; and

(b) the shorter period is authorised by an officer of at least the rank of inspector.

(4)  Where an authorisation is given under sub-paragraph (3)(b) above—

(a) the fact of the authorisation, and

(b) the reasons for giving it,

shall be recorded as soon as practicable after it has been given.

(5)  If the constable giving a requirement under this Schedule and the person to whom it is given so agree, it may be varied so as to specify any period within which, or date or time at which, the person must attend; but a variation shall not have effect unless confirmed by the constable in writing.

*Enforcement*

17 A constable may arrest without warrant a person who has failed to comply with a requirement under this Schedule.

# Criminal Justice Act 1988

(1988, c. 33)

## PART III  OTHER PROVISIONS ABOUT EVIDENCE IN CRIMINAL PROCEEDINGS

### 30  Expert reports

(1)  An expert report shall be admissible as evidence in criminal proceedings, whether or not the person making it attends to give oral evidence in those proceedings.

(2)  If it is proposed that the person making the report shall not give oral evidence, the report shall only be admissible with the leave of the court.

(3)  For the purpose of determining whether to give leave the court shall have regard—

(a) to the contents of the report;

(b) to the reasons why it is proposed that the person making the report shall not give oral evidence;

(c) to any risk, having regard in particular to whether it is likely to be possible to controvert statements in the report if the person making it does not attend to give oral evidence in the proceedings, that its admission or exclusion will result in unfairness to the accused or, if there is more than one, to any of them; and

(d) to any other circumstances that appear to the court to be relevant.

(4)  An expert report, when admitted, shall be evidence of any fact or opinion of which the person making it could have given oral evidence.

(4A)  . . .

(5) In this section 'expert report' means a written report by a person dealing wholly or mainly with matters on which he is (or would if living be) qualified to give expert evidence.

## 31  Form of evidence and glossaries

For the purpose of helping members of juries to understand complicated issues of fact or technical terms Criminal Procedure Rules may make provision:

(a) as to the furnishing of evidence in any form, notwithstanding the existence of admissible material from which the evidence to be given in that form would be derived; and

(b) as to the furnishing of glossaries for such purposes as may be specified;

in any case where the court gives leave for, or requires, evidence or a glossary to be so furnished.

## 32  Evidence through television links

(1) A person other than the accused may give evidence through a live television link in proceedings to which subsection (1A) below applies if—

(a) the witness is outside the United Kingdom;

but evidence may not be so given without the leave of the court.

(1A) This subsection applies—

(a) to trials on indictment, appeals to the criminal division of the Court of Appeal and hearings of references under section 9 of the Criminal Appeal Act 1995; and

(b) to proceedings in youth courts, appeals to the Crown Court arising out of such proceedings and hearings of references under section 11 of the Criminal Appeal Act 1995 so arising.

(3) A statement made on oath by a witness outside the United Kingdom and given in evidence through a link by virtue of this section shall be treated for the purposes of section 1 of the Perjury Act 1911 as having been made in the proceedings in which it is given in evidence.

(4) Without prejudice to the generality of any enactment conferring power to make Criminal Procedure Rules to which this subsection applies, such rules may make such provision as appears to the authority making them to be necessary or expedient for the purposes of this section.

## 34  Abolition of requirement of corroboration for unsworn evidence of children

(2) Any requirement whereby at a trial on indictment it is obligatory for the court to give the jury a warning about convicting the accused on the uncorroborated evidence of a child is abrogated.

(3) Unsworn evidence admitted by virtue of section 56 of the Youth Justice and Criminal Evidence Act 1999 may corroborate evidence (sworn or unsworn) given by any other person.

# Road Traffic Offenders Act 1988

(1988, c. 53)

## 11  Evidence by certificate as to driver, user or owner

(1) In any proceedings in England and Wales for an offence to which this section applies, a certificate in the prescribed form, purporting to be signed by a constable and certifying that a person specified in the certificate stated to the constable—

(a) that a particular mechanically propelled vehicle was being driven or used by, or belonged to, that person on a particular occasion, or

(b) that a particular mechanically propelled vehicle on a particular occasion was used by, or belonged to, a firm and that he was, at the time of the statement, a partner in that firm, or

(c) that a particular mechanically propelled vehicle on a particular occasion was used by, or belonged to, a corporation and that he was, at the time of the statement, a director, officer or employee of that corporation, shall be admissible as evidence for the purpose of determining by whom the vehicle was being driven or used, or to whom it belonged, as the case may be, on that occasion.

(2) Nothing in subsection (1) above makes a certificate admissible as evidence in proceedings for an offence except in a case where and to the like extent to which oral evidence to the like effect would have been admissible in those proceedings.

(3) Nothing in subsection (1) above makes a certificate admissible as evidence in proceedings for an offence—

    (a) unless a copy of it has, not less than seven days before the hearing or trial, been served in the prescribed manner on the person charged with the offence, or

    (b) if that person, not later than three days before the hearing or trial or within such further time as the court in special circumstances allow, serves a notice in the prescribed form and manner on the prosecutor requiring the attendance at the trial of the person who signed the certificate.

(4) In this section 'prescribed' means prescribed by rules made by the Secretary of State by statutory instrument.

(5) Schedule 1 to this Act shows the offences to which this section applies.

## 12 Proof, in summary proceedings, of identity of driver of vehicle

(1) Where on the summary trial in England and Wales of an information for an offence to which this subsection applies—

    (a) it is proved to the satisfaction of the court, on oath or in manner prescribed by Criminal Procedure Rules, that a requirement under section 172(2) of the Road Traffic Act 1988 to give information as to the identity of the driver of a particular vehicle on the particular occasion to which the information relates has been served on the accused by post, and

    (b) a statement in writing is produced to the court purporting to be signed by the accused that the accused was the driver of that vehicle on that occasion,

the court may accept that statement as evidence that the accused was the driver of that vehicle on that occasion.

(2) Schedule 1 to this Act shows the offences to which subsection (1) above applies.

(3) Where on the summary trial in England and Wales of an information for an offence to which section 112 of the Road Traffic Regulation Act 1984 applies—

    (a) it is proved to the satisfaction of the court, on oath or in manner prescribed by Criminal Procedure Rules, that a requirement under section 112(2) of the Road Traffic Regulation Act 1984 to give information as to the identity of the driver of a particular vehicle on the particular occasion to which the information relates has been served on the accused by post, and

    (b) a statement in writing is produced to the court purporting to be signed by the accused that the accused was the driver of that vehicle on that occasion,

the court may accept that statement as evidence that the accused was the driver of that vehicle on that occasion.

## 13 Admissibility of records as evidence

(1) This section applies to a statement contained in a document purporting to be—

    (a) a part of the records maintained by the Secretary of State in connection with any functions exercisable by him by virtue of Part III of the Road Traffic Act 1988 or a part of any other records maintained by the Secretary of State with respect to vehicles or of any records maintained with respect to vehicles by an approved testing authority in connection with the exercise by that authority of any functions conferred on such authority, or on that authority as such an authority, by or under any enactment or of any records maintained with respect to vehicles by an approved testing authority in connection with the exercise by that authority of any functions conferred on such authorities, or on that authority as such an authority, by or under any enactment, or

    (b) a copy of a document forming part of those records, or

    (c) a note of any information contained in those records,

and to be authenticated by a person authorised in that behalf by the Secretary of State or (as the case may be) the approved testing authority.

(2) A statement to which this section applies shall be admissible in any proceedings as evidence . . . of any fact stated in it to the same extent as oral evidence of that fact is admissible in those proceedings.

(3) In the preceding subsections, . . .

'copy', in relation to a document, means anything onto which information recorded in the document has been copied, by whatever means and whether directly or indirectly;

'document' means anything in which information of any description is recorded; and

'statement' means any representation of fact, however made.

(3A) In any case where—

 (a) a person is convicted by a magistrates' court of a summary offence under the Traffic Acts or the Road Traffic (Driver Licensing and Information Systems) Act 1989,

 (b) a statement to which this section applies is produced to the court in the proceedings,

 (c) the statement specifies an alleged previous conviction of the accused of an offence involving obligatory endorsement or an order made on the conviction, and

 (d) the accused is not present in person before the court when the statement is produced,

the court may take account of the previous conviction or order as if the accused had appeared and admitted it.

(3B) Section 104 of the Magistrates' Courts Act 1980 (under which the previous convictions may be adduced in the absence of the accused after giving him seven days' notice of them) does not limit the effect of subsection (3A) above.

(4) In any case where—

 (a) a statement to which this section applies is produced to a magistrates' court in any proceedings for an offence involving obligatory or discretionary disqualification other than a summary offence under any of the enactments mentioned in subsection (3A) above,

 (b) the statement specifies an alleged previous conviction of an accused person of any such offence or any order made on the conviction,

 (c) it is proved to the satisfaction of the court, on oath or in such manner as may be prescribed by Criminal Procedure Rules, that not less than seven days before the statement is so produced a notice was served on the accused, in such form and manner as may be so prescribed, specifying the previous conviction or order and stating that it is proposed to bring it to the notice of the court in the event of or, as the case may be, in view of his conviction, and

 (d) the accused is not present in person before the court when the statement is so produced,

the court may take account of the previous conviction or order as if the accused had appeared and admitted it.

(5) Nothing in the preceding provisions of this section enables evidence to be given in respect of any matter other than a matter of a description prescribed by regulations made by the Secretary of State.

(6) The power to make regulations under this section shall be exercisable by statutory instrument, which shall be subject to annulment in pursuance of a resolution of either House of Parliament.

## 16 Documentary evidence as to specimens in such proceedings

(1) Evidence of the proportion of alcohol or a drug in a specimen of breath, blood or urine may, subject to subsections (3) and (4) below and to section 15(5) and (5A) of this Act, be given by the production of a document or documents purporting to be whichever of the following is appropriate, that is to say—

 (a) a statement automatically produced by the device by which the proportion of alcohol in a specimen of breath was measured and a certificate signed by a constable (which may but need not be contained in the same document as the statement) that the statement relates to a specimen provided by the accused at the date and time shown in the statement, and

 (b) a certificate signed by an authorised analyst as to the proportion of alcohol or any drug found in a specimen of blood or urine identified in the certificate.

(2) Subject to subsections (3) and (4) below, evidence that a specimen of blood was taken from the accused with his consent by a medical practitioner or a registered health care professional may be given by the production of a document purporting to certify that fact and to be signed by a medical practitioner or registered health care professional.

(3) Subject to subsection (4) below—

(a) a document purporting to be such a statement or such a certificate (or both such a statement and such a certificate) as is mentioned in subsection (1)(a) above is admissible in evidence on behalf of the prosecution in pursuance of this section only if a copy of it either has been handed to the accused when the document was produced or has been served on him not later than seven days before the hearing, and

(b) any other document is so admissible only if a copy of it has been served on the accused not later than seven days before the hearing.

(4) A document purporting to be a certificate (or so much of a document as purports to be a certificate) is not so admissible if the accused, not later than three days before the hearing or within such further time as the court may in special circumstances allow, has served notice on the prosecutor requiring the attendance at the hearing of the person by whom the document purports to be signed.

(5) ...*

(6) A copy of a certificate required by this section to be served on the accused or a notice required by this section to be served on the prosecutor may be served personally or sent by registered post or recorded delivery service.

(7) In this section 'authorised analyst' means—

(a) any person possessing the qualifications prescribed by regulations made under section 27 of the Food Safety Act 1990 as qualifying persons for appointment as public analysts under those Acts, and

(b) any other person authorised by the Secretary of State to make analyses for the purposes of this section.

## 18    Evidence by certificate as to registration of driving instructors etc.

(1) A certificate signed by the Registrar and stating that, on any date—

(a)    a person's name was, or was not, in the register,

(b)    the entry of a person's name was made in the register or a person's name was removed from it,

(ba)  a person's registration was, or was not, suspended,

(c)    a person was, or was not, the holder of a current licence under section 129 of the Road Traffic Act 1988, or

(d)    a licence under that section granted to a person came into force or ceased to be in force, shall be evidence, ... of the facts stated in the certificate in pursuance of this section.

(2) A certificate so stating and purporting to be signed by the Registrar shall be deemed to be so signed unless the contrary is proved.

(3) In this section 'current licence', 'Registrar', 'registered' and 'registration' have the same meanings as in Part V of the Road Traffic Act 1988.

## 20    Speeding offences etc.: admissibility of certain evidence

(1) Evidence . . . of a fact relevant to proceedings for an offence to which this section applies may be given by the production of—

(a) a record produced by a prescribed device, and

(b) (in the same or another document) a certificate as to the circumstances in which the record was produced signed by a constable or by a person authorised by or on behalf of the chief officer of police for the police area in which the offence is alleged to have been committed;

---

\* **Editor's Note:** Applies to Scotland only.

but subject to the following provisions of this section.

(2)  This section applies to—

(a)   an offence under section 16 of the Road Traffic Regulation Act 1984 consisting in the contravention of a restriction on the speed of vehicles imposed under section 14 of that Act;

(b)   an offence under subsection (4) of section 17 of that Act consisting in the contravention of a restriction on the speed of vehicles imposed under that section;

(ba)  an offence under subsection (4) of section 17 of that Act consisting in a contravention of regulation 9 of the Motorways Traffic (England and Wales) Regulations 1982(1) (restriction on the use of hard shoulders) by the driving of a vehicle on the hard shoulder of a motorway; and

(c)   an offence under section 88(7) of that Act (temporary minimum speed limits);

(d)   an offence under section 89(1) of that Act (speeding offences generally);

(e)   an offence under section 36(1) of the Road Traffic Act 1988 consisting in the failure to comply with an indication given by a light signal that vehicular traffic is not to proceed;

(ea)  an offence under section 36(1) of that Act consisting in the failure to comply with an indication given by a light signal to vehicular traffic not to enter, or proceed in, a traffic lane; and

(f)   an offence under Part I or II of the Road Traffic Regulation Act 1984 of contravening or failing to comply with an order or regulations made under either of those Parts relating to the use of an area of road which is described as a bus lane or a route for use by buses only;

(g)   an offence under section 29(1) of the Vehicle Excise and Registration Act 1994 (using or keeping an unlicensed vehicle on a public road);

(h)   an offence under section 11(1) of the HGV Road User Levy Act 2013 (using or keeping heavy goods vehicle if levy not paid).

(3)  The Secretary of State may by order amend subsection (2) above by making additions to or deletions from the list of offences for the time being set out there; and an order under this subsection may make such transitional provision as appears to him to be necessary or expedient.

(4)  A record produced or measurement made by a prescribed device shall not be admissible as evidence of a fact relevant to proceedings for an offence to which this section applies unless—

(a)  the device is of a type approved by the Secretary of State, and

(b)  any conditions subject to which the approval was given are satisfied.

(5)  Any approval given by the Secretary of State for the purposes of this section may be given subject to conditions as to the purposes for which, and the manner and other circumstances in which, any device of the type concerned is to be used.

(6)  In proceedings for an offence to which this section applies, evidence (which in Scotland shall be sufficient evidence)—

(a)  of a measurement made by a device, or of the circumstances in which it was made, or

(b)  that a device was of a type approved for the purposes of this section, or that any conditions subject to which an approval was given were satisfied,

may be given by the production of a document which is signed as mentioned in subsection (1) above and which, as the case may be, gives particulars of the measurement or of the circumstances in which it was made, or states that the device was of such a type or that, to the best of the knowledge and belief of the person making the statement, all such conditions were satisfied.

(7)  For the purposes of this section a document purporting to be a record of the kind mentioned in subsection (1) above, or to be a certificate or other document signed as mentioned in that subsection or in subsection (6) above, shall be deemed to be such a record, or to be so signed, unless the contrary is proved.

(8)  Nothing in subsection (1) or (6) above makes a document admissible as evidence in proceedings for an offence unless a copy of it has, not less than seven days before the hearing or trial, been served on the person charged with the offence; and nothing in those subsections makes a document admissible as evidence of anything other than the matters shown on a record produced by a prescribed device if that person, not less than three days before the hearing or trial or within such further

time as the court may in special circumstances allow, serves a notice on the prosecutor requiring attendance at the hearing or trial of the person who signed the document.

(9) In this section 'prescribed device' means device of a description specified in an order made by the Secretary of State.

(10) The powers to make orders under subsections (3) and (9) above shall be exercisable by statutory instrument, which shall be subject to annulment in pursuance of a resolution of either House of Parliament.

# Road Traffic Act 1988

**(1992, c. 52)**

### 172   Duty to give information as to identity of driver etc. in certain circumstances

(1) This section applies—

   (a) to any offence under the preceding provisions of this Act except—

      (i) an offence under Part V, or

      (ii) an offence under section 13, 16, 51(2), 61(4), 67(9), 68(4), 96 or 120, and to an offence under section 178 of this Act,

   (b) to any offence under sections 25, 26 or 27 of the Road Traffic Offenders Act 1988,

   (c) to any offence against any other enactment relating to the use of vehicles on roads, and

   (d) to manslaughter . . . by the driver of a motor vehicle.

(2) Where the driver of a vehicle is alleged to be guilty of an offence to which this section applies—

   (a) the person keeping the vehicle shall give such information as to the identity of the driver as he may be required to give by or on behalf of a chief officer of police or the Chief Constable of the British Transport Police Force, and

   (b) any other person shall if required as stated above give any information which it is in his power to give and may lead to identification of the driver.

(3) Subject to the following provisions, a person who fails to comply with a requirement under subsection (2) above shall be guilty of an offence.

(4) A person shall not be guilty of an offence by virtue of paragraph (a) of subsection (2) above if he shows that he did not know and could not with reasonable diligence have ascertained who the driver of the vehicle was.

(5) Where a body corporate is guilty of an offence under this section and the offence is proved to have been committed with the consent or connivance of, or to be attributable to neglect on the part of, a director, manager, secretary or other similar officer of the body corporate, or a person who was purporting to act in any such capacity, he, as well as the body corporate, is guilty of that offence and liable to be proceeded against and punished accordingly.

(6) Where the alleged offender is a body corporate . . . or the proceedings are brought against him by virtue of subsection (5) above or subsection (11) below, subsection (4) above shall not apply unless, in addition to the matters there mentioned, the alleged offender shows that no record was kept of the persons who drove the vehicle and that the failure to keep a record was reasonable.

(7) A requirement under subsection (2) may be made by written notice served by post; and where it is so made—

   (a) it shall have effect as a requirement to give the information within the period of 28 days beginning with the day on which the notice is served, and

   (b) the person on whom the notice is served shall not be guilty of an offence under this section if he shows either that he gave the information as soon as reasonably practicable after the end of that period or that it has not been reasonably practicable for him to give it.

(8) Where the person on whom a notice under subsection (7) above is to be served is a body corporate, the notice is duly served if it is served on the secretary or clerk of that body.

(9) For the purposes of section 7 of the Interpretation Act 1978 as it applies for the purposes of this section the proper address of any person in relation to the service on him of a notice under subsection (7) above is—

(a) in the case of the secretary or clerk of a body corporate, that of the registered or principal office of that body or (if the body corporate is the registered keeper of the vehicle concerned) the registered address, and

(b) in any other case, his last known address at the time of service.

(10) in this section—

'registered address', in relation to the registered keeper of a vehicle, means the address recorded in the record kept under the Vehicles Excise and Registration Act 1994 with respect to that vehicle as being that person's address, and

'registered keeper', in relation to a vehicle, means the person in whose name the vehicle is registered under that Act;

and references to the driver of a vehicle include references to the rider of a cycle.

# Sexual Offences (Amendment) Act 1992

(1992, c. 34)

## 1  Anonymity of victims of certain offences

(1) Where an allegation has been made that an offence to which this Act applies has been committed against a person, no matter relating to that person shall during that person's lifetime be included in any publication if it is likely to lead members of the public to identify that person as the person against whom the offence is alleged to have been committed.

(2) Where a person is accused of an offence to which this Act applies, no matter likely to lead members of the public to identify a person as the person against whom the offence is alleged to have been committed ('the complainant') shall during the complainant's lifetime be included in any publication.

(3) This section—

(a) does not apply in relation to a person by virtue of subsection (1) at any time after a person has been accused of the offence, and

(b) in its application in relation to a person by virtue of subsection (2), has effect subject to any direction given under section 3.

(3A) The matters relating to a person in relation to which the restrictions imposed by subsection (1) or (2) apply (if their inclusion in any publication is likely to have the result mentioned in that subsection) include in particular—

(a) the person's name,

(b) the person's address,

(c) the identity of any school or other educational establishment attended by the person,

(d) the identity of any place of work, and

(e) any still or moving picture of the person.

(4) Nothing in this section prohibits the inclusion in a publication of matter consisting only of a report of criminal proceedings other than proceedings at, or intended to lead to, or on an appeal arising out of, a trial at which the accused is charged with the offence.

## 2  Offences to which this Act applies

(1) This Act applies to the following offences against the law of England and Wales—

(aa) rape;

(ab) burglary with intent to rape;

(a)   any offence under any of the provisions of the Sexual Offences Act 1956 mentioned in subsection (2);

(b)   any offence under section 128 of the Mental Health Act 1959 (intercourse with mentally handicapped person by hospital staff etc.);

(c)   any offence under section 1 of the Indecency with Children Act 1960 (indecent conduct towards young child);

(d)   any offence under section 54 of the Criminal Law Act 1977 (incitement by man of his grand-daughter, daughter or sister under the age of 16 to commit incest with him);

(da)  any offence under any of the provisions of Part 1 of the Sexual Offences Act 2003 except section 64, 65, 69 or 71;

(db)  any offence under section 2 of the Modern Slavery Act 2015 (human trafficking);

(e)   any attempt to commit any of the offences mentioned in paragraphs (aa) to (db);

(f)   any conspiracy to commit any of those offences;

(g)   any incitement of another to commit any of those offences;

(h)   aiding, abetting, counselling or procuring the commission of any of the offences mentioned in paragraphs (aa) to (e) and (g);

(2) The provisions of the Act of 1956 are—

(a)  section 2 (procurement of a woman by threats);

(b)  section 3 (procurement of a woman by false pretences);

(c)  section 4 (administering drugs to obtain intercourse with a woman);

(d)  section 5 (intercourse with a girl under the age of 13);

(e)  section 6 (intercourse with a girl between the ages of 13 and 16);

(f)  section 7 (intercourse with a mentally handicapped person);

(g)  section 9 (procurement of a mentally handicapped person);

(h)  section 10 (incest by a man);

(i)  section 11 (incest by a woman);

(j)  section 12 (buggery);

(k)  section 14 (indecent assault on a woman);

(l)  section 15 (indecent assault on a man);

(m) section 16 (assault with intent to commit buggery);

(n)  section 17 (abduction of woman by force).

(3) . . .*

(4) . . .**

# Criminal Justice and Public Order Act 1994

**(1994, c. 33)**

*Corroboration*

### 32   Abolition of corroboration rules

(1)  Any requirement whereby at a trial on indictment it is obligatory for the court to give the jury a warning about convicting the accused on the uncorroborated evidence of a person merely because that person is—

(a)  an alleged accomplice of the accused, or

(b)  where the offence charged is a sexual offence, the person in respect of whom it is alleged to have been committed,

is hereby abrogated.

---

* **Editor's Note:** Applies to Northern Ireland.
** **Editor's Note:** Applies to armed forces.

(2) . . .

(3) Any requirement that—

    (a) is applicable at the summary trial of a person for an offence, and

    (b) corresponds to the requirement mentioned in subsection (1) above or that mentioned in section 34(2) of the Criminal Justice Act 1988,

is hereby abrogated.

(4) Nothing in this section applies in relation to—

    (a) any trial, or

    (b) any proceedings before a magistrates' court as examining justices,

which began before the commencement of this section.

## 33 Abolition of corroboration requirements under Sexual Offences Act 1956

(1) The following provisions of the Sexual Offences Act 1956 (which provide that a person shall not be convicted of the offence concerned on the evidence of one witness only unless the witness is corroborated) are hereby repealed—

    (a) section 2(2) (procurement of woman by threats),

    (b) section 3(2) (procurement of woman by false pretences),

    (c) section 4(2) (administering drugs to obtain or facilitate intercourse),

    (d) section 22(2) (causing prostitution of women), and

    (e) section 23(2) (procuration of girl under twenty-one).

(2) Nothing in this section applies in relation to—

    (a) any trial, or

    (b) any proceedings before a magistrates' court as examining justices,

which began before the commencement of this section.

### *Inferences from accused's silence*

## 34 Effect of accused's failure to mention facts when questioned or charged

(1) Where, in any proceedings against a person for an offence, evidence is given that the accused—

    (a) at any time before he was charged with the offence, on being questioned under caution by a constable trying to discover whether or by whom the offence had been committed, failed to mention any fact relied on in his defence in those proceedings; or

    (b) on being charged with the offence or officially informed that he might be prosecuted for it, failed to mention any such fact, or

    (c) . . .*

being a fact which in the circumstances existing at the time the accused could reasonably have been expected to mention when so questioned, charged or informed, as the case may be, subsection (2) below applies.

(2) Where this subsection applies—

    (a) . . .

    (b) a judge, in deciding whether to grant an application made by the accused under—

        (i) paragraph 2 of Schedule 3 to the Crime and Disorder Act 1998;

    (c) the court, in determining whether there is a case to answer; and

    (d) the court or jury, in determining whether the accused is guilty of the offence charged,

may draw such inferences from the failure as appear proper.

(2A) Where the accused was at an authorised place of detention at the time of failure, subsections (1) and (2) above do not apply if he had not been allowed an opportunity to consult a solicitor prior to being questioned, charged or informed as mentioned in subsection (1) above.

(3) Subject to any directions by the court, evidence tending to establish the failure may be given before or after evidence tending to establish the fact which the accused is alleged to have failed to mention.

---

\* **Editor's Note:** Applies to terrorism.

(4)  This section applies in relation to questioning by persons (other than constables) charged with the duty of investigating offences or charging offenders as it applies in relation to questioning by constables; and in subsection (1) above 'officially informed' means informed by a constable or any such person.

(5)  This section does not—

(a)  prejudice the admissibility in evidence of the silence or other reaction of the accused in the face of anything said in his presence relating to the conduct in respect of which he is charged, in so far as evidence thereof would be admissible apart from this section; or

(b)  preclude the drawing of any inference from any such silence or other reaction of the accused which could properly be drawn apart from this section.

(6)  This section does not apply in relation to a failure to mention a fact if the failure occurred before the commencement of this section.

### 35   Effect of accused's silence at trial

(1)  At the trial of any person for an offence, subsections (2) and (3) below apply unless—

(a)  the accused's guilt is not in issue; or

(b)  it appears to the court that the physical or mental condition of the accused makes it undesirable for him to give evidence;

but subsection (2) below does not apply if, at the conclusion of the evidence for the prosecution, his legal representative informs the court that the accused will give evidence or, where he is unrepresented, the court ascertains from him that he will give evidence.

(2)  Where this subsection applies, the court shall, at the conclusion of the evidence for the prosecution, satisfy itself (in the case of proceedings on indictment with a jury, in the presence of the jury) that the accused is aware that the stage has been reached at which evidence can be given for the defence and that he can, if he wishes, give evidence and that, if he chooses not to give evidence, or having been sworn, without good cause refuses to answer any question, it will be permissible for the court or jury to draw such inferences as appear proper from his failure to give evidence or his refusal, without good cause, to answer any question.

(3)  Where this subsection applies, the court or jury, in determining whether the accused is guilty of the offence charged, may draw such inferences as appear proper from the failure of the accused to give evidence or his refusal, without good cause, to answer any question.

(4)  This section does not render the accused compellable to give evidence on his own behalf, and he shall accordingly not be guilty of contempt of court by reason of a failure to do so.

(5)  For the purposes of this section a person who, having been sworn, refuses to answer any question shall be taken to do so without good cause unless—

(a)  he is entitled to refuse to answer the question by virtue of any enactment, whenever passed or made, or on the ground of privilege; or

(b)  the court in the exercise of its general discretion excuses him from answering it.

(7)  This section applies—

(a)  in relation to proceedings on indictment for an offence, only if the person charged with the offence is arraigned on or after the commencement of this section;

(b)  in relation to proceedings in a magistrates' court, only if the time when the court begins to receive evidence in the proceedings falls after the commencement of this section.

### 36   Effect of accused's failure or refusal to account for objects, substances or marks

(1)  Where—

(a)  a person is arrested by a constable, and there is—

(i)   on his person; or

(ii)  in or on his clothing or footwear; or

(iii) otherwise in his possession; or

(iv)  in any place in which he is at the time of his arrest,

any object, substance or mark, or there is any mark on any such object; and

(b) that or another constable investigating the case reasonably believes that the presence of the object, substance or mark may be attributable to the participation of the person arrested in the commission of an offence specified by the constable; and

(c) the constable informs the person arrested that he so believes, and requests him to account for the presence of the object, substance or mark; and

(d) the person fails or refuses to do so,

then if, in any proceedings against the person for the offence so specified, evidence of those matters is given, subsection (2) below applies.

(2) Where this subsection applies—

(a) . . .

(b) a judge, in deciding whether to grant an application made by the accused under—

(i) paragraph 2 of Schedule 3 to the Crime and Disorder Act 1998;

(c) the court, in determining whether there is a case to answer; and

(d) the court or jury, in determining whether the accused is guilty of the offence charged,

may draw such inferences from the failure or refusal as appear proper.

(3) Subsections (1) and (2) above apply to the condition of clothing or footwear as they apply to a substance or mark thereon.

(4) Subsections 1 and 2 above do not apply unless the accused was told in ordinary language by the constable when making the request mentioned in subsection (1)(c) above what the effect of this section would be if he failed or refused to comply with the request.

(4A) Where the accused was at an authorised place of detention at the time of the failure or refusal, subsections (1) and (2) above do not apply if he had not been allowed an opportunity to consult a solicitor prior to the request being made.

(5) This section applies in relation to officers of customs and excise as it applies in relation to constables.

(6) This section does not preclude the drawing of any inference from a failure or refusal of the accused to account for the presence of an object, substance or mark or from the condition of clothing or footwear which could properly be drawn apart from this section.

(7) This section does not apply in relation to a failure or refusal which occurred before the commencement of this section.

## 37 Effect of accused's failure or refusal to account for presence at a particular place

(1) Where—

(a) a person arrested by a constable was found by him at a place at or about the time the offence for which he was arrested is alleged to have been committed; and

(b) that or another constable investigating the offence reasonably believes that the presence of the person at that place and at that time may be attributable to his participation in the commission of the offence; and

(c) the constable informs the person that he so believes, and requests him to account for that presence; and

(d) the person fails or refuses to do so, then if, in any proceedings against the person for the offence, evidence of those matters is given, subsection (2) below applies.

(2) Where this subsection applies—

(a) . . .

(b) a judge, in deciding whether to grant an application made by the accused under—

(i) paragraph 2 of Schedule 3 to the Crime and Disorder Act 1998;

(c) the court, in determining whether there is a case to answer, and

(d) the court or jury, in determining whether the accused is guilty of the offence charged,

may draw such inferences from the failure or refusal as appear proper.

(3) Subsections (1) and (2) do not apply unless the accused was told in ordinary language by the constable when making the request mentioned in subsection (1)(c) above what the effect of this section would be if he failed or refused to comply with the request.

(3A) Where the accused was at an authorised place of detention at the time of the failure or refusal, subsections (1) and (2) do not apply if he had not been allowed an opportunity to consult a solicitor prior to the request being made.

(4) This section applies in relation to officers of customs and excise as it applies in relation to constables.

(5) This section does not preclude the drawing of any inference from a failure or refusal of the accused to account for his presence at a place which could properly be drawn apart from this section.

(6) This section does not apply in relation to a failure or refusal which occurred before the commencement of this section.

## 38 Interpretation and savings for sections 34, 35, 36 and 37

(1) In sections 34, 35, 36 and 37 of this Act—

'legal representative' means a person who, for the purposes of the Legal Services Act 2007, is an authorised person in relation to an activity which constitutes the exercise of a right of audience or the conduct of litigation (within the meaning of that Act); and

'place' includes any building or part of a building, any vehicle, vessel, aircraft or hovercraft and any other place whatsoever.

(2) In sections 34(2), 35(3), 36(2) and 37(2), references to an offence charged include references to any other offence of which the accused could lawfully be convicted on that charge.

(2A) In each of sections 34(2A), 36(4A) and 37(3A) 'authorised place of detention' means—

(a) a police station; or

(b) any other place prescribed for the purpose of that provision by the Secretary of State;

and the power to make an order under this subsection shall be exercisable by statutory instrument which shall be subject to annulment on pursuance of a resolution of either House of Parliament.

(3) A person shall not have the proceedings against him transferred to the Crown Court for trial, have a case to answer or be convicted of an offence solely on an inference drawn from such a failure or refusal as is mentioned in section 34(2), 35(3), 36(2) or 37(2).

(4) A judge shall not refuse to grant such an application as is mentioned in section 34(2)(b), 36(2)(b) and 37(2)(b) solely on an inference drawn from such a failure as is mentioned in section 34(2), 36(2) or 37(2).

(5) Nothing in sections 34, 35, 36 or 37 prejudices the operation of a provision of an enactment which provides (in whatever words) that any answer or evidence given by a person in specified circumstances shall not be admissible in evidence against him or some other person in any proceedings or class of proceedings (however described, and whether civil or criminal).

In this subsection, the reference to giving evidence is a reference to giving evidence in any manner, whether by furnishing information, making discovery, producing documents or otherwise.

(6) Nothing in sections 34, 35, 36 or 37 prejudices any power of a court, in any proceedings, to exclude evidence (whether by preventing questions being put or otherwise) at its discretion.

# Criminal Evidence (Amendment) Act 1997

(1997, c. 17)

*Extension of power to take non-intimate body samples without consent*

## 1 Persons imprisoned or detained by virtue of pre-existing conviction for sexual offence etc.

(1) This section has effect for removing, in relation to persons to whom this section applies, the restriction on the operation of section 63(3B) of the Police and Criminal Evidence Act 1984 (power to take non-intimate samples without the appropriate consent from persons convicted of recordable offences)—

(a) which is imposed by the subsection (10) inserted in section 63 by section 55(6) of the Criminal Justice and Public Order Act 1994, and

(b) by virtue of which section 63(3B) does not apply to persons convicted before 10 April 1995.

(2) . . .\*

(3) This section applies to a person who was convicted of a recordable offence before 10 April 1995 if—

(a) that offence was one of the offences listed in Schedule 1 to this Act (which lists certain sexual, violent and other offences), and

(b) he has at any time served or at the relevant time he is serving a sentence of imprisonment in respect of that offence.

(4) This section also applies to a person who was convicted of a recordable offence before 10 April 1995 if—

(a) that offence was one of the offences listed in Schedule 1 to this Act, and

(b) he has at any time been detained or at the relevant time he is detained under Part III of the Mental Health Act 1983 in pursuance of—

(i) a hospital order or interim hospital order made following that conviction.

Expressions used in this subsection and in the Mental Health Act 1983 have the same meaning as in that Act.

(5) Where a person convicted of a recordable offence before 10 April 1995 was, following his conviction for that and any other offence or offences, sentenced to two or more terms of imprisonment (whether taking effect consecutively or concurrently), he shall be treated for the purposes of this section as serving a sentence of imprisonment in respect of that offence at any time when serving any of those terms.

(6) For the purposes of this section, references to a person serving a sentence of imprisonment include references—

(a) to his being detained in any institution to which the Prison Act 1952 applies in pursuance of any other sentence or order for detention imposed by a court in criminal proceedings, or

(b) to his being detained (otherwise than in any such institution) in pursuance of directions of the Secretary of State under section 92 of the Powers of Criminal Courts (Sentencing) Act 2000;

and any reference to a term of imprisonment shall be construed accordingly.

## 2  Persons detained following acquittal on grounds of insanity or finding of unfitness to plead

(1) This section has effect for enabling non-intimate samples to be taken from persons under section 63 of the 1984 Act without the appropriate consent where they are persons to whom this section applies.

(3) This section applies to a person if—

(a) he has at any time been detained or at the relevant time he is detained under Part III of the Mental Health Act 1983 in pursuance of an order made under—

(i) section 5(2)(a) of the Criminal Procedure (Insanity) Act 1964 or section 6 or 14 of the Criminal Appeal Act 1968 (finding of insanity or unfitness to plead), or

(ii) section 37(3) of the Mental Health Act 1983 (power of magistrates' court to make hospital order without convicting accused); and

(b) that order was made on or after the date of the passing of this Act in respect of a recordable offence.

(4) This section also applies to a person if—

---

\* **Editor's Note:** Amends Police and Criminal Evidence Act 1984 section 63(3)(B) for limited purposes of subsection (1) above.

      (a)  he has at any time been detained or at the relevant time he is detained under Part III of the Mental Health Act 1983 in pursuance of an order made under—

         (i)   any of the provisions mentioned in subsection (3)(a), or

         (ii)   section 5(1) of the Criminal Procedure (Insanity) Act 1964 as originally enacted; and

      (b)  that order was made before the date of the passing of this Act in respect of any offence listed in Schedule 1 to this Act.

    (5)  Subsection (4)(a)(i) does not apply to any order made under section 14(2) of the Criminal Appeal Act 1968 as originally enacted.

    (6)  For the purposes of this section an order falling within subsection (3) or (4) shall be treated as having been made in respect of an offence of a particular description—

      (a)  if, where the order was made following—

         (i)   a finding of not guilty by reason of insanity, or

         (ii)   a finding that the person in question was under a disability and did the act or made the omission charged against him, or

         (iii)   a finding for the purposes of section 37(3) of the Mental Health Act 1983 that the person in question did the act or made the omission charged against him, or

         (iv)   (in the case of an order made under section 5(1) of the Criminal Procedure (Insanity) Act 1964 as originally enacted) a finding that he was under a disability,

        that finding was recorded in respect of an offence of that description; or

      (b)  if, where the order was made following the Court of Appeal forming such opinion as is mentioned in section 6(1) or 14(1) of the Criminal Appeal Act 1968, that opinion was formed on an appeal brought in respect of an offence of that description.

    (7)  In this section any reference to an Act 'as originally enacted' is a reference to that Act as it had effect without any of the amendments made by the Criminal Procedure (Insanity and Unfitness to Plead) Act 1991.

*Supplementary*

### 5  Interpretation

In this Act—

   'the 1984 Act' means the Police and Criminal Evidence Act 1984;

   'appropriate consent' has the meaning given by section 65 of the 1984 Act;

   'non-intimate sample' has the meaning given by section 65 of the 1984 Act;

   'recordable offence' means any offence to which regulations under section 27 of the 1984 Act (fingerprinting) apply;

   'the relevant time' means, in relation to the exercise of any power to take a non-intimate sample from a person, the time when it is sought to take the sample.

# SCHEDULE 1
# LIST OF OFFENCES

*Sexual offences and offences of indecency*

    1.  Any offence under the Sexual Offences Act 1956, other than an offence under section 30, 31 or 33 to 36 of that Act.

    2.  Any offence under section 128 of the Mental Health Act 1959 (intercourse with mentally handicapped person by hospital staff etc.).

    3.  Any offence under section 1 of the Indecency with Children Act 1960 (indecent conduct towards young child).

    4.  Any offence under section 54 of the Criminal Law Act 1977 (incitement by man of his granddaughter, daughter or sister under the age of 16 to commit incest with him).

    5.  Any offence under section 1 of the Protection of Children Act 1978.

## Violent and other offences

6. Any of the following offences—
   (a) murder;
   (b) manslaughter;
   (c) false imprisonment; and
   (d) kidnapping.

7. Any offence under any of the following provisions of the Offences Against the Person Act 1861—
   (a) section 4 (conspiring or soliciting to commit murder);
   (b) section 16 (threats to kill);
   (c) section 18 (wounding with intent to cause grievous bodily harm);
   (d) section 20 (causing grievous bodily harm);
   (e) section 21 (attempting to choke etc. in order to commit or assist in the committing of any indictable offence);
   (f) section 22 (using chloroform etc. to commit or assist in the committing of any indictable offence);
   (g) section 23 (maliciously administering poison etc. so as to endanger life or inflict grievous bodily harm);
   (h) section 24 (maliciously administering poison etc. with intent to injure etc.); and
   (i) section 47 (assault occasioning actual bodily harm).

8. Any offence under either of the following provisions of the Explosive Substances Act 1883—
   (a) section 2 (causing explosion likely to endanger life or property); and
   (b) section 3 (attempt to cause explosion, or making or keeping explosive with intent to endanger life or property).

9. Any offence under section 1 of the Children and Young Persons Act 1933 (cruelty to person under 16).

10. Any offence under section 4(1) of the Criminal Law Act 1967 (assisting offender) committed in relation to the offence of murder.

11. Any offence under any of the following provisions of the Firearms Act 1968—
    (a) section 16 (possession of firearm with intent to injure);
    (b) section 17 (use of firearm to resist arrest); and
    (c) section 18 (carrying firearm with criminal intent).

12. Any offence under either of the following provisions of the Theft Act 1968—
    (a) section 9 (burglary); and
    (b) section 10 (aggravated burglary);
and any offence under section 12A of that Act (aggravated vehicle-taking) involving an accident which caused the death of any person.

13. Any offence under section 1 of the Criminal Damage Act 1971 (destroying or damaging property) required to be charged as arson.

14. Any offence under section 2 of the Child Abduction Act 1984 (abduction of child by person other than parent).

## Conspiracy, incitement and attempts

15. Any offence under section 1 of the Criminal Law Act 1977 of conspiracy to commit any of the offences mentioned in paragraphs 1 to 14.

16. Any offence under section 1 of the Criminal Attempts Act 1981 of attempting to commit any of those offences.

17. Any offence of inciting another to commit any of those offences.

# Youth Justice and Criminal Evidence Act 1999

**(1999, c. 23)**

## PART II  GIVING OF EVIDENCE OR INFORMATION FOR PURPOSES OF CRIMINAL PROCEEDINGS

### Chapter I  Special measures directions in case of vulnerable and intimidated witnesses

*Preliminary*

**16  Witnesses eligible for assistance on grounds of age or incapacity**

(1)  For the purposes of this Chapter a witness in criminal proceedings (other than the accused) is eligible for assistance by virtue of this section—

    (a)  if under the age of 18 at the time of the hearing; or

    (b)  if the court considers that the quality of evidence given by the witness is likely to be diminished by reason of any circumstances falling within subsection (2).

(2)  The circumstances falling within this subsection are—

    (a)  that the witness—

        (i)  suffers from mental disorder within the meaning of the Mental Health Act 1983, or

        (ii)  otherwise has a significant impairment of intelligence and social functioning;

    (b)  that the witness has a physical disability or is suffering from a physical disorder.

(3)  In subsection (1)(a) 'the time of the hearing', in relation to a witness, means the time when it falls to the court to make a determination for the purposes of section 19(2) in relation to the witness.

(4)  In determining whether a witness falls within subsection (1)(b) the court must consider any views expressed by the witness.

(5)  In this Chapter references to the quality of a witness's evidence are to its quality in terms of completeness, coherence and accuracy; and for this purpose 'coherence' refers to a witness's ability in giving evidence to give answers which address the questions put to the witness and can be understood both individually and collectively.

**17  Witnesses eligible for assistance on grounds of fear or distress about testifying**

(1)  For the purposes of this Chapter a witness in criminal proceedings (other than the accused) is eligible for assistance by virtue of this subsection if the court is satisfied that the quality of evidence given by the witness is likely to be diminished by reason of fear or distress on the part of the witness in connection with testifying in the proceedings.

(2)  In determining whether a witness falls within subsection (1) the court must take into account, in particular—

    (a)  the nature and alleged circumstances of the offence to which the proceedings relate;

    (b)  the age of the witness;

    (c)  such of the following matters as appear to the court to be relevant, namely—

        (i)  the social and cultural background and ethnic origins of the witness,

        (ii)  the domestic and employment circumstances of the witness, and

        (iii)  any religious beliefs or political opinions of the witness;

    (d)  any behaviour towards the witness on the part of—

        (i)  the accused,

        (ii)  members of the family or associates of the accused, or

        (iii)  any other person who is likely to be an accused or a witness in the proceedings.

(3)  In determining that question the court must in addition consider any views expressed by the witness.

(4)  Where the complainant in respect of a sexual offence or an offence under section 1 or 2 of the Modern Slavery Act 2015 is a witness in proceedings relating to that offence (or to that offence and any other offences), the witness is eligible for assistance in relation to those proceedings by virtue of this subsection unless the witness has informed the court of the witness's wish not to be so eligible by virtue of this subsection.

(5)  A witness in proceedings relating to a relevant offence (or to a relevant offence and any other offences) is eligible for assistance in relation to those proceedings by virtue of this subsection unless the witness has informed the court of the witness's wish not to be so eligible by virtue of this subsection.

(6)  For the purposes of subsection (5) an offence is a relevant offence if it is an offence described in Schedule 1A.

(7)  The Secretary of State may by order amend Schedule 1A.

## 18  Special measures available to eligible witnesses

(1)  For the purposes of this Chapter—

    (a)  the provision which may be made by a special measures direction by virtue of each of sections 23 to 30 is a special measure available in relation to a witness eligible for assistance by virtue of section 16; and

    (b)  the provision which may be made by such a direction by virtue of each of sections 23 to 28 is a special measure available in relation to a witness eligible for assistance by virtue of section 17;

but this subsection has effect subject to subsection (2).

(2)  Where (apart from this subsection) a special measure would, in accordance with subsection (1)(a) or (b), be available in relation to a witness in any proceedings, it shall not be taken by a court to be available in relation to the witness unless—

    (a)  the court has been notified by the Secretary of State that relevant arrangements may be made available in the area in which it appears to the court that the proceedings will take place, and

    (b)  the notice has not been withdrawn.

(3)  In subsection (2) 'relevant arrangements' means arrangements for implementing the measure in question which cover the witness and the proceedings in question.

(4)  The withdrawal of a notice under that subsection relating to a special measure shall not affect the availability of that measure in relation to a witness if a special measures direction providing for that measure to apply to the witness's evidence has been made by the court before the notice is withdrawn.

(5)  The Secretary of State may by order make such amendments of this Chapter as he considers appropriate for altering the special measures which, in accordance with subsection (1)(a) or (b), are available in relation to a witness eligible for assistance by virtue of section 16 or (as the case may be) section 17, whether—

    (a)  by modifying the provisions relating to any measure for the time being available in relation to such a witness,

    (b)  by the addition—

        (i)   (with or without modifications) of any measure which is for the time being available in relation to a witness eligible for assistance virtue of the other of those sections, or

        (ii)  of any new measure, or

    (c)  by the removal of any measure.

*Special measures directions*

## 19  Special measures direction relating to eligible witness

(1)  This section applies where in any criminal proceedings—

    (a)  a party to the proceedings makes an application for the court to give a direction under this section in relation to a witness in the proceedings other than the accused, or

    (b)  the court of its own motion raises the issue whether such a direction should be given.

(2) Where the court determines that the witness is eligible for assistance by virtue of section 16 or 17, the court must then—

(a) determine whether any of the special measures available in relation to the witness (or any combination of them) would, in its opinion, be likely to improve the quality of evidence given by the witness; and

(b) if so—

(i) determine which of those measures (or combination of them) would, in its opinion, be likely to maximise so far as practicable the quality of such evidence; and

(ii) give a direction under this section providing for the measure or measures so determined to apply to evidence given by the witness.

(3) In determining for the purposes of this Chapter whether any special measure or measures would or would not be likely to improve, or to maximise so far as practicable, the quality of evidence given by the witness, the court must consider all the circumstances of the case, including in particular—

(a) any views expressed by the witness; and

(b) whether the measure or measures might tend to inhibit such evidence being effectively tested by a party to the proceedings.

(4) A special measures direction must specify particulars of the provision made by the direction in respect of each special measure which is to apply to the witness's evidence.

(5) In this Chapter 'special measures direction' means a direction under this section.

(6) Nothing in this Chapter is to be regarded as affecting any power of a court to make an order or give leave of any description (in the exercise of its inherent jurisdiction or otherwise)—

(a) in relation to a witness who is not an eligible witness, or

(b) in relation to an eligible witness where (as, for example, in a case where a foreign language interpreter is to be provided) the order is made or the leave is given otherwise than by reason of the fact that the witness is an eligible witness.

## 20   Further provisions about directions: general

(1) Subject to subsection (2) and section 21(8), a special measures direction has binding effect from the time it is made until the proceedings for the purposes of which it is made are either—

(a) determined (by acquittal, conviction or otherwise), or

(b) abandoned,

in relation to the accused or (if there is more than one) in relation to each of the accused.

(2) The court may discharge or vary (or further vary) a special measures direction if it appears to the court to be in the interests of justice to do so, and may do so either—

(a) on an application made by a party to the proceedings, if there has been a material change of circumstances since the relevant time, or

(b) of its own motion.

(3) In subsection (2) 'the relevant time' means—

(a) the time when the direction was given, or

(b) if a previous application has been made under that subsection, the time when the application (or last application) was made.

(4) Nothing in section 24(2) and (3), 27(4) to (7) or 28(4) to (6) is to be regarded as affecting the power of the court to vary or discharge a special measures direction under subsection (2).

(5) The court must state in open court its reasons for—

(a) giving or varying,

(b) refusing an application for, or for the variation or discharge of, or

(c) discharging,

a special measures direction and, if it is a magistrates' court, must cause them to be entered in the register of its proceedings.

(6) Criminal Procedure Rules may make provision—

(a) for uncontested applications to be determined by the court without a hearing;

(b) for preventing the renewal of an unsuccessful application for a special measures direction except where there has been a material change of circumstances;

    (c) for expert evidence to be given in connection with an application for, or for varying or discharging, such a direction;

    (d) for the manner in which confidential or sensitive information is to be treated in connection with such an application and in particular as to its being disclosed to, or withheld from, a party to the proceedings.

## 21 Special provisions relating to child witnesses

(1) For the purposes of this section—

    (a) a witness in criminal proceedings is a 'child witness' if he is an eligible witness by reason of section 16(1)(a) (whether or not he is an eligible witness by reason of any other provision of section 16 or 17); and

    (c) a 'relevant recording', in relation to a child witness, is a video recording of an interview of the witness made with a view to its admission as evidence in chief of the witness.

(2) Where the court, in making a determination for the purposes of section 19(2), determines that a witness in criminal proceedings is a child witness, the court must—

    (a) first have regard to subsections (3) to (4C) below; and

    (b) then have regard to section 19(2);

and for the purposes of section 19(2), as it then applies to the witness, any special measures required to be applied in relation to him by virtue of this section shall be treated as if they were measures determined by the court, pursuant to section 19(2)(a) and (b)(i), to be ones that (whether on their own or with any other special measures) would be likely to maximise, so far as practicable, the quality of his evidence.

(3) The primary rule in the case of a child witness is that the court must give a special measures direction in relation to the witness which complies with the following requirements—

    (a) it must provide for any relevant recording to be admitted under section 27 (video recorded evidence in chief); and

    (b) it must provide for any evidence given by the witness in the proceedings which is not given by means of a video recording (whether in chief or otherwise) to be given by means of a live link in accordance with section 24.

(4) The primary rule is subject to the following limitations—

    (a) the requirement contained in subsection (3)(a) or (b) has effect subject to the availability (within the meaning of section 18(2)) of the special measure in question in relation to the witness;

    (b) the requirement contained in subsection (2)(a) also has effect subject to section 27(2);

    (ba) if the witness informs the court of the witness's wish that the rule should not apply or should apply only in part, the rule does not apply to the extent that the court is satisfied that not complying with the rule would not diminish the quality of the witness's evidence; and

    (c) the rule does not apply to the extent that the court is satisfied that compliance with it would not be likely to maximise the quality of the witness's evidence so far as practicable (whether because the application to that evidence of one or more other special measures available in relation to the witness would have that result or for any other reason).

(4A) Where as a consequence of all or part of the primary rule being disapplied under subsection (4)(ba) a witness's evidence or any part of it would fall to be given as testimony in court, the court must give a special measures direction making such provision as is described in section 23 for the evidence or that part of it.

(4B) The requirement in subsection (4A) is subject to the following limitations—

    (a) if the witness informs the court of the witness's wish that the requirement in subsection (4A) should not apply, the requirement does not apply to the extent that the court is satisfied that not complying with it would not diminish the quality of the witness's evidence; and

    (b) the requirement does not apply to the extent that the court is satisfied that making such a provision would not be likely to maximise the quality of the witness's evidence so far as practicable (whether because the application to that evidence of one or more other special measures available in relation to the witness would have that result or for any other reason).

(4C) In making a decision under subsection (4)(ba) or (4B)(a), the court must take into account the following factors (and any others it considers relevant)—

    (a) the age and maturity of the witness;

    (b) the ability of the witness to understand the consequences of giving evidence otherwise than in accordance with the requirements in subsection (3) or (as the case may be) in accordance with the requirement in subsection (4A);

    (c) the relationship (if any) between the witness and the accused;

    (d) the witness's social and cultural background and ethnic origins;

    (e) the nature and alleged circumstances of the offence to which the proceedings relate.

(8) Where a special measures direction is given in relation to a child witness who is an eligible witness by reason only of section 16(1)(a), then—

    (a) subject to subsection (9) below, and

    (b) except where the witness has already begun to give evidence in the proceedings,

the direction shall cease to have effect at the time when the witness attains the age of 18.

(9) Where a special measures direction is given in relation to a child witness who is an eligible witness by reason only of section 16(1)(a) and—

    (a) the direction provides—

        (i) for any relevant recording to be admitted under section 27 as evidence in chief of the witness, or

        (ii) for the special measure available under section 28 to apply in relation to the witness, and

    (b) if it provides for that special measure to so apply, the witness is still under the age of 18 when the video recording is made for the purposes of section 28,

then, so far as it provides as mentioned in paragraph (a)(i) or (ii) above, the direction shall continue to have effect in accordance with section 20(1) even though the witness subsequently attains that age.

## 22 Extension of provisions of section 21 to certain witness over 18

(1) For the purposes of this section—

    (a) a witness in criminal proceedings (other than the accused) is a 'qualifying witness' if he—

        (i) is not an eligible witness at the time of the hearing (as defined by section 16(3)), but

        (ii) was under the age of 18 when a relevant recording was made; and

    (c) a 'relevant recording', in relation to a witness, is a video recording of an interview of the witness made with a view to its admission as evidence in chief of the witness.

(2) Subsections (2) to (4) and (4C) of section 21, so far as relating to the giving of a direction complying with the requirement contained in section 21(3)(a), apply to a qualifying witness in respect of the relevant recording as they apply to a child witness (within the meaning of that section).

## 22A Special provisions relating to sexual offences

(1) This section applies where in criminal proceedings relating to a sexual offence (or to a sexual offence and other offences) the complainant in respect of that offence is a witness in the proceedings.

(2) This section does not apply if the place of trial is a magistrates' court.

(3) This section does not apply if the complainant is an eligible witness by reason of section 16(1)(a) (whether or not the complainant is an eligible witness by reason of any other provision of section 16 or 17).

(4) If a party to the proceedings makes an application under section 19(1)(a) for a special measures direction in relation to the complainant, the party may request that the direction provide for any relevant recording to be admitted under section 27 (video recorded evidence in chief).

(5) Subsection (6) applies if—

    (a) a party to the proceedings makes a request under subsection (4) with respect to the complainant, and

    (b) the court determines for the purposes of section 19(2) that the complainant is eligible for assistance by virtue of section 16(1)(b) or 17.

(6) The court must—

(a) first have regard to subsections (7) to (9); and

(b) then have regard to section 19(2);

and for the purposes of section 19(2), as it then applies to the complainant, any special measure required to be applied in relation to the complainant by virtue of this section is to be treated as if it were a measure determined by the court, pursuant to section 19(2)(a) and (b)(i), to be one that (whether on its own or with any other special measures) would be likely to maximise, so far as practicable, the quality of the complainant's evidence.

(7) The court must give a special measures direction in relation to the complainant that provides for any relevant recording to be admitted under section 27.

(8) The requirement in subsection (7) has effect subject to section 27(2).

(9) The requirement in subsection (7) does not apply to the extent that the court is satisfied that compliance with it would not be likely to maximise the quality of the complainant's evidence so far as practicable (whether because the application to that evidence of one or more other special measures available in relation to the complainant would have that result or for any other reason).

(10) In this section 'relevant recording', in relation to a complainant, is a video recording of an interview of the complainant made with a view to its admission as the evidence in chief of the complainant.

### Special measures

## 23  Screening witness from accused

(1) A special measures direction may provide for the witness, while giving testimony or being sworn in court, to be prevented by means of a screen or other arrangement from seeing the accused.

(2) But the screen or other arrangement must not prevent the witness from being able to see, and to be seen by—

(a) the judge or justices (or both) and the jury (if there is one);

(b) legal representatives acting in the proceedings; and

(c) any interpreter or other person appointed (in pursuance of the direction or otherwise) to assist the witness.

(3) Where two or more legal representatives are acting for a party to the proceedings, subsection (2)(b) is to be regarded as satisfied in relation to those representatives if the witness is able to all material times to see and be seen by at least one of them.

## 24  Evidence by live link

(1) A special measures direction may provide for the witness to give evidence by means of a live link.

(1A) Such a direction may also provide for a specified person to accompany the witness while the witness is giving evidence by live link.

(1B) In determining who may accompany the witness, the court must have regard to the wishes of the witness.

(2) Where a direction provides for the witness to give evidence by means of a live link, the witness may not give evidence in any other way without the permission of the court.

(3) The court may give permission for the purposes of subsection (2) if it appears to the court to be in the interests of justice to do so, and may do so either—

(a) on an application by a party to the proceedings, if there has been a material change of circumstances since the relevant time, or

(b) of its own motion.

(4) In subsection (3) 'the relevant time' means—

(a) the time when the direction was given, or

(b) if a previous application has been made under that subsection, the time when the application (or last application) was made.

(8)  In this Chapter 'live link' means a live television link or other arrangement whereby a witness, while absent from the courtroom or other place where the proceedings are being held, is able to see and hear a person there and to be such and heard by the persons specified in section 23(2)(a) to (c).

## 25  Evidence given in private

(1)  A special measures direction may provide for the exclusion from the court, during the giving of the witness's evidence, of persons of any description specified in the direction.

(2)  The persons who may be so excluded do not include—

(a)  the accused,

(b)  legal representatives acting in the proceedings, or

(c)  any interpreter or other person appointed (in pursuance of the direction or otherwise) to assist the witness.

(3)  A special measures direction providing for representatives of news gathering or reporting organisations to be so excluded shall be expressed not to apply to one named person who—

(a)  is a representative of such an organisation, and

(b)  has been nominated for the purpose by one or more such organisations,

unless it appears to the court that no such nomination has been made.

(4)  A special measures direction may only provide for the exclusion of persons under this section where—

(a)  the proceedings relate to a sexual offence or an offence under section 1 or 2 of the Modern Slavery Act 2015; or

(b)  it appears to the court that there are reasonable grounds for believing that any person other than the accused has sought, or will seek, to intimidate the witness in connection with testifying in the proceedings.

(5)  Any proceedings from which persons are excluded under this section (whether or not those persons include representatives of news gathering or reporting organisations) shall nevertheless be taken to be held in public for the purposes of any privilege or exemption from liability available in respect of fair, accurate and contemporaneous reports of legal proceedings held in public.

## 26  Removal of wigs and gowns

A special measures direction may provide for the wearing of wigs or gowns to be dispensed with during the giving of the witness's evidence.

## 27  Video recorded evidence in chief

(1)  A special measures direction may provide for a video recording of an interview of the witness to be admitted as evidence in chief of the witness.

(2)  A special measures direction may, however, not provide for a video recording, or a part of such a recording, to be admitted under this section if the court is of the opinion, having regard to all the circumstances of the case, that in the interests of justice the recording, or that part of it, should not be so admitted.

(3)  In considering for the purposes of subsection (2) whether any part of a recording should not be admitted under this section, the court must consider whether any prejudice to the accused which might result from that part being so admitted is outweighed by the desirability of showing the whole, or substantially the whole, of the recorded interview.

(4)  Where a special measures direction provides for a recording to be admitted under this section, the court may nevertheless subsequently direct that it is not to be so admitted if—

(a)  it appears to the court that—

(i)  the witness will not be available for cross-examination (whether conducted in the ordinary way or in accordance with any such direction), and

(ii)  the parties to the proceedings have not agreed that there is no need for the witness to be so available; or

(b)  any Criminal Procedure Rules requiring disclosure of the circumstances in which the recording was made have not been complied with to the satisfaction of the court.

(5)  Where a recording is admitted under this section—

    (a)  the witness must be called by the party tendering it in evidence, unless—

        (i)  a special measures direction provides for the witness's evidence on cross-examination to be given in any recording admissible under section 28, or

        (ii)  the parties to the proceedings have agreed as mentioned in subsection (4)(a)(ii); and

    (b)  the witness may not without the permission of the court give evidence in chief otherwise than by means of the recording as to any matter which, in the opinion of the court, is dealt with in the witness's recorded testimony.

(6)  Where in accordance with subsection (2) a special measures direction provides for part only of a recording to be admitted under this section, references in subsection (4) and (5) to the recording or to the witness's recorded testimony are references to the part of the recording or testimony which is to be so admitted.

(7)  The court may give permission for the purposes of subsection (5)(b) if it appears to the court to be in the interests of justice to do so, and may do so either—

    (a)  on an application by a party to the proceedings, or

    (b)  of its own motion.

(9)  The court may, in giving permission for the purposes of subsection (5)(b), direct that the evidence in question is to be given by the witness by means of a live link; and, if the court so directs, subsections (5) to (7) of section 24 shall apply in relation to that evidence as they apply in relation to evidence which is to be given in accordance with a special measures direction.

(9A)  If the court directs under subsection (9) that evidence is to be given by live link, it may also make such provision in that direction as it could make under section 24(1A) in a special measures direction.

(11)  Nothing in this section affects the admissibility of any video recording which would be admissible apart from this section.

## 28  Video recorded cross-examination or re-examination

(1)  Where a special measures direction provides for a video recording to be admitted under section 27 as evidence in chief of the witness, the direction may also provide—

    (a)  for any cross-examination of the witness, and any re-examination, to be recorded by means of a video recording; and

    (b)  for such a recording to be admitted, so far as it relates to any such cross-examination or re-examination, as evidence of the witness under cross-examination or on re-examination, as the case may be.

(2)  Such a recording must be made in the presence of such persons as Criminal Procedure Rules or the direction may provide and in the absence of the accused, but in circumstances in which—

    (a)  the judge or justices (or both) and legal representatives acting in the proceedings are able to see and hear the examination of the witness and to communicate with the persons in whose presence the recording is being made, and

    (b)  the accused is able to see and hear any such examination and to communicate with any legal representative acting for him.

(3)  Where two or more legal representatives are acting for a party to the proceedings, subsection (2)(a) and (b) are to be regarded as satisfied in relation to those representatives if at all material times they are satisfied in relation to at least one of them.

(4)  Where a special measures direction provides for a recording to be admitted under this section, the court may nevertheless subsequently direct that it is not to be so admitted if any requirement of subsection (2) or Criminal Procedure Rules or the direction has not been complied with to the satisfaction of the court.

(5)  Where in pursuance of subsection (1) a recording has been made of any examination of the witness, the witness may not be subsequently cross-examined or re-examined in respect of any evidence given by the witness in the proceedings (whether in any recording admissible under section 27

or this section or otherwise than in such a recording) unless the court gives a further special measures direction making such provision as is mentioned in subsection (1)(a) and (b) in relation to any subsequent cross-examination, and re-examination, of the witness.

(6) The court may only give such a further direction if it appears to the court—

(a) that the proposed cross-examination is sought by a party to the proceedings as a result of that party having become aware, since the time when the original recording was made in pursuance of subsection (1), of a matter which that party could not with reasonable diligence have ascertained by then, or

(b) that for any other reason it is in the interests of justice to give the further direction.

(7) Nothing in this section shall be read as applying in relation to any cross-examination of the witness by the accused in person (in a case where the accused is to be able to conduct any such cross-examination).

### 29   Examination of witness through intermediary

(1) A special measures direction may provide for any examination of the witness (however and wherever conducted) to be conducted through an interpreter or other person approved by the court for the purposes of this section ('an intermediary').

(2) The function of an intermediary is to communicate—

(a) to the witness, questions put to the witness, and

(b) to any person asking such questions, the answers given by the witness in reply to them,

and to explain such questions or answers so far as necessary to enable them to be understood by the witness or person in question.

(3) Any examination of the witness in pursuance of subsection (1) must take place in the presence of such persons as Criminal Procedure Rules or the direction may provide, but in circumstances in which—

(a) the judge or justices (or both) and legal representatives acting in the proceedings are able to see and hear the examination of the witness and to communicate with the intermediary, and

(b) (except in the case of a video recorded examination) the jury (if there is one) are able to see and hear the examination of the witness.

(4) Where two or more legal representatives are acting for a party to the proceedings, subsection (3)(a) is to be regarded as satisfied in relation to those representatives if at all material times it is satisfied in relation to at least one of them.

(5) A person may not act as an intermediary in a particular case except after making a declaration, in such form as may be prescribed by Criminal Procedure Rules, that he will faithfully perform his function as intermediary.

(6) Subsection (1) does not apply to an interview of the witness which is recorded by means of a video recording with a view to its admission as evidence in chief of the witness; but a special measures direction may provide for such a recording to be admitted under section 27 if the interview was conducted through an intermediary and—

(a) that person complied with subsection (5) before the interview began, and

(b) the court's approval for the purposes of this action is given before the direction is given.

(7) Section 1 of the Perjury Act 1911 (perjury) shall apply in relation to a person acting as an intermediary as it applies in relation to a person lawfully sworn as an interpreter in a judicial proceeding; and for this purpose, where a person acts as an intermediary in any proceeding which is not a judicial proceeding for the purposes of that section, that proceeding shall be taken to be part of the judicial proceeding in which the witness's evidence is given.

### 30   Aids to communication

A special measures direction may provide for the witness, while giving evidence (whether by testimony in court or otherwise), to be provided with such device as the court considers appropriate with a view to enabling questions or answers to be communicated to or by the witness despite any disability or disorder or other impairment which the witness has or suffers from.

*Supplementary*

## 31   Status of evidence given under Chapter 1

(1)  Subsections (2) to (4) apply to a statement made by a witness in criminal proceedings which, in accordance with a special measures direction, is not made by the witness in direct oral testimony in court but forms part of the witness's evidence in those proceedings.

(2)  The statement shall be treated as if made by the witness in direct oral testimony in court; and accordingly—

(a)  it is admissible evidence of any fact of which such testimony from the witness would be admissible;

(b)  it is not capable of corroborating any other evidence given by the witness.

(3)  Subsection (2) applies to a statement admitted under section 27 or 28 which is not made by the witness on oath even though it would have been required to be made on oath if made by the witness in direct oral testimony in court.

(4)  In estimating the weight (if any) to be attached to the statement, the court must have regard to all the circumstances from which an inference can reasonably be drawn (as to the accuracy of the statement or otherwise).

(5)  Nothing in this Chapter (apart from subsection (3)) affects the operation of any rule of law relating to evidence in criminal proceedings.

(6)  Where any statement made by a person on oath in any proceeding which is not a judicial proceeding for the purposes of section 1 of the Perjury Act 1911 (perjury) is received in evidence in pursuance of a special measures direction, that proceeding shall be taken for the purposes of that section to be part of the judicial proceeding in which the statement is so received in evidence.

(7)  Where in any proceeding which is not a judicial proceeding for the purposes of that Act—

(a)  a person wilfully makes a false statement otherwise than on oath which is subsequently received in evidence in pursuance of a special measures direction, and

(b)  the statement is made in such circumstances that had it been given on oath in any such judicial proceeding that person would have been guilty of perjury, he shall be guilty of an offence and liable to any punishment which might be imposed on conviction of an offence under section 57(2) (giving of false unsworn evidence in criminal proceedings).

(8)  In this section 'statement' includes any representation of fact, whether made in words or otherwise.

## 32   Warning to jury

Where on a trial on indictment with a jury evidence has been given in accordance with a special measures direction, the judge must give the jury such warning (if any) as the judge considers necessary to ensure that the fact that the direction was given in relation to the witness does not prejudice the accused.

## 33   Interpretation etc. of Chapter 1

(1)  In this Chapter—

'eligible witness' means a witness eligible for assistance by virtue of section 16 or 17;

'live link' has the meaning given by section 24(8);

'quality', in relation to the evidence of a witness, shall be construed in accordance with section 16(5);

'special measures direction' means (in accordance with section 19(5)) a direction under section 19.

(2)  In this Chapter references to the special measures available in relation to a witness shall be construed in accordance with section 18.

(3)  In this Chapter references to a person being able to see or hear, or be seen or heard by, another person are to be read as not applying to the extent that either of them is unable to see or hear by reason of any impairment of eyesight or hearing.

(4)  In the case of any proceedings in which there is more than one accused—

(a) any reference to the accused in sections 23 to 28 may be taken by a court, in connection with the giving of a special measures direction, as a reference to all or any of the accused, as the court may determine, and

(b) any such direction may be given on the basis of any such determination.

(5) For the purposes of this Chapter as it applies in relation to a witness who is the complainant in respect of a relevant offence, where the age of the witness is uncertain and there are reasons to believe that the witness is under the age of 18, that witness is presumed to be under the age of 18.

(6) In subsection (5) 'relevant offence' means—

(a) a sexual offence;

(b) an offence under section 1 of the Protection of Children Act 1978;

(c) an offence under section 160 of the Criminal Justice Act 1988;

(d) an offence under section 1 or 2 of the Modern Slavery Act 2015.

## Chapter 1A  Use of live link and intermediary for evidence of certain accused persons

### 33A    Live link directions

(1) This section applies to any proceedings (whether in a magistrates' court or before the Crown Court) against a person for an offence.

(2) The court may, on the application of the accused, give a live link direction if it is satisfied—

(a) that the conditions in subsection (4) or, as the case may be, subsection (5) are met in relation to the accused, and

(b) that it is in the interests of justice for the accused to give evidence through a live link.

(3) A live link direction is a direction that any oral evidence to be given before the court by the accused is to be given through a live link.

(4) Where the accused is aged under 18 when the application is made, the conditions are that—

(a) his ability to participate effectively in the proceedings as a witness giving oral evidence in court is compromised by his level of intellectual ability or social functioning, and

(b) use of a live link would enable him to participate more effectively in the proceedings as a witness (whether by improving the quality of his evidence or otherwise).

(5) Where the accused has attained the age of 18 at that time, the conditions are that—

(a) he suffers from a mental disorder (within the meaning of the Mental Health Act 1983) or otherwise has a significant impairment of intelligence and social function,

(b) he is for that reason unable to participate effectively in the proceedings as a witness giving oral evidence in court, and

(c) use of a live link would enable him to participate more effectively in the proceedings as a witness (whether by improving the quality of his evidence or otherwise).

(6) While a live link direction has effect the accused may not give oral evidence before the court in the proceedings otherwise than through a live link.

(7) The court may discharge a live link direction at any time before or during any hearing to which it applies if it appears to the court to be in the interests of justice to do so (but this does not affect the power to give a further live link direction in relation to the accused).

The court may exercise this power of its own motion or on an application by a party.

(8) The court must state in open court its reasons for—

(a) giving or discharging a live link direction, or

(b) refusing an application for or for the discharge of a live link direction,

and, if it is a magistrates' court, it must cause those reasons to be entered in the register of its proceedings.

### 33B    Section 33A: meaning of 'live link'

(1) In section 33A 'live link' means an arrangement by which the accused, while absent from the place where the proceedings are being held, is able—

(a) to see and hear a person there, and

(b) to be seen and heard by the persons mentioned in subsection (2), and for this purpose any impairment of eyesight or hearing is to be disregarded.

(2) The persons are—

(a) the judge or justices (or both) and the jury (if there is one),

(b) where there are two or more accused in the proceedings, each of the other accused,

(c) legal representatives acting in the proceedings, and

(d) any interpreter or other person appointed by the court to assist the accused.

## 33BA   Examination of accused through intermediary

(1) This section applies to any proceedings (whether in a magistrates' court or before the Crown Court) against a person for an offence.

(2) The court may, on the application of the accused, give a direction under subsection (3) if it is satisfied—

(a) that the condition in subsection (5) is or, as the case may be, the conditions in subsection (6) are met in relation to the accused, and

(b) that making the direction is necessary in order to ensure that the accused receives a fair trial.

(3) A direction under this subsection is a direction that provides for any examination of the accused to be conducted through an interpreter or other person approved by the court for the purposes of this section ('an intermediary').

(4) The function of an intermediary is to communicate—

(a) to the accused, questions put to the accused, and

(b) to any person asking such questions, the answers given by the accused in reply to them,

and to explain such questions or answers so far as necessary to enable them to be understood by the accused or the person in question.

(5) Where the accused is aged under 18 when the application is made the condition is that the accused's ability to participate effectively in the proceedings as a witness giving oral evidence in court is compromised by the accused's level of intellectual ability or social functioning.

(6) Where the accused has attained the age of 18 when the application is made the conditions are that—

(a) the accused suffers from a mental disorder (within the meaning of the Mental Health Act 1983) or otherwise has a significant impairment of intelligence and social function, and

(b) the accused is for that reason unable to participate effectively in the proceedings as a witness giving oral evidence in court.

(7) Any examination of the accused in pursuance of a direction under subsection (3) must take place in the presence of such persons as Criminal Procedure Rules or the direction may provide and in circumstances in which—

(a) the judge or justices (or both) and legal representatives acting in the proceedings are able to see and hear the examination of the accused and to communicate with the intermediary,

(b) the jury (if there is one) are able to see and hear the examination of the accused, and

(c) where there are two or more accused in the proceedings, each of the other accused is able to see and hear the examination of the accused.

For the purposes of this subsection any impairment of eyesight or hearing is to be disregarded.

(8) Where two or more legal representatives are acting for a party to the proceedings, subsection (7)(a) is to be regarded as satisfied in relation to those representatives if at all material times it is satisfied in relation to at least one of them.

(9) A person may not act as an intermediary in a particular case except after making a declaration, in such form as may be prescribed by Criminal Procedure Rules, that the person will faithfully perform the function of an intermediary.

(10) Section 1 of the Perjury Act 1911 (perjury) applies in relation to a person acting as an intermediary as it applies in relation to a person lawfully sworn as an interpreter in a judicial proceeding.

### 33BB    Further provision as to directions under section 33BA(3)

(1)  The court may discharge a direction given under section 33BA(3) at any time before or during the proceedings to which it applies if it appears to the court that the direction is no longer necessary in order to ensure that the accused receives a fair trial (but this does not affect the power to give a further direction under section 33BA(3) in relation to the accused).

(2)  The court may vary (or further vary) a direction given under section 33BA(3) at any time before or during the proceedings to which it applies if it appears to the court that it is necessary for the direction to be varied in order to ensure that the accused receives a fair trial.

(3)  The court may exercise the power in subsection (1) or (2) of its own motion or on an application by a party.

(4)  The court must state in open court its reasons for—

(a)  giving, varying or discharging a direction under section 33BA(3), or

(b)  refusing an application for, or for the variation or discharge of, a direction under section 33BA(3),

and, if it is a magistrates' court, it must cause those reasons to be entered in the register of its proceedings.

### 33C    Saving

Nothing in this Chapter affects—

(a)  any power of a court to make an order, give directions or give leave of any description in relation to any witness (including an accused), or

(b)  the operation of any rule of law relating to evidence in criminal proceedings.

## Chapter II  Protection of witnesses from cross-examination by accused in person

### *General prohibitions*

### 34    Complainants in proceedings for sexual offences

No person charged with a sexual offence may in any criminal proceedings cross-examine in person a witness who is the complainant, either—

(a)  in connection with that offence, or

(b)  in connection with any other offence (or whatever nature) with which that person is charged in the proceedings.

### 35    Child complainants and other child witnesses

(1)  No person charged with an offence to which this section applies may in any criminal proceedings cross-examine in person a protected witness, either—

(a)  in connection with that offence, or

(b)  in connection with any other offence (of whatever nature) with which that person is charged in the proceedings.

(2)  For the purposes of subsection (1) a 'protected witness' is a witness who—

(a)  either is the complainant or is alleged to have been a witness to the commission of the offence to which this section applies, and

(b)  either is a child or falls to be cross-examined after giving evidence in chief (whether wholly or in part)—

(i)    by means of a video recording made (for the purposes of section 27) at a time when the witness was a child, or

(ii)   in any other way at any such time.

(3)  The offences to which this section applies are—

(a)  any offence under—

(iva)  any of sections 33 to 36 of the Sexual Offences Act 1956

(v)   the Protection of Children Act 1978; or

(vi)   Part I of the Sexual Offences Act 2003 or any relevant superseded enactment.

(vii)   sections 1 and 2 of the Modern Slavery Act 2015.

(b) kidnapping, false imprisonment or an offence under section 1 or 2 of the Child Abduction Act 1984;

(c) any offence under section 1 of the Children and Young Persons Act 1933;

(d) any offence (not within any of the preceding paragraphs) which involves an assault on, or injury or a threat of injury to, any person.

(3A)  In subsection (3)(a)(vi) 'relevant superseded enactment' means—

(a) any of sections 1 to 32 of the Sexual Offences Act 1956;

(b) the Indecency with Children Act 1960;

(c) the Sexual Offences Act 1967;

(d) section 54 of the Criminal Law Act 1977.

(4)  In this section 'child' means—

(a) where the offence falls within subsection (3)(a), a person under the age of 18; or

(b) where the offence falls within subsection (3)(b), (c) or (d), a person under the age of 14.

(5)  For the purposes of this section 'witness' includes a witness who is charged with an offence in the proceedings.

### *Prohibition imposed by court*

## 36   **Direction prohibiting accused from cross-examining particular witness**

(1)  This section applies where, in a case where neither of sections 34 and 35 operates to prevent an accused in any criminal proceedings from cross-examining a witness in person—

(a) the prosecutor makes an application for the court to give a direction under this section in relation to the witness, or

(b) the court of its own motion raises the issue whether such a direction should be given.

(2)  If it appears to the court—

(a) that the quality of evidence given by the witness on cross-examination—

(i)   is likely to be diminished if the cross-examination (or further cross-examination) is conducted by the accused in person, and

(ii)   would be likely to be improved if a direction were given under this section,

and

(b) that it would not be contrary to the interests of justice to give such a direction, the court may give a direction prohibiting the accused from cross-examining (or further cross-examining) the witness in person.

(3)  In determining whether subsection (2)(a) applies in the case of a witness the court must have regard, in particular, to—

(a) any views expressed by the witness as to whether or not the witness is content to be cross-examined by the accused in person;

(b) the nature of the questions likely to be asked, having regard to the issues in the proceedings and the defence case advanced so far (if any);

(c) any behaviour on the part of the accused at any stage of the proceedings, both generally and in relation to the witness;

(d) any relationship (of whatever nature) between the witness and the accused;

(e) whether any person (other than the accused) is or has at any time been charged in the proceedings with a sexual offence or an offence to which section 35 applies, and (if so) whether section 34 or 35 operates or would have operated to prevent that person from cross-examining the witness in person;

(f) any direction under section 19 which the court has given, or proposes to give, in relation to the witness.

(4)  For the purposes of this section—

(a) 'witness', in relation to an accused, does not include any other person who is charged with an offence in the proceedings; and

(b) any reference to the quality of a witness's evidence shall be construed in accordance with section 16(5).

### 37   Further provisions about directions under section 36

(1)   Subject to subsection (2), a direction has binding effect from the time it is made until the witness to whom it applies is discharged.

In this section 'direction' means a direction under section 36.

(2)   The court may discharge a direction if it appears to the court to be in the interests of justice to do so, and may do so either—

(a) on an application made by a party to the proceedings, if there has been a material change of circumstances since the relevant time, or

(b) of its own motion.

(3)   In subsection (2) 'the relevant time' means—

(a) the time when the direction was given, or

(b) if a previous application has been made under that subsection, the time when the application (or last application) was made.

(4)   The court must state in open court its reasons for—

(a) giving, or

(b) refusing an application for, or for the discharge of, or

(c) discharging,

a direction and, if it is a magistrates' court, must cause them to be entered in the register of its proceedings.

(5)   Criminal Procedure Rules may make provision—

(a) for uncontested applications to be determined by the court without a hearing;

(b) for preventing the renewal of an unsuccessful application for a direction except where there has been a material change of circumstances;

(c) for expert evidence to be given in connection with an application for, or for discharging, a direction;

(d) for the manner in which confidential or sensitive information is to be treated in connection with such an application and in particular as to its being disclosed to, or withheld from, a party to the proceedings.

*Cross-examination on behalf of accused*

### 38   Defence representation for purposes of cross-examination

(1)   This section applies where an accused is prevented from cross-examining a witness in person by virtue of section 34, 35 or 36.

(2)   Where it appears to the court that this section applies, it must—

(a) invite the accused to arrange for a legal representative to act for him for the purpose of cross-examining the witness; and

(b) require the accused to notify the court, by the end of such period as it may specify, whether a legal representative is to act for him for that purpose.

(3)   If by the end of the period mentioned in subsection (2)(b) either—

(a) the accused has notified the court that no legal representative is to act for him for the purpose of cross-examining the witness, or

(b) no notification has been received by the court and it appears to the court that no legal representative is to so act,

the court must consider whether it is necessary in the interests of justice for the witness to be cross-examined by a legal representative appointed to represent the interests of the accused.

(4) If the court decides that it is necessary in the interests of justice for the witness to be so cross-examined, the court must appoint a qualified legal representative (chosen by the court) to cross-examine the witness in the interests of the accused.

(5) A person so appointed shall not be responsible to the accused.

(6) Criminal Procedure Rules may make provision—

    (a) as to the time when, and the manner in which, subsection (2) is to be complied with;

    (b) in connection with the appointment of a legal representative under subsection (4), and in particular for securing that a person so appointed is provided with evidence or other material relating to the proceedings.

(7) Criminal Procedure Rules made in pursuance of subsection (6)(b) may make provision for the application, with such modifications as are specified in the rules, of any of the provisions of—

    (a) Part I of the Criminal Procedure and Investigations Act 1996 (disclosure of material in connection with criminal proceedings), or

    (b) the Sexual Offences (Protected Material) Act 1997.

(8) For the purposes of this section—

    (a) any reference to cross-examination includes (in a case where a direction is given under section 36 after the accused has begun cross-examining the witness) a reference to further cross-examination; and

    (b) 'qualified legal representative' means a legal representative who has a right of audience (within the meaning of the Courts and Legal Services Act 1990) in relation to the proceedings before the court.

### 39 Warning to jury

(1) Where on a trial on indictment with a jury an accused is prevented from cross-examining a witness in person by virtue of section 34, 35 or 36, the judge must give the jury such warning (if any) as the judge considers necessary to ensure that the accused is not prejudiced—

    (a) by any inferences that might be drawn from the fact that the accused has been prevented from cross-examining the witness in person;

    (b) where the witness has been cross-examined by a legal representative appointed under section 38(4), by the fact that the cross-examination was carried out by such a legal representative and not by a person acting as the accused's own legal representative.

(2) Subsection (8)(a) of section 38 applies for the purposes of this section as it applies for the purposes of section 38.

## Chapter III  Protection of complainants in proceedings for sexual offences

### 41  Restriction on evidence or questions about complainant's sexual history

(1) If at a trial a person is charged with a sexual offence, then, except with the leave of the court—

    (a) no evidence may be adduced, and

    (b) no question may be asked in cross-examination,

by or on behalf of any accused at the trial, about any sexual behaviour of the complainant.

(2) The court may give leave in relation to any evidence or question only on an application made by or on behalf of an accused, and may not give such leave unless it is satisfied—

    (a) that subsection (3) or (5) applies, and

    (b) that a refusal of leave might have the result of rendering unsafe a conclusion of the jury or (as the case may be) the court on any relevant issue in the case.

(3) This subsection applies if the evidence or question relates to a relevant issue in the case and either—

    (a) that issue is not an issue of consent; or

    (b) it is an issue of consent and the sexual behaviour of the complainant to which the evidence or question relates is alleged to have taken place at or about the same time as the event which is the subject matter of the charge against the accused; or

(c) it is an issue of consent and the sexual behaviour of the complainant to which the evidence or question relates is alleged to have been, in any respect, so similar—

    (i) to any sexual behaviour of the complainant which (according to evidence adduced or to be adduced by or on behalf of the accused) took place as part of the event which is the subject matter of the charge against the accused, or

    (ii) to any other sexual behaviour of the complainant which (according to such evidence) took place at or about the same time as the event,

that the similarity cannot reasonably be explained as a coincidence.

(4) For the purposes of subsection (3) no evidence or question shall be regarded as relating to a relevant issue in the case if it appears to the court to be reasonable to assume that the purpose (or main purpose) for which it would be adduced or asked is to establish or elicit material for impugning the credibility of the complainant as a witness.

(5) This subsection applies if the evidence or question—

(a) relates to any evidence adduced by the prosecution about any sexual behaviour of the complainant; and

(b) in the opinion of the court, would go no further than is necessary to enable the evidence adduced by the prosecution to be rebutted or explained by or on behalf of the accused.

(6) For the purposes of subsections (3) and (5) the evidence or question must relate to a specific instance (or specific instances) of alleged sexual behaviour on the part of the complainant (and accordingly nothing in those subsections is capable of applying in relation to the evidence or question to the extent that it does not so relate).

(7) Where this section applies in relation to a trial by virtue of the fact that one or more of a number of persons charged in the proceedings is or are charged with a sexual offence—

(a) it shall cease to apply in relation to the trial if the prosecutor decides not to proceed with the case against that person or those persons in respect of that charge; but

(b) it shall not cease to do so in the event of that person or those persons pleading guilty to, or being convicted of, that charge.

(8) Nothing in this section authorises any evidence to be adduced or any question to be asked which cannot be adduced or asked apart from this section.

### 42   Interpretation and application of section 41

(1) In section 41—

(a) 'relevant issue in the case' means any issue falling to be proved by the prosecution or defence in the trial of the accused;

(b) 'issue of consent' means any issue whether the complainant in fact consented to the conduct constituting the offence with which the accused is charged (and accordingly does not include any issue as to the belief of the accused that the complainant so consented);

(c) 'sexual behaviour' means any sexual behaviour or other sexual experience, whether or not involving any accused or other person, but excluding (except in section 41(3)(c)(i) and (5)(a)) anything alleged to have taken place as part of the event which is the subject matter of the charge against the accused; and

(d) subject to any other made under subsection (2), 'sexual offence' shall be construed in accordance with section 62.

(2) The Secretary of State may by order make such provision as he considers appropriate for adding or removing, for the purposes of section 41, any offence to or from the offences which are sexual offences for the purposes of this Act by virtue of section 62.

(3) Section 41 applies in relation to the following proceedings as it applies to a trial, namely—

(c) the hearing of an application under paragraph 2(1) of Schedule 3 to the Crime and Disorder Act 1998 (application to dismiss charge by person sent for trial under section 51 or 51A of that Act),

    (d) any hearing held, between conviction and sentencing, for the purpose of determining matters relevant to the court's decision as to how the accused is to be dealt with, and

    (e) the hearing of an appeal,

and references (in section 41 or this section) to a person charged with an offence accordingly include a person convicted of an offence.

## 43   Procedure on applications under section 41

    (1) An application for leave shall be heard in private and in the absence of the complainant.

In this section 'leave' means leave under section 41.

    (2) Where such an application has been determined, the court must state in open court (but in the absence of the jury, if there is one)—

    (a) its reasons for giving, or refusing, leave, and

    (b) if it gives leave, the extent to which evidence may be adduced or questions asked in pursuance of the leave,

and, if it is a magistrates' court, must cause those matters to be entered in the register of its proceedings.

    (3) Criminal Procedure Rules may make provision—

    (a) requiring applications for leave to specify, in relation to each item of evidence or question to which they relate, particulars of the grounds on which it is asserted that leave should be given by virtue of subsection (3) or (5) or section 41;

    (b) enabling the court to request a party to the proceedings to provide the court with information which it considers would assist it in determining an application for leave;

    (c) for the manner in which confidential or sensitive information is to be treated in connection with such an application, and in particular as to its being disclosed to, or withheld from, parties to the proceedings.

## Chapter IV   Reporting restrictions

*Reports relating to persons under 18*

## 44   Restrictions on reporting alleged offences involving persons under 18

    (1) This section applies (subject to subsection (3)) where a criminal investigation has begun in respect of—

    (a) an alleged offence against the law of—

      (i) England and Wales, or

      (ii) . . .

    (2) No matter relating to any person involved in the offence shall while he is under the age of 18 be included in any publication if it is likely to lead members of the public to identify him as a person involved in the offence.

    (3) The restrictions imposed by subsection (2) cease to apply once there are proceedings in a court . . . in respect of the offence.

    (4) For the purposes of subsection (2) any reference to a person involved in the offence is to—

    (a) a person by whom the offence is alleged to have been committed; or

    (b) if this paragraph applies to the publication in question by virtue of subsection (5)—

      (i) a person against or in respect of whom the offence is alleged to have been committed, or

      (ii) a person who is alleged to have been a witness to the commission of the offence;

except that paragraph (b)(i) does not include a person in relation to whom section 1 of the Sexual Offences (Amendment) Act 1992 (anonymity of victims of certain sexual offences) applies in connection with the offence.

    (5) Subsection (4)(b) applies to a publication if—

    (a) where it is a relevant programme, it is transmitted, or

    (b) in the case of any other publication, it is published,

on or after such date as may be specified in an order made by the Secretary of State.

(6) The matters relating to a person in relation to which the restrictions imposed by subsection (2) apply (if their inclusion in any publication is likely to have the result mentioned in that subsection) include in particular—

    (a) his name,

    (b) his address,

    (c) the identity of an school or other educational establishment attended by him,

    (d) the identity of any place of work, and

    (e) any still or moving picture of him.

(7) Any appropriate criminal court may by order dispense, to any extent specified in the order, with the restrictions imposed by subsection (2) in relation to a person if it is satisfied that it is necessary in the interests of justice to do so.

(8) However, when deciding whether to make such an order dispensing (to any extent) with the restrictions imposed by subsection (2) in relation to a person, the court shall have regard to the welfare of that person.

(9) In subsection (7) 'appropriate criminal court' means—

    (a) in a case where this section applies by virtue of subsection (1)(a)(i) or (ii), any court . . . which has any jurisdiction in, or in relation to, any criminal proceedings (but not a service court unless the offence is alleged to have been committed by a person subject to service law);

    (b) in a case where this section applies by virtue of subsection (1)(b), any court falling within paragraph (a) or a service court.

(10) The power under subsection (7) of a magistrates' court may be exercised by a single justice.

(11) In the case of a decision of a magistrates' court . . . to make or refuse to make an order under subsection (7), the following persons, namely—

    (a) any person who was a party to the proceedings on the application for the order, and

    (b) with the leave of the Crown Court, any other person,

may, in accordance with Criminal Procedure Rules, appeal to the Crown Court against that decision or appear or be represented at the hearing of such an appeal.

(12) On such an appeal the Crown Court—

    (a) may make such order as is necessary to give effect to its determination of the appeal; and

    (b) may also make such incidental or consequential orders as appear to it to be just.

(13) In this section—

    (a) 'civil offence' means an act or omission which, if committed in England and Wales, would be an offence against the law of England and Wales;

    (b) any reference to a criminal investigation, in relation to an alleged offence, is to an investigation conducted by police officers, or other persons charged with the duty of investigation offences, with a view to it being ascertained whether a person should be charged with the offence;

    (c) . . .

## 45 Power to restrict reporting of criminal proceedings involving persons under 18

(1) This section applies (subject to subsection (2)) in relation to—

    (a) any criminal proceedings in any court (other than a service court) . . . ; and

    (b) . . .

(2) This section does not apply in relation to any proceedings to which section 49 of the Children and Young Persons Act 1933 applies.

(3) The court may direct that no matter relating to any person concerned in the proceedings shall while he is under the age of 18 be included in any publication if it is likely to lead members of the public to identify him as a person concerned in the proceedings.

(4) The court or an appellate court may by direction ('an excepting direction') dispense, to any extent specified in the excepting direction, with the restrictions imposed by a direction under subsection (3) if it is satisfied that it is necessary in the interests of justice to do so.

(5) The court or an appellate court may also by direction ('an excepting direction') dispense, to any extent specified in the excepting direction, with the restrictions imposed by a direction under subsection (3) if it is satisfied—

  (a) that their effect is to impose a substantial and unreasonable restriction on the reporting of the proceedings, and

  (b) that it is in the public interest to remove or relax that restriction;

but no excepting direction shall be given under this subsection by reason only of the fact that the proceedings have been determined in any way or have been abandoned.

(6) When deciding whether to make—

  (a) a direction under subsection (3) in relation to a person, or

  (b) an expecting direction under subsection (4) or (5) by virtue of which the restrictions imposed by a direction under subsection (3) would be dispensed with (to any extent) in relation to a person,

the court or (as the case may be) the appellate court shall have regard to the welfare of that person.

(7) For the purposes of subsection (3) any reference to a person concerned in the proceedings is to a person—

  (a) against or in respect of whom the proceedings are taken, or

  (b) who is a witness in the proceedings.

(8) the matters relating to a person in relation to which the restrictions imposed by a direction under subsection (3) apply (if their inclusion in any publication is likely to have the result mentioned in that subsection) include in particular—

  (a) his name,

  (b) his address,

  (c) the identity of any school or other educational establishment attended by him,

  (d) the identity of any place of work, and

  (e) any still or moving picture of him.

(9) A direction under subsection (3) may be revoked by the court or an appellate court.

(10) An excepting direction—

  (a) may be given at the time the direction under subsection (3) is given or subsequently; and

  (b) may be varied or revoked by the court or an appellate court.

(11) In this section 'appellate court', in relation to any proceedings in a court, means a court dealing with an appeal (including an appeal by way of case stated) arising out of the proceedings or with any further appeal.

## 45A Power to restrict reporting of criminal proceedings for lifetime of witnesses and victims under 18

(1) This section applies in relation to—

  (a) any criminal proceedings in any court (other than a service court) . . . , and

  (b) . . .

(2) The court may make a direction ('a reporting direction') that no matter relating to a person mentioned in subsection (3) shall during that person's lifetime be included in any publication if it is likely to lead members of the public to identify that person as being concerned in the proceedings.

(3) A reporting direction may be made only in respect of a person who is under the age of 18 when the proceedings commence and who is—

  (a) a witness, other than an accused, in the proceedings;

  (b) a person against whom the offence, which is the subject of the proceedings, is alleged to have been committed.

(4) For the purposes of subsection (2), matters relating to a person in respect of whom the reporting direction is made include—

  (a) the person's name,

  (b) the person's address,

  (c) the identity of any school or other educational establishment attended by the person,

(d)  the identity of any place of work of the person, and

(e)  any still or moving picture of the person.

(5)  The court may make a reporting direction in respect of a person only if it is satisfied that—

(a)  the quality of any evidence given by the person, or

(b)  the level of co-operation given by the person to any party to the proceedings in connection with that party's preparation of its case,

is likely to be diminished by reason of fear or distress on the part of the person in connection with being identified by members of the public as a person concerned in the proceedings.

(6)  In determining whether subsection (5) is satisfied, the court must in particular take into account—

(a)  the nature and alleged circumstances of the offence to which the proceedings relate;

(b)  the age of the person;

(c)  such of the following as appear to the court to be relevant—

(i)   the social and cultural background and ethnic origins of the person,

(ii)  the domestic, educational and employment circumstances of the person, and

(iii) any religious beliefs or political opinions of the person;

(d)  any behaviour towards the person on the part of—

(i)   an accused,

(ii)  members of the family or associates of an accused, or

(iii) any other person who is likely to be an accused or a witness in the proceedings.

(7)  In determining that question the court must in addition consider any views expressed—

(a)  by the person in respect of whom the reporting restriction may be made, and

(b)  where that person is under the age of 16, by an appropriate person other than an accused.

(8)  In determining whether to make a reporting direction in respect of a person, the court must have regard to—

(a)  the welfare of that person,

(b)  whether it would be in the interests of justice to make the direction, and

(c)  the public interest in avoiding the imposition of a substantial and unreasonable restriction on the reporting of the proceedings.

(9)  A reporting direction may be revoked by the court or an appellate court.

(10)  The court or an appellate court may by direction ('an excepting direction') dispense, to any extent specified in the excepting direction, with the restrictions imposed by a reporting direction.

(11)  The court or an appellate court may only make an excepting direction if—

(a)  it is satisfied that it is necessary in the interests of justice to do so, or

(b)  it is satisfied that—

(i)   the effect of the reporting direction is to impose a substantial and unreasonable restriction on the reporting of the proceedings, and

(ii)  it is in the public interest to remove or relax that restriction.

(12)  No excepting direction shall be given under subsection (11)(b) by reason only of the fact that the proceedings have been determined in any way or have been abandoned.

(13)  In determining whether to make an excepting direction in respect of a person, the court or the appellate court must have regard to the welfare of that person.

(14)  An excepting direction—

(a)  may be given at the time the reporting direction is given or subsequently, and

(b)  may be varied or revoked by the court or an appellate court.

(15)  For the purposes of this section—

(a)  criminal proceedings in a court . . . commence when proceedings are instituted for the purposes of Part 1 of the Prosecution of Offences Act 1985, in accordance with section 15(2) of that Act;

(b)  . . .

(16)  In this section—

(a) 'appellate court', in relation to any proceedings in a court, means a court dealing with an appeal (including an appeal by way of case stated) arising out of the proceedings or with any further appeal;

(b) 'appropriate person' has the same meaning as in section 50;

(c) references to the quality of evidence given by a person are to its quality in terms of completeness, coherence and accuracy (and for this purpose 'coherence' refers to a person's ability in giving evidence to give answers which address the questions put to the person and can be understood both individually and collectively);

(d) references to the preparation of the case of a party to any proceedings include, where the party is the prosecution, the carrying out of investigations into any offence at any time charged in the proceedings.

*Reports relating to adult witnesses*

## 46   Power to restrict reports about certain adult witnesses in criminal proceedings

(1) This section applies where—

(a) in any criminal proceedings in any court (other than a service court) or

(b) . . .

a party to the proceedings makes an application for the court to give a reporting direction in relation to a witness in the proceedings (other than the accused) who has attained the age of 18.

In this section 'reporting direction' has the meaning given by subsection (6).

(2) If the court determines—

(a) that the witness is eligible for protection, and

(b) that giving a reporting direction in relation to the witness is likely to improve—

(i)   the quality of evidence given by the witness, or

(ii)   the level of co-operation given by the witness to any party to the proceedings in connection with that party's preparation of its case,

the court may give a reporting direction in relation to the witness.

(3) For the purposes of this section a witness is eligible for protection if the court is satisfied—

(a) that the quality of evidence given by the witness, or

(b) the level of co-operation given by the witness to any party to the proceedings in connection with that party's preparation of its case,

is likely to be diminished by reason of fear or distress on the part of the witness in connection with being identified by members of the public as a witness in the proceedings.

(4) In determining whether a witness is eligible for protection the court must take into account, in particular—

(a) the nature and alleged circumstances of the offence to which the proceedings relate;

(b) the age of the witness;

(c) such of the following matters as appear to the court to be relevant, namely—

(i)   the social and cultural background and ethnic origins of the witness,

(ii)   the domestic and employment circumstances of the witness, and

(iii)   any religious beliefs or political opinions of the witness;

(d) any behaviour towards the witness on the part of—

(i)   the accused,

(ii)   members of the family or associates of the accused, or

(iii)   any other person who is likely to be an accused or a witness in the proceedings.

(5) In determining that question the court must in addition consider any views expressed by the witness.

(6) For the purposes of this section a reporting direction in relation to a witness is a direction that no matter relating to the witness shall during the witness's lifetime be included in any publication if it is likely to lead members of the public to identify him as being a witness in the proceedings.

(7)  The matters relating to a witness in relation to which the restrictions imposed by a reporting direction apply (if their inclusion in any publication is likely to have the result mentioned in subsection (6)) include in particular—

(a)  the witness's name,

(b)  the witness's address,

(c)  the identity of any educational establishment attended by the witness,

(d)  the identity of any place of work, and

(e)  any still or moving picture of the witness.

(8)  In determining whether to give a reporting direction the court shall consider—

(a)  whether it would be in the interests of justice to do so, and

(b)  the public interest in avoiding the imposition of a substantial and unreasonable restriction on the reporting of the proceedings.

(9)  The court or an appellate court may by direction ('an excepting direction') dispense, to any extent specified in the excepting direction, with the restrictions imposed by a reporting direction if—

(a)  it is satisfied that it is necessary in the interests of justice to do so, or

(b)  it is satisfied—

(i)   that the effect of those restrictions is to impose a substantial and unreasonable restriction on the reporting of the proceedings, and

(ii)  that it is in the public interest to remove or relax that restriction;

but no excepting direction shall be given under paragraph (b) by reason only of the fact that the proceedings have been determined in any way or have been abandoned.

(10)  A reporting direction may be revoked by the court or an appellate court.

(11)  An excepting direction—

(a)  may be given at the time the reporting direction is given or subsequently; and

(b)  may be varied or revoked by the court or an appellate court.

(12)  In this section—

(a)  'appellate court', in relation to any proceedings in a court, means a court dealing with an appeal (including an appeal by way of case stated) arising out of the proceedings or with any further appeal;

(b)  references to the quality of a witness's evidence are to its quality in terms of completeness, coherence and accuracy (and for this purpose 'coherence' refers to a witness's ability in giving evidence to give answers which address the questions put to the witness and can be understood both individually and collectively);

(c)  references to the preparation of the case of a party to any proceedings include, where the party is the prosecution, the carrying out of investigations into any offence at any time charged in the proceedings.

*Reports relating to directions under Chapter 1, 1A or 2*

**47  Restrictions on reporting directions under Chapter 1A or 2**

(1)  Except as provided by this section, no publication shall include a report of a matter falling within subsection (2).

(2)  The matters falling within this subsection are—

(a)  a direction under section 19, 33A or 36 or an order discharging, or (in the case of a direction under section 19) varying, such a direction;

(b)  proceedings—

(i)   on an application for such a direction or order, or

(ii)  where the court acts of its own motion to determine whether to give or make any such direction or order.

(3)  The court dealing with a matter falling within subsection (2) may order that subsection (1) is not to apply, or is not to apply to a specified extent, to a report of that matter.

(4) Where—

    (a) there is only one accused in the relevant proceedings, and

    (b) he objects to the making of an order under subsection (3),

the court shall make the order if (and only if) satisfied after hearing the representations of the accused that it is in the interests of justice to do so; and if the order is made it shall not apply to the extent that a report deals with any such objections or representations.

(5) Where—

    (a) there are two or more accused in the relevant proceedings, and

    (b) one or more of them object to the making of an order under subsection (3),

the court shall make the order if (and only if) satisfied after hearing the representations of each of the accused that it is in the interests of justice to do so; and if the order is made it shall not apply to the extent that a report deals with any such objections or representations.

(6) Subsection (1) does not apply to the inclusion in a publication of a report of matters after the relevant proceedings are either—

    (a) determined (by acquittal, conviction or otherwise), or

    (b) abandoned,

in relation to the accused or (if there is more than one) in relation to each of the accused.

(7) In this section 'the relevant proceedings' means the proceedings to which any such direction as is mentioned in subsection (2) relates or would relate.

(8) Nothing in this section affects any prohibition or restriction by virtue of any other enactment on the inclusion of matter in a publication.

*Other restrictions*

## 48   Amendments relating to other reporting restrictions

Schedule 2, which contains amendments relating to reporting restrictions under—

    (a) the Children and Young Persons Act 1933,

    (b) the Sexual Offences (Amendment) Act 1976,

    (d) the Sexual Offences (Amendment) Act 1992,

shall have effect.

*Offences*

## 49   Offences under Chapter IV

(1) This section applies if a publication—

    (a) includes any matter in contravention of section 44(2) or of a direction under section 45(3) or 46(2); or

    (b) includes a report in a contravention of section 47.

(2) Where the publication is a newspaper or periodical, any proprietor, any editor and any publisher of the newspaper or periodical is guilty of an offence.

(3) Where the publication is a relevant programme—

    (a) any body corporate . . . engaged in providing the programme service in which the programme is included, and

    (b) any person having functions in relation to the programme corresponding to those of an editor of a newspaper,

is guilty of an offence.

(4) In the case of any other publication, any person publishing it is guilty of an offence.

(5) A person guilty of an offence under this section is liable on summary conviction to a fine not exceeding level 5 on the standard scale.

(6) Proceedings for an offence under this section in respect of a publication falling within subsection (1)(b) may not be instituted—

    (a) in England and Wales otherwise than by or with the consent of the Attorney General,

(7) Schedule 2A makes special provision in connection with the operation of this section, so far as it relates to a publication that includes matter in contravention of a direction under section 45A(2), in relation to persons providing information society services.

## 50 Defences

(1) Where a person is charged with an offence under section 49 it shall be a defence to prove that at the time of the alleged offence he was not aware, and neither suspected nor had reason to suspect, that the publication included in the matter or report in question.

(2) Where—

(a) a person is charged with an offence under section 49, and

(b) the offence relates to the inclusion of any matter in a publication in contravention of section 44(2),

it shall be a defence to prove that at the time of the alleged offence he was not aware, and neither suspected nor had reason to suspect, that the criminal investigation in question had begun.

(3) Where—

(a) paragraphs (a) and (b) or subsection (2) apply, and

(b) the contravention of section 44(2) does not relate to either—

(i) the person by whom the offence mentioned in that provision is alleged to have been committed, or

(ii) (where that offence is one in relation to which section 1 of the Sexual Offences (Amendment) Act 1992 applies) a person who is alleged to be a witness to the commission of the offence,

it shall be a defence to show to the satisfaction of the court that the inclusion in the publication of the matter in question was in the public interest on the ground that, to the extent that they operated to prevent that matter from being so included, the effect of the restrictions imposed by section 44(2) was to impose a substantial and unreasonable restriction on the reporting of matters connected with that offence.

(4) Subsection (5) applies where—

(a) paragraphs (a) and (b) of subsection (2) apply, and

(b) the contravention of section 44(2) relates to a person ('the protected person') who is neither—

(i) the person mentioned in subsection (3)(b)(i), nor

(ii) a person within subsection (3)(b)(ii) who is under the age of 16.

(5) In such a case it shall be a defence, subject to subsection (6), to prove that written consent to the inclusion of the matter in question in the publication had been given—

(a) by an appropriate person, if at the time when the consent was given the protected person was under the age of 16, or

(b) by the protected person, if that person was aged 16 or 17 at that time,

and (where the consent was given by an appropriate person) that written notice had been previously given to that person drawing to his attention the need to consider the welfare of the protected person when deciding whether to give consent.

(6) The defence provided by subsection (5) is not available if—

(a) (where the consent was given by an appropriate person) it is proved that written or other notice withdrawing the consent—

(i) was given to the appropriate recipient by any other appropriate person or by the protected person, and

(ii) was so given in sufficient time to enable the inclusion in the publication of the matter in question to be prevented; or

(b) subsection (8) applies.

(6A) Where—

(a) a person is charged with an offence under section 49, and

(b) the offence relates to the inclusion of any matter in a publication in contravention of a direction under section 45A(2), it shall be a defence, unless subsection (6B) or (8) applies, to prove that the person in relation to whom the direction was given had given written consent to the inclusion of that matter in the publication.

(6B)  Written consent is not a defence by virtue of subsection (6A) if the person was under the age of 18 at the time the consent was given.

(7)  Where—

(a)  a person is charged with an offence under section 49, and

(b)  the offence relates to the inclusion of any matter in a publication in contravention of a direction under section 46(2),

it shall be a defence, unless subsection (8) applies, to prove that the person in relation to whom the direction was given had given written consent to the inclusion of that matter in the publication.

(8)  Written consent is not a defence by virtue of subsections (5) to (7) if it is proved that any person interfered—

(a)  with the peace or comfort of the person giving the consent, or

(b)  (where the consent was given by an appropriate person) with the peace or comfort of either that person or the protected person,

with intent to obtain the consent.

(9)  In this section—

'an appropriate person' means (subject to subsections (10) to (12))—

(a)  . . . a person who is a parent or guardian of the protected person,

'guardian', in relation to the protected person, means any person who is not a parent of the protected person but who has parental responsibility for the protected person within the meaning of—

(a)  . . . the Children Act 1989, or

(b)  . . .

(10)  Where the protected person is (within the meaning of the Children Act 1989) a child who is looked after by a local authority, 'an appropriate person' means a person who is—

(a)  a representative of that authority, or

(b)  a parent or guardian of the protected person with whom the protected person is allowed to live.

(13)  However, no person by whom the offence mentioned in section 44(2) is alleged to have been committed is, by virtue of subsection (9) to (10), an appropriate person for the purposes of this section.

(14)  In this section 'the appropriate recipient', in relation to a notice under subsection (6)(a), means—

(a)  the person to whom the notice giving consent was given,

(b)  (if different) the person by whom the matter in question was published, or

(c)  any other person exercising, on behalf of the person mentioned in paragraph (b), any responsibility in relation to the publication of that matter;

and for this purpose 'person' includes a body of persons and a partnership.

### 51  Offences committed by bodies corporate

(1)  If an offence under section 49 committed by a body corporate is proved—

(a)  to have been committed with the consent or connivance of, or

(b)  to be attributable to any neglect on the part of,

an officer, the officer as well as the body corporate is guilty of the offence and liable to be proceeded against and punished accordingly.

(2)  In subsection (1) 'officer' means a director, manager, secretary or other similar officer of the body, or a person purporting to act in any such capacity.

(3)  If the affairs of a body corporate are managed by its members, 'director' in subsection (2) means a member of that body.

*Supplementary*

### 52   Decisions as to public interest for purposes of Chapter IV

(1) Where for the purposes of any provision of this Chapter it falls to a court to determine whether anything is (or, as the case may be, was) in the public interest, the court must have regard, in particular, to the matters referred to in subsection (2) (so far as relevant).

(2) Those matters are—

    (a) the interest in each of the following—

        (i)   the open reporting of crime,

        (ii)  the open reporting of matters relating to human health or safety, and

        (iii) the prevention and exposure of miscarriages of justice;

    (b) the welfare of any person in relation to whom the relevant restrictions imposed by or under this Chapter apply or would apply (or, as the case may be, applied); and

    (c) any views expressed—

        (i)   by an appropriate person on behalf of a person within paragraph (b) who is under the age of 16 ('the protected person'), or

        (ii)  by a person within that paragraph who has attained that age.

(3) In subsection (2) 'an appropriate person', in relation to the protected person, has the same meaning as it has for the purposes of section 50.

## Chapter V   Competence of witnesses and capacity to be sworn

*Competence of witnesses*

### 53   Competence of witnesses to give evidence

(1) At every stage in criminal proceedings all persons are (whatever their age) competent to give evidence.

(2) Subsection (1) has effect subject to subsections (3) and (4).

(3) A person is not competent to give evidence in criminal proceedings if it appears to the court that he is not a person who is able to—

    (a) understand questions put to him as a witness, and

    (b) give answers to them which can be understood.

(4) A person charged in criminal proceedings is not competent to give evidence in the proceedings for the prosecution (whether he is the only person, or is one of two or more persons, charged in the proceedings).

(5) In subsection (4) the reference to a person charged in criminal proceedings does not include a person who is not, or is no longer, liable to be convicted of any offence in the proceedings (whether as a result of pleading guilty or for any other reason).

### 54   Determining competence of witnesses

(1) Any question whether a witness in criminal proceedings is competent to give evidence in the proceedings, whether raised—

    (a) by a party to the proceedings, or

    (b) by the court of its own motion,

shall be determined by the court in accordance with this section.

(2) It is for the party calling the witness to satisfy the court that, on a balance of probabilities, the witness is competent to give evidence in the proceedings.

(3) In determining the question mentioned in subsection (1) the court shall treat the witness as having the benefit of any directions under section 19 which the court has given, or proposes to give, in relation to the witness.

(4) Any proceedings held for the determination of the question shall take place in the absence of the jury (if there is one).

(5) Expert evidence may be received on the question.

(6) Any questioning of the witness (where the court considers that necessary) shall be conducted by the court in the presence of the parties.

*Giving of sworn or unsworn evidence*

## 55   Determining whether witness to be sworn

(1) Any question whether a witness in criminal proceedings may be sworn for the purpose of giving evidence on oath, whether raised—

    (a) by a party to the proceedings, or

    (b) by the court of its own motion,

shall be determined by the court in accordance with this section.

(2) The witness may not be sworn for that purpose unless—

    (a) he has attained the age of 14, and

    (b) he has a sufficient appreciation of the solemnity of the occasion and of the particular responsibility to tell the truth which is involved in taking an oath.

(3) The witness shall, if he is able to give intelligible testimony, be presumed to have a sufficient appreciation of those matters if no evidence tending to show the contrary is adduced (by any party).

(4) If any such evidence is adduced, it is for the party seeking to have the witness sworn to satisfy the court that, on a balance of probabilities, the witness has attained the age of 14 and has a sufficient appreciation of the matters mentioned in subsection (2)(b).

(5) Any proceedings held for the determination of the question mentioned in subsection (1) shall take place in the absence of the jury (if there is one).

(6) Expert evidence may be received on the question.

(7) Any questioning of the witness (where the court considers that necessary) shall be conducted by the court in the presence of the parties.

(8) For the purposes of this section a person is able to give intelligible testimony if he is able to—

    (a) understand questions put to him as a witness, and

    (b) give answers to them which can be understood.

## 56   Reception of unsworn evidence

(1) Subsections (2) and (3) apply to a person (of any age) who—

    (a) is competent to give evidence in criminal proceedings, but

    (b) (by virtue of section 55(2)) is not permitted to be sworn for the purpose of giving evidence on oath in such proceedings.

(2) The evidence in criminal proceedings of a person to whom this subsection applies shall be given unsworn.

(3) A deposition of unsworn evidence given by a person to whom this subsection applies may be taken for the purposes of criminal proceedings as if that evidence had been given on oath.

(4) A court in criminal proceedings shall accordingly receive in evidence any evidence given unsworn in pursuance of subsection (2) or (3).

(5) Where a person ('the witness') who is competent to give evidence in criminal proceedings gives evidence in such proceedings unsworn, no conviction, verdict or finding in those proceedings shall be taken to be unsafe for the purposes of any of sections 2(1), 13(1) and 16(1) of the Criminal Appeal Act 1968 (grounds for allowing appeals) by reason only that it appears to the Court of Appeal that the witness was a person falling within section 55(2) (and should accordingly have given his evidence on oath).

## 57   Penalty for giving false unsworn evidence

(1) This section applies where a person gives unsworn evidence in criminal proceedings in pursuance of section 56(2) or (3).

(2)  If such a person wilfully gives false evidence in such circumstances that, had the evidence been given on oath, he would have been guilty of perjury, he shall be guilty of an offence and liable on summary conviction to—

    (a)  imprisonment for a term not exceeding 6 months, or

    (b)  a fine not exceeding £1,000,

or both.

(3)  In relation to a person under the age of 14, subsection (2) shall have effect as if for the words following 'on summary conviction' there were substituted 'to a fine not exceeding £250'.

### 59   Restriction on use of answers etc. obtained under compulsion

Schedule 3, which amends enactments providing for the use of answers and statements given under compulsion so as to restrict in criminal proceedings their use in evidence against the persons giving them, shall have effect.

## Chapter VII   General

### 62   Meaning of 'sexual offence' and other references to offences

(1)  In this Part 'sexual offence' means any offence under—

    (a)  Part 1 of the Sexual Offences Act 2003 or any relevant superseded offence; or

    (b)  section 2 of the Modern Slavery Act 2015 (human trafficking) committed with a view to exploitation that consists of or includes behaviour within section 3(3) of that Act (sexual exploitation).

(1A)  In subsection (1) 'relevant superseded offence' means—

    (a)  rape or burglary with intent to rape;

    (b)  an offence under any of sections 2 to 12 and 14 to 17 of the Sexual Offences Act 1956 (unlawful intercourse, indecent assault, forcible abduction etc.);

    (c)  an offence under section 128 of the Mental Health Act 1959 (unlawful intercourse with person receiving treatment for mental disorder by member of hospital staff etc.);

    (d)  an offence under section 1 of the Indecency with Children Act 1960 (indecent conduct towards child under 14);

    (e)  an offence under section 54 of the Criminal Law Act 1977 (incitement of child under 16 to commit incest).

(2)  In this part any reference (including a reference having effect by virtue of this subsection) to an offence of any description ('the substantive offence') is to be taken to include a reference to an offence which consists of attempting or conspiring to commit, or of aiding, abetting, counselling, procuring or inciting* the commission of, the substantive offence.

### 63   General interpretation etc. of Part II

(1)  In this Part (except where the context otherwise requires)—

'accused', in relation to any criminal proceedings, means any person charged with an offence to which the proceedings relate (whether or not he has been convicted);

'the complainant', in relation to any offence (or alleged offence), means a person against or in relation to whom the offence was (or is alleged to have been) committed;

'court' (except in Chapter IV or V or subsection (2)) means a magistrates' court, the Crown Court or criminal division of the Court of Appeal;

'legal representative' means a person who, for the purposes of the Legal Services Act 2007, is a person who, for the purposes of the Legal Services Act 2007, is an authorised person in relation to an activity which constitutes the exercise of a right of audience or the conduct of litigation (within the meaning of that Act);

---

\* **Editor's Note:** The common law offence of inciting a crime was abolished by the Serious Crime Act 2007. Schedule 6 Part 1 section 37 applies to subsection (2) above.

'picture' includes a likeness however produced;

'the prosecutor' means any person acting as prosecutor, whether an individual or body;

'publication' includes any speech, writing, relevant programme or other communication in whatever form, which is addressed to the public at large or any section of the public (and for this purpose every relevant programme shall be taken to be so addressed), but does not include an indictment or other document prepared for use in particular legal proceedings;

'relevant programme' means a programme included in a programme service, within the meaning of the Broadcasting Act 1990;

'service court' means—

. . .

'video recording' means any recording, on any medium, from which a moving image may by any means be produced, and includes the accompanying sound-track;

'witness', in relation to any criminal proceedings, means any person called, or proposed to be called, to give evidence in the proceedings.

(2) Nothing in this Part shall affect any power of a court to exclude evidence at its discretion (whether by preventing questions being put or otherwise) which is exercisable apart from this Part.

# SCHEDULE 1A

# RELEVANT OFFENCES FOR THE PURPOSES OF SECTION 17

### Murder and manslaughter

1 Murder in a case where it is alleged that a firearm or knife was used to cause the death in question.

2 Manslaughter in a case where it is alleged that a firearm or knife was used to cause the death in question.

3 Murder or manslaughter in a case (other than a case falling within paragraph 1 or 2) where it is alleged that—

(a) the accused was carrying a firearm or knife at any time during the commission of the offence, and

(b) a person other than the accused knew or believed at any time during the commission of the offence that the accused was carrying a firearm or knife.

### Offences against the Person Act 1861

4 An offence under section 18 of the Offences against the Person Act 1861 (wounding with intent to cause grievous bodily harm etc.) in a case where it is alleged that a firearm or knife was used to cause the wound or harm in question.

5 An offence under section 20 of that Act (malicious wounding) in a case where it is alleged that a firearm or knife was used to cause the wound or inflict the harm in question.

6 An offence under section 38 of that Act (assault with intent to resist arrest) in a case where it is alleged that a firearm or knife was used to carry out the assault in question.

7 An offence under section 47 of the Offences against the Person Act 1861 (assault occasioning actual bodily harm) in a case where it is alleged that a firearm or knife was used to inflict the harm in question.

8 An offence under section 18, 20, 38 or 47 of the Offences against the Person Act 1861 in a case (other than a case falling within any of paragraphs 4 to 7) where it is alleged that—

(a) the accused was carrying a firearm or knife at any time during the commission of the offence, and

(b) a person other than the accused knew or believed at any time during the commission of the offence that the accused was carrying a firearm or knife.

### Prevention of Crime Act 1953

9  An offence under section 1 of the Prevention of Crime Act 1953 (having an offensive weapon in a public place).

9A  An offence under section 1A (threatening with offensive weapon in public).

### Firearms Act 1968

10  An offence under section 1 of the Firearms Act 1968 (requirement of firearm certificate).

11  An offence under section 2(1) of that Act (possession etc. of a shot gun without a certificate).

12  An offence under section 3 of that Act (business and other transactions with firearms and ammunition).

13  An offence under section 4 of that Act (conversion of weapons).

14  An offence under section 5(1) of that Act (weapons subject to general prohibition).

15  An offence under section 5(1A) of that Act (ammunition subject to general prohibition).

16  An offence under section 16 of that Act (possession with intent to injure).

17  An offence under section 16A of that Act (possession with intent to cause fear of violence).

18  An offence under section 17 of that Act (use of firearm to resist arrest).

19  An offence under section 18 of that Act (carrying firearm with criminal intent).

20  An offence under section 19 of that Act (carrying firearm in a public place).

21  An offence under section 20 of that Act (trespassing with firearm).

22  An offence under section 21 of that Act (possession of firearms by person previously convicted of crime).

23  An offence under section 21A of that Act (firing an air weapon beyond premises).

24  An offence under section 24A of that Act (supplying imitation firearms to minors).

### Criminal Justice Act 1988

25  An offence under section 139 of the Criminal Justice Act 1988 (having article with blade or point in public place).

26  An offence under section 139A of that Act (having article with blade or point (or offensive weapon) on school premises).

26A  An offence under section 139AA of that Act (threatening with article with blade or point or offensive weapon).

### Violent Crime Reduction Act 2006

27  An offence under section 28 of the Violent Crime Reduction Act 2006 (using someone to mind a weapon).

28  An offence under section 32 of that Act (sales of air weapons by way of trade or business to be face to face).

29  An offence under section 36 of that Act (manufacture, import and sale of realistic imitation firearms).

### General

30  A reference in any of paragraphs 1 to 8 to an offence ('offence A') includes—

    (a) a reference to an attempt to commit offence A in a case where it is alleged that it was attempted to commit offence A in the manner or circumstances described in that paragraph,

    (b) a reference to a conspiracy to commit offence A in a case where it is alleged that the conspiracy was to commit offence A in the manner or circumstances described in that paragraph,

    (c) a reference to an offence under Part 2 of the Serious Crime Act 2007 in relation to which offence A is the offence (or one of the offences) which the person intended or believed would be committed in a case where it is alleged that the person intended or believed offence A would be committed in the manner or circumstances described in that paragraph, and

    (d) a reference to aiding, abetting, counselling or procuring the commission of offence A in a case where it is alleged that offence A was committed, or the act or omission charged in respect of offence A was done or made, in the manner or circumstances described in that paragraph.

31  A reference in any of paragraphs 9 to 29 to an offence ('offence A') includes—

 (a)  a reference to an attempt to commit offence A,

 (b)  a reference to a conspiracy to commit offence A,

 (c)  a reference to an offence under Part 2 of the Serious Crime Act 2007 in relation to which offence A is the offence (or one of the offences) which the person intended or believed would be committed, and

 (d)  a reference to aiding, abetting, counselling or procuring the commission of offence A.

*Interpretation*

32  In this Schedule—

'firearm' has the meaning given by section 57 of the Firearms Act 1968;

'knife' has the meaning given by section 10 of the Knives Act 1997.

# Criminal Cases Review (Insanity) Act 1999

(1999, c. 25)

## 1  Reference of former verdict of guilty but insane

(1)  Where a verdict was returned . . . to the effect that a person was guilty of the act or omission charged against him but was insane at the time, the Criminal Cases Review Commission may at any time refer the verdict to the Court of Appeal if subsection (2) below applies.

(2)  This subsection applies if the commission consider that there is a real possibility that the verdict would not be upheld were the reference to be made and either—

 (a)  the Commission so consider because of an argument, or evidence, not raised in the proceedings which led to the verdict, or

 (b)  it appears to the Commission that there are exceptional circumstances which justify the making of the reference.

(3)  Section 14 of the Criminal Appeal Act 1995 (supplementary provision about the reference of a verdict) shall apply in relation to a reference under subsection (1) above as it applies in relation to references under section 9 or 10 of that Act.

## 2  Reference treated as appeal: England and Wales

(1)  A reference under section 1(1) above of a verdict returned . . . in the case of a person shall be treated for all purposes as an appeal by the person under section 12 of the Criminal Appeal Act 1968.

(2)  In their application to such a reference by virtue of subsection (1) above, sections 13 and 14 of that Act shall have effect—

 (a)  as if references to the verdict of not guilty by reason of insanity were to the verdict referred under section 1(1) above, and

 (b)  as if, in section 14(1)(b), for the words from the beginning to 'that he' there were substituted 'the accused was under a disability and'.

# Terrorism Act 2000

(1996, c. 25)

## 118  Defences

(1)  Subsection (2) applies where in accordance with a provision mentioned in subsection (5) it is a defence for a person charged with an offence to prove a particular matter.

(2) If the person adduces evidence which is sufficient to raise an issue with respect to the matter the court or jury shall assume that the defence is satisfied unless the prosecution proves beyond reasonable doubt that it is not.

(3) Subsection (4) applies where in accordance with a provision mentioned in subsection (5) a court—

> (a) may make an assumption in relation to a person charged with an offence unless a particular matter is proved, or
>
> (b) may accept a fact as sufficient evidence unless a particular matter is proved.

(4) If evidence is adduced which is sufficient to raise an issue with respect to the matter mentioned in subsection (3)(a) or (b) the court shall treat it as proved unless the prosecution disproves it beyond reasonable doubt.

(5) The provisions in respect of which subsections (2) and (4) apply are—

> (a) sections 12(4), 39(5)(a), 54, 57, 58, 58A, 77 and 103 of this Act,

### 120   Evidence

(1) A document which purports to be—

> (a) a notice or direction given or order made by the Secretary of State for the purposes of a provision of this Act, and
>
> (b) signed by him or on his behalf,

shall be received in evidence and shall, until the contrary is proved, be deemed to have been given or made by the Secretary of State.

(2) A document bearing a certificate which—

> (a) purports to be signed by or on behalf of the Secretary of State, and
>
> (b) states that the document is a true copy of a notice or direction given or order made by the Secretary of State for the purposes of a provision of this Act,

shall be evidence . . . of the document in legal proceedings.

(3) In subsections (1) and (2) a reference to an order does not include a reference to an order made by statutory instrument.

(4) The Documentary Evidence Act 1868 shall apply to an authorisation given in writing by the Secretary of State for the purposes of this Act as it applies to an order made by him.

## Sexual Offences Act 2003

(2003, c. 42)

### 75   Evidential presumptions about consent

(1) If in proceedings for an offence to which this section applies it is proved—

> (a) that the defendant did the relevant act,
>
> (b) that any of the circumstances specified in subsection (2) existed, and
>
> (c) that the defendant knew that those circumstances existed,

the complainant is to be taken not to have consented to the relevant act unless sufficient evidence is adduced to raise an issue as to whether he consented, and the defendant is to be taken not to have reasonably believed that the complainant consented unless sufficient evidence is adduced to raise an issue as to whether he reasonably believed it.

(2) The circumstances are that—

> (a) any person was, at the time of the relevant act or immediately before it began, using violence against the complainant or causing the complainant to fear that immediate violence would be used against him;
>
> (b) any person was, at the time of the relevant act or immediately before it began, causing the complainant to fear that violence was being used, or that immediate violence would be used, against another person;

(c) the complainant was, and the defendant was not, unlawfully detained at the time of the relevant act;

(d) the complainant was asleep or otherwise unconscious at the time of the relevant act;

(e) because of the complainant's physical disability, the complainant would not have been able at the time of the relevant act to communicate to the defendant whether the complainant consented;

(f) any person had administered to or caused to be taken by the complainant, without the complainant's consent, a substance which, having regard to when it was administered or taken, was capable of causing or enabling the complainant to be stupefied or overpowered at the time of the relevant act.

(3) In subsection (2)(a) and (b), the reference to the time immediately before the relevant act began is, in the case of an act which is one of a continuous series of sexual activities, a reference to the time immediately before the first sexual activity began.

## 76 Conclusive presumptions about consent

(1) If in proceedings for an offence to which this section applies it is proved that the defendant did the relevant act and that any of the circumstances specified in subsection (2) existed, it is to be conclusively presumed—

(a) that the complainant did not consent to the relevant act, and

(b) that the defendant did not believe that the complainant consented to the relevant act.

(2) The circumstances are that—

(a) the defendant intentionally deceived the complainant as to the nature or purpose of the relevant act;

(b) the defendant intentionally induced the complainant to consent to the relevant act by impersonating a person known personally to the complainant.

## 77 Sections 75 and 76: relevant acts

In relation to an offence to which sections 75 and 76 apply, references in those sections to the relevant act and to the complainant are to be read as follows—

| Offence | Relevant Act |
| --- | --- |
| An offence under section 1 (rape). | The defendant intentionally penetrating, with his penis, the vagina, anus or mouth of another person ('the complainant'). |
| An offence under section 2 (assault by penetration). | The defendant intentionally penetrating, with a part of his body or anything else, the vagina or anus of another person ('the complainant'), where the penetration is sexual. |
| An offence under section 3 (sexual assault). | The defendant intentionally touching another person ('the complainant'), where the touching is sexual. |
| An offence under section 4 (causing a person to engage in sexual activity without consent). | The defendant intentionally causing another person ('the complainant') to engage in an activity, where the activity is sexual. |

## 78 'Sexual'

For the purposes of this Part (except sections 15A and 71), penetration, touching or any other activity is sexual if a reasonable person would consider that—

(a) whatever its circumstances or any person's purpose in relation to it, it is because of its nature sexual, or

(b) because of its nature it may be sexual and because of its circumstances or the purpose of any person in relation to it (or both) it is sexual.

### 79   Part 1: general interpretation

(1)  The following apply for the purposes of this Part.

(2)  Penetration is a continuing act from entry to withdrawal.

(3)  References to a part of the body include references to a part surgically constructed (in particular, through gender reassignment surgery).

(4)  'Image' means a moving or still image and includes an image produced by any means and, where the context permits, a three-dimensional image.

(5)  References to an image of a person include references to an image of an imaginary person.

(6)  'Mental disorder' has the meaning given by section 1 of the Mental Health Act 1983.

(7)  References to observation (however expressed) are to observation whether direct or by looking at an image.

(8)  Touching includes touching—

  (a)  with any part of the body,

  (b)  with anything else,

  (c)  through anything,

and in particular includes touching amounting to penetration.

(9)  'Vagina' includes vulva.

(10)  In relation to an animal, references to the vagina or anus include references to any similar part.

## Criminal Justice Act 2003

(2003, c. 44)

## PART 8   LIVE LINKS

### 51   Live links in criminal proceedings

(1)  A witness (other than the defendant) may, if the court so directs, give evidence through a live link in the following criminal proceedings.

(2)  They are—

  (a)  a summary trial,

  (b)  an appeal to the Crown Court arising out of such a trial,

  (c)  a trial on indictment,

  (d)  an appeal to the criminal division of the Court of Appeal,

  (e)  the hearing of a reference under section 9 or 11 of the Criminal Appeal Act 1995,

  (f)  a hearing before a magistrates' court or the Crown Court which is held after the defendant has entered a plea of guilty, and

  (g)  a hearing before the Court of Appeal under section 80 of this Act.

(3)  A direction may be given under this section—

  (a)  on an application by a party to the proceedings, or

  (b)  of the court's own motion.

(4)  But a direction may not be given under this section unless—

  (a)  the court is satisfied that it is in the interests of the efficient or effective administration of justice for the person concerned to give evidence in the proceedings through a live link,

  (b)  it has been notified by the Secretary of State that suitable facilities for receiving evidence through a live link are available in the area in which it appears to the court that the proceedings will take place, and

  (c)  that notification has not been withdrawn.

(5)  The withdrawal of such a notification is not to affect a direction given under this section before that withdrawal.

(6)  In deciding whether to give a direction under this section the court must consider all the circumstances of the case.

(7) Those circumstances include in particular—
  (a) the availability of the witness,
  (b) the need for the witness to attend in person,
  (c) the importance of the witness's evidence to the proceedings,
  (d) the views of the witness,
  (e) the suitability of the facilities at the place where the witness would give evidence through a live link,
  (f) whether a direction might tend to inhibit any party to the proceedings from effectively testing the witness's evidence.

(8) The court must state in open court its reasons for refusing an application for a direction under this section and, if it is a magistrates' court, must cause them to be entered in the register of its proceedings.

## 52 Effect of, and rescission of, direction

(1) Subsection (2) applies where the court gives a direction under section 51 for a person to give evidence through a live link in particular proceedings.

(2) The person concerned may not give evidence in those proceedings after the direction is given otherwise than through a live link (but this is subject to the following provisions of this section).

(3) The court may rescind a direction under section 51 if it appears to the court to be in the interests of justice to do so.

(4) Where it does so, the person concerned shall cease to be able to give evidence in the proceedings through a live link, but this does not prevent the court from giving a further direction under section 51 in relation to him.

(5) A direction under section 51 may be rescinded under subsection (3)—
  (a) on an application by a party to the proceedings, or
  (b) of the court's own motion.

(6) But an application may not be made under subsection (5)(a) unless there has been a material change of circumstances since the direction was given.

(7) The court must state in open court its reasons—
  (a) for rescinding a direction under section 51, or
  (b) for refusing an application to rescind such a direction,
and, if it is a magistrates' court, must cause them to be entered in the register of its proceedings.

## 53 Magistrates' courts permitted to sit at other locations

(1) This section applies where—
  (a) a magistrates' court is minded to give a direction under section 51 for evidence to be given through a live link in proceedings before the court, and
  (b) suitable facilities for receiving such evidence are not available at any place at which the court can (apart from subsection (2)) lawfully sit.

(2) The court may sit for the purposes of the whole or any part of the proceedings at any place at which such facilities are available and which has been authorised by a direction under section 30 of the Courts Act 2003.

(3) If the place mentioned in subsection (2) is outside the local justice area in which the justices act it shall be deemed to be in that area for the purpose of the jurisdiction of the justices acting in that area.

## 54 Warning to jury

(1) This section applies where, as a result of a direction under section 51, evidence has been given through a live link in proceedings before the Crown Court.

(2) The judge may give the jury (if there is one) such direction as he thinks necessary to ensure that the jury gives the same weight to the evidence as if it had been given by the witness in the court-room or other place where the proceedings are held.

## 55   Rules of court

(1) Criminal Procedure Rules may make such provision as appears to the Criminal Procedure Rules Authority to be necessary or expedient for the purposes of this Part.

(2) Criminal Procedure Rules may in particular make provision—

(a) as to the procedure to be followed in connection with applications under section 51 or 52, and

(b) as to the arrangements or safeguards to be put in place in connection with the operation of live links.

(3) The provision which may be made by virtue of subsection (2)(a) includes provision—

(a) for uncontested applications to be determined by the court without a hearing,

(b) for preventing the renewal of an unsuccessful application under section 51 unless there has been a material change of circumstances,

(c) for the manner in which confidential or sensitive information is to be treated in connection with an application under section 51 or 52 and in particular as to its being disclosed to, or withheld from, a party to the proceedings.

(4) Nothing in this section is to be taken as affecting the generality of any enactment conferring power to make Criminal Procedure Rules.

## 56   Interpretation of Part 8

(1) In this Part—

'legal representative' means a person who, for the purposes of the Legal Services Act 2007, is an authorised person in relation to an activity which constitutes the exercise of a right of audience or the conduct of litigation (within the meaning of that Act),

'local justice area' has the same meaning as in the Courts Act 2003,

'witness', in relation to any criminal proceedings, means a person called, or proposed to be called, to give evidence in the proceedings.

(2) In this Part 'live link' means a live television link or other arrangement by which a witness, while at a place in the United Kingdom which is outside the building where the proceedings are being held, is able to see and hear a person at the place where the proceedings are being held and to be seen and heard by the following persons.

(3) They are—

(a) the defendant or defendants,

(b) the judge or justices (or both) and the jury (if there is one),

(c) legal representatives acting in the proceedings, and

(d) any interpreter or other person appointed by the court to assist the witness.

(4) The extent (if any) to which a person is unable to see or hear by reason of any impairment of eyesight or hearing is to be disregarded for the purposes of subsection (2).

(5) Nothing in this Part is to be regarded as affecting any power of a court—

(a) to make an order, give directions or give leave of any description in relation to any witness (including the defendant or defendants), or

(b) to exclude evidence at its discretion (whether by preventing questions being put or otherwise).

# PART 9   PROSECUTION APPEALS

*Introduction*

## 57   Introduction

(1) In relation to a trial on indictment, the prosecution is to have the rights of appeal for which provision is made by this Part.

(2) But the prosecution is to have no right of appeal under this Part in respect of—

    (a) a ruling that a jury be discharged, or

    (b) a ruling from which an appeal lies to the Court of Appeal by virtue of any other enactment.

(3) An appeal under this Part is to lie to the Court of Appeal.

(4) Such an appeal may be brought only with the leave of the judge or the Court of Appeal.

### *General right of appeal in respect of rulings*

## 58   **General right of appeal in respect of rulings**

(1) This section applies where a judge makes a ruling in relation to a trial on indictment at an applicable time and the ruling relates to one or more offences included in the indictment.

(2) The prosecution may appeal in respect of the ruling in accordance with this section.

(3) The ruling is to have no effect whilst the prosecution is able to take any steps under subsection (4).

(4) The prosecution may not appeal in respect of the ruling unless—

    (a) following the making of the ruling, it—

        (i) informs the court that it intends to appeal, or

        (ii) requests an adjournment to consider whether to appeal, and

    (b) if such an adjournment is granted, it informs the court following the adjournment that it intends to appeal.

(5) If the prosecution requests an adjournment under subsection (4)(a)(ii), the judge may grant such an adjournment.

(6) Where the ruling relates to two or more offences—

    (a) any one or more of those offences may be the subject of the appeal, and

    (b) if the prosecution informs the court in accordance with subsection (4) that it intends to appeal, it must at the same time inform the court of the offence or offences which are the subject of the appeal.

(7) Where—

    (a) the ruling is a ruling that there is no case to answer, and

    (b) the prosecution, at the same time that it informs the court in accordance with subsection (4) that it intends to appeal, nominates one or more other rulings which have been made by a judge in relation to the trial on indictment at an applicable time and which relate to the offence or offences which are the subject of the appeal,

that other ruling, or those other rulings, are also to be treated as the subject of the appeal.

(8) The prosecution may not inform the court in accordance with subsection (4) that it intends to appeal, unless, at or before that time, it informs the court that it agrees that, in respect of the offence or each offence which is the subject of the appeal, the defendant in relation to that offence should be acquitted of that offence if either of the conditions mentioned in subsection (9) is fulfilled.

(9) Those conditions are—

    (a) that leave to appeal to the Court of Appeal is not obtained, and

    (b) that the appeal is abandoned before it is determined by the Court of Appeal.

(10) If the prosecution informs the court in accordance with subsection (4) that it intends to appeal, the ruling mentioned in subsection (1) is to continue to have no effect in relation to the offence or offences which are the subject of the appeal whilst the appeal is pursued.

(11) If and to the extent that a ruling has no effect in accordance with this section—

    (a) any consequences of the ruling are also to have no effect,

    (b) the judge may not take any steps in consequence of the ruling, and

    (c) if he does so, any such steps are also to have no effect.

(12) Where the prosecution has informed the court of its agreement under subsection (8) and either of the conditions mentioned in subsection (9) is fulfilled, the judge or the Court of Appeal must order that the defendant in relation to the offence or each offence concerned be acquitted of that offence.

(13) In this section 'applicable time', in relation to a trial on indictment, means any time (whether before or after the commencement of the trial) before the judge starts his summing-up to the jury.

(14) The reference in subsection (13) to the time when the judge starts his summing-up to the jury includes the time when the judge would start his summing-up to the jury but for the making of an order under Part 7.

### 59   Expedited and non-expedited appeals

(1) Where the prosecution informs the court in accordance with section 58(4) that it intends to appeal, the judge must decide whether or not the appeal should be expedited.

(2) If the judge decides that the appeal should be expedited, he may order an adjournment.

(3) If the judge decides that the appeal should not be expedited, he may—

    (a) order an adjournment, or

    (b) discharge the jury (if one has been sworn).

(4) If he decides that the appeal should be expedited, he or the Court of Appeal may subsequently reverse that decision and, if it is reversed, the judge may act as mentioned in subsection (3)(a) or (b).

### 60   Continuation of proceedings for offences not affected by ruling

(1) This section applies where the prosecution informs the court in accordance with section 58(4) that it intends to appeal.

(2) Proceedings may be continued in respect of any offence which is not the subject of the appeal.

### 61   Determination of appeal by court of appeal

(1) On an appeal under section 58, the Court of Appeal may confirm, reverse or vary any ruling to which the appeal relates.

(2) Subsections (3) to (5) apply where the appeal relates to a single ruling.

(3) Where the Court of Appeal confirms the ruling, it must, in respect of the offence or each offence which is the subject of the appeal, order that the defendant in relation to that offence be acquitted of that offence.

(4) Where the Court of Appeal reverses or varies the ruling, it must, in respect of the offence or each offence which is the subject of the appeal, do any of the following—

    (a) order that proceedings for that offence may be resumed in the Crown Court,

    (b) order that a fresh trial may take place in the Crown Court for that offence,

    (c) order that the defendant in relation to that offence be acquitted of that offence.

(5) But the Court of Appeal may not make an order under subsection (4)(a) or (b) in respect of an offence unless it considers that the defendant could not receive a fair trial if an order were made under subsection (4)(a) or (b).

(6) Subsections (7) and (8) apply where the appeal relates to a ruling that there is no case to answer and one or more other rulings.

(7) Where the Court of Appeal confirms the ruling that there is no case to answer, it must, in respect of the offence or each offence which is the subject of the appeal, order that the defendant in relation to that offence be acquitted of that offence.

(8) Where the Court of Appeal reverses or varies the ruling that there is no case to answer, it must in respect of the offence or each offence which is the subject of the appeal, make any of the orders mentioned in subsection (4)(a) to (c) (but subject to subsection (5)).

*Right of appeal in respect of evidentiary rulings*

### 62   Right of appeal in respect of evidentiary rulings

(1) The prosecution may, in accordance with this section and section 63, appeal in respect of—

    (a) a single qualifying evidentiary ruling, or

    (b) two or more qualifying evidentiary rulings.

(2) A 'qualifying evidentiary ruling' is an evidentiary ruling of a judge in relation to a trial on indictment which is made at any time (whether before or after the commencement of the trial) before the opening of the case for the defence.

(3) The prosecution may not appeal in respect of a single qualifying evidentiary ruling unless the ruling relates to one or more qualifying offences (whether or not it relates to any other offence).

(4) The prosecution may not appeal in respect of two or more qualifying evidentiary rulings unless each ruling relates to one or more qualifying offences (whether or not it relates to any other offence).

(5) If the prosecution intends to appeal under this section, it must before the opening of the case for the defence inform the court—

    (a) of its intention to do so, and

    (b) of the ruling or rulings to which the appeal relates.

(6) In respect of the ruling, or each ruling, to which the appeal relates—

    (a) the qualifying offence, or at least one of the qualifying offences, to which the ruling relates must be the subject of the appeal, and

    (b) any other offence to which the ruling relates may, but need not, be the subject of the appeal.

(7) The prosecution must, at the same time that it informs the court in accordance with subsection (5), inform the court of the offence or offences which are the subject of the appeal.

(8) For the purposes of this section, the case for the defence opens when, after the conclusion of the prosecution evidence, the earliest of the following events occurs—

    (a) evidence begins to be adduced by or on behalf of a defendant,

    (b) it is indicated to the court that no evidence will be adduced by or on behalf of a defendant,

    (c) a defendant's case is opened, as permitted by section 2 of the Criminal Procedure Act 1865.

(9) In this section—

'evidentiary ruling' means a ruling which relates to the admissibility or exclusion of any prosecution evidence,

'qualifying offence' means an offence described in Part 1 of Schedule 4.

(10) The Secretary of State may by order amend that Part by doing any one or more of the following—

    (a) adding a description of offence,

    (b) removing a description of offence for the time being included,

    (c) modifying a description of offence for the time being included.

(11) Nothing in this section affects the right of the prosecution to appeal in respect of an evidentiary ruling under section 58.

### 63  Condition that evidentiary ruling significantly weakens prosecution case

(1) Leave to appeal may not be given in relation to an appeal under section 62 unless the judge or, as the case may be, the Court of Appeal is satisfied that the relevant condition is fulfilled.

(2) In relation to an appeal in respect of a single qualifying evidentiary ruling, the relevant condition is that the ruling significantly weakens the prosecution's case in relation to the offence or offences which are the subject of the appeal.

(3) In relation to an appeal in respect of two or more qualifying evidentiary rulings, the relevant condition is that the rulings taken together significantly weaken the prosecution's case in relation to the offence or offences which are the subject of the appeal.

### 64  Expedited and non-expedited appeals

(1) Where the prosecution informs the court in accordance with section 62(5), the judge must decide whether or not the appeal should be expedited.

(2) If the judge decides that the appeal should be expedited, he may order an adjournment.

(3) If the judge decides that the appeal should not be expedited, he may—

    (a) order an adjournment, or

    (b) discharge the jury (if one has been sworn).

(4) If he decides that the appeal should be expedited, he or the Court of Appeal may subsequently reverse that decision and, if it is reversed, the judge may act as mentioned in subsection (3)(a) or (b).

### 65   Continuation of proceedings for offences not affected by ruling

(1) This section applies where the prosecution informs the court in accordance with section 62(5).

(2) Proceedings may be continued in respect of any offence which is not the subject of the appeal.

### 66   Determination of appeal by court of appeal

(1) On an appeal under section 62, the Court of Appeal may confirm, reverse or vary any ruling to which the appeal relates.

(2) In addition, the Court of Appeal must, in respect of the offence or each offence which is the subject of the appeal, do any of the following—

    (a) order that proceedings for that offence be resumed in the Crown Court,

    (b) order that a fresh trial may take place in the Crown Court for that offence,

    (c) order that the defendant in relation to that offence be acquitted of that offence.

(3) But no order may be made under subsection (2)(c) in respect of an offence unless the prosecution has indicated that it does not intend to continue with the prosecution of that offence.

### 67   Reversal of rulings

The Court of Appeal may not reverse a ruling on an appeal under this Part unless it is satisfied—

    (a) that the ruling was wrong in law,

    (b) that the ruling involved an error of law or principle, or

    (c) that the ruling was a ruling that it was not reasonable for the judge to have made.

## PART 10   RETRIAL FOR SERIOUS OFFENCES

*Cases that may be retried*

### 75   Cases that may be retried

(1) This Part applies where a person has been acquitted of a qualifying offence in proceedings—

    (a) on indictment in England and Wales,

    (b) on appeal against a conviction, verdict or finding in proceedings on indictment in England and Wales, or

    (c) on appeal from a decision on such an appeal.

(2) A person acquitted of an offence in proceedings mentioned in subsection (1) is treated for the purposes of that subsection as also acquitted of any qualifying offence of which he could have been convicted in the proceedings because of the first-mentioned offence being charged in the indictment, except an offence—

    (a) of which he has been convicted,

    (b) of which he has been found not guilty by reason of insanity, or

    (c) in respect of which, in proceedings where he has been found to be under a disability (as defined by section 4 of the Criminal Procedure (Insanity) Act 1964), a finding has been made that he did the act or made the omission charged against him.

(3) References in subsections (1) and (2) to a qualifying offence do not include references to an offence which, at the time of the acquittal, was the subject of an order under section 77(1) or (3).

(4) This Part also applies where a person has been acquitted, in proceedings elsewhere than in the United Kingdom, of an offence under the law of the place where the proceedings were held, if the

commission of the offence as alleged would have amounted to or included the commission (in the United Kingdom or elsewhere) of a qualifying offence.

(5) Conduct punishable under the law in force elsewhere than in the United Kingdom is an offence under that law for the purposes of subsection (4), however it is described in that law.

(6) This Part applies whether the acquittal was before or after the passing of this Act.

(7) References in this Part to acquittal are to acquittal in circumstances within subsection (1) or (4).

(8) In this Part 'qualifying offence' means an offence listed in Part 1 of Schedule 5.

### Application for retrial

## 76    Application to court of appeal

(1) A prosecutor may apply to the Court of Appeal for an order—

(a) quashing a person's acquittal in proceedings within section 75(1), and

(b) ordering him to be retried for the qualifying offence.

(2) A prosecutor may apply to the Court of Appeal, in the case of a person acquitted elsewhere than in the United Kingdom, for—

(a) a determination whether the acquittal is a bar to the person being tried in England and Wales for the qualifying offence, and

(b) if it is, an order that the acquittal is not to be a bar.

(3) A prosecutor may make an application under subsection (1) or (2) only with the written consent of the Director of Public Prosecutions.

(4) The Director of Public Prosecutions may give his consent only if satisfied that—

(a) there is evidence as respects which the requirements of section 78 appear to be met,

(b) it is in the public interest for the application to proceed, and

(c) any trial pursuant to an order on the application would not be inconsistent with obligations of the United Kingdom under Article 31 or 34 of the Treaty on European Union (as it had effect before 1 December 2009) or Article 82, 83 or 85 of the Treaty on the Functioning of the European Union relating to the principle of *ne bis in idem*.

(5) Not more than one application may be made under subsection (1) or (2) in relation to an acquittal.

## 77    Determination by court of appeal

(1) On an application under section 76(1), the Court of Appeal—

(a) if satisfied that the requirements of sections 78 and 79 are met, must make the order applied for;

(b) otherwise, must dismiss the application.

(2) Subsections (3) and (4) apply to an application under section 76(2).

(3) Where the Court of Appeal determines that the acquittal is a bar to the person being tried for the qualifying offence, the court—

(a) if satisfied that the requirements of sections 78 and 79 are met, must make the order applied for;

(b) otherwise, must make a declaration to the effect that the acquittal is a bar to the person being tried for the offence.

(4) Where the Court of Appeal determines that the acquittal is not a bar to the person being tried for the qualifying offence, it must make a declaration to that effect.

## 78    New and compelling evidence

(1) The requirements of this section are met if there is new and compelling evidence against the acquitted person in relation to the qualifying offence.

(2) Evidence is new if it was not adduced in the proceedings in which the person was acquitted (nor, if those were appeal proceedings, in earlier proceedings to which the appeal related).

(3) Evidence is compelling if—

(a) it is reliable,

(b) it is substantial, and

(c) in the context of the outstanding issues, it appears highly probative of the case against the acquitted person.

(4) The outstanding issues are the issues in dispute in the proceedings in which the person was acquitted and, if those were appeal proceedings, any other issues remaining in dispute from earlier proceedings to which the appeal related.

(5) For the purposes of this section, it is irrelevant whether any evidence would have been admissible in earlier proceedings against the acquitted person.

### 79   Interests of justice

(1) The requirements of this section are met if in all the circumstances it is in the interests of justice for the court to make the order under section 77.

(2) That question is to be determined having regard in particular to—

(a) whether existing circumstances make a fair trial unlikely;

(b) for the purposes of that question and otherwise, the length of time since the qualifying offence was allegedly committed;

(c) whether it is likely that the new evidence would have been adduced in the earlier proceedings against the acquitted person but for a failure by an officer or by a prosecutor to act with due diligence or expedition;

(d) whether, since those proceedings or, if later, since the commencement of this Part, any officer or prosecutor has failed to act with due diligence or expedition.

(3) In subsection (2) references to an officer or prosecutor include references to a person charged with corresponding duties under the law in force elsewhere than in England and Wales.

(4) Where the earlier prosecution was conducted by a person other than a prosecutor, subsection (2)(c) applies in relation to that person as well as in relation to a prosecutor.

### 80   Procedure and evidence

(1) A prosecutor who wishes to make an application under section 76(1) or (2) must give notice of the application to the Court of Appeal.

(2) Within two days beginning with the day on which any such notice is given, notice of the application must be served by the prosecutor on the person to whom the application relates, charging him with the offence to which it relates or, if he has been charged with it in accordance with section 87(4), stating that he has been so charged.

(3) Subsection (2) applies whether the person to whom the application relates is in the United Kingdom or elsewhere, but the Court of Appeal may, on application by the prosecutor, extend the time for service under that subsection if it considers it necessary to do so because of that person's absence from the United Kingdom.

(4) The Court of Appeal must consider the application at a hearing.

(5) The person to whom the application relates—

(a) is entitled to be present at the hearing, although he may be in custody, unless he is in custody elsewhere than in England and Wales or Northern Ireland, and

(b) is entitled to be represented at the hearing, whether he is present or not.

(6) For the purposes of the application, the Court of Appeal may, if it thinks it necessary or expedient in the interests of justice—

(a) order the production of any document, exhibit or other thing, the production of which appears to the court to be necessary for the determination of the application, and

(b) order any witness who would be a compellable witness in proceedings pursuant to an order or declaration made on the application to attend for examination and be examined before the court.

(7) The Court of Appeal may at one hearing consider more than one application (whether or not relating to the same person), but only if the offences concerned could be tried on the same indictment.

# PART 11

## Chapter 1  Evidence of bad character

### *Introductory*

**98  'Bad character'**

References in this Chapter to evidence of a person's 'bad character' are to evidence of, or of a disposition towards, misconduct on his part, other than evidence which—

(a) has to do with the alleged facts of the offence with which the defendant is charged, or

(b) is evidence of misconduct in connection with the investigation or prosecution of that offence.

**99  Abolition of common law rules**

(1) The common law rules governing the admissibility of evidence of bad character in criminal proceedings are abolished.

(2) Subsection (1) is subject to section 118(1) in so far as it preserves the rule under which in criminal proceedings a person's reputation is admissible for the purposes of proving his bad character.

### *Persons other than defendants*

**100  Non-defendant's bad character**

(1) In criminal proceedings evidence of the bad character of a person other than the defendant is admissible if and only if—

(a) it is important explanatory evidence,

(b) it has substantial probative value in relation to a matter which—

(i) is a matter in issue in the proceedings, and

(ii) is of substantial importance in the context of the case as a whole,

or

(c) all parties to the proceedings agree to the evidence being admissible.

(2) For the purposes of subsection (1)(a) evidence is important explanatory evidence if—

(a) without it, the court or jury would find it impossible or difficult properly to understand other evidence in the case, and

(b) its value for understanding the case as a whole is substantial.

(3) In assessing the probative value of evidence for the purposes of subsection (1)(b) the court must have regard to the following factors (and to any others it considers relevant)—

(a) the nature and number of the events, or other things, to which the evidence relates;

(b) when those events or things are alleged to have happened or existed;

(c) where—

(i) the evidence is evidence of a person's misconduct, and

(ii) it is suggested that the evidence has probative value by reason of similarity between that misconduct and other alleged misconduct,

the nature and extent of the similarities and the dissimilarities between each of the alleged instances of misconduct;

(d) where—

(i) the evidence is evidence of a person's misconduct,

(ii) it is suggested that that person is also responsible for the misconduct charged, and

(iii) the identity of the person responsible for the misconduct charged is disputed, the extent to which the evidence shows or tends to show that the same person was responsible each time.

(4) Except where subsection (1)(c) applies, evidence of the bad character of a person other than the defendant must not be given without leave of the court.

*Defendants*

### 101   Defendant's bad character

(1) In criminal proceedings evidence of the defendant's bad character is admissible if, but only if—

(a) all parties to the proceedings agree to the evidence being admissible,

(b) the evidence is adduced by the defendant himself or is given in answer to a question asked by him in cross-examination and intended to elicit it,

(c) it is important explanatory evidence,

(d) it is relevant to an important matter in issue between the defendant and the prosecution,

(e) it has substantial probative value in relation to an important matter in issue between the defendant and a co-defendant,

(f) it is evidence to correct a false impression given by the defendant, or

(g) the defendant has made an attack on another person's character.

(2) Sections 102 to 106 contain provision supplementing subsection (1).

(3) The court must not admit evidence under subsection (1)(d) or (g) if, on an application by the defendant to exclude it, it appears to the court that the admission of the evidence would have such an adverse effect on the fairness of the proceedings that the court ought not to admit it.

(4) On an application to exclude evidence under subsection (3) the court must have regard, in particular, to the length of time between the matters to which that evidence relates and the matters which form the subject of the offence charged.

### 102   'Important explanatory evidence'

For the purposes of section 101(1)(c) evidence is important explanatory evidence if—

(a) without it, the court or jury would find it impossible or difficult properly to understand other evidence in the case, and

(b) its value for understanding the case as a whole is substantial.

### 103   'Matter in issue between the defendant and the prosecution'

(1) For the purposes of section 101(1)(d) the matters in issue between the defendant and the prosecution include—

(a) the question whether the defendant has a propensity to commit offences of the kind with which he is charged, except where his having such a propensity makes it no more likely that he is guilty of the offence;

(b) the question whether the defendant has a propensity to be untruthful, except where it is not suggested that the defendant's case is untruthful in any respect.

(2) Where subsection (1)(a) applies, a defendant's propensity to commit offences of the kind with which he is charged may (without prejudice to any other way of doing so) be established by evidence that he has been convicted of—

(a) an offence of the same description as the one with which he is charged, or

(b) an offence of the same category as the one with which he is charged.

(3) Subsection (2) does not apply in the case of a particular defendant if the court is satisfied, by reason of the length of time since the conviction or for any other reason, that it would be unjust for it to apply in his case.

(4) For the purposes of subsection (2)—

(a) two offences are of the same description as each other if the statement of the offence in a written charge or indictment would, in each case, be in the same terms;

(b) two offences are of the same category as each other if they belong to the same category of offences prescribed for the purposes of this section by an order made by the Secretary of State.

(5) A category prescribed by an order under subsection (4)(b) must consist of offences of the same type.

(6) Only prosecution evidence is admissible under section 101(1)(d).

(7)–(11) . . .*

## 104  'Matter in issue between the defendant and a co-defendant'

(1) Evidence which is relevant to the question whether the defendant has a propensity to be untruthful is admissible on that basis under section 101(1)(e) only if the nature or conduct of his defence is such as to undermine the co-defendant's defence.

(2) Only evidence—

(a) which is to be (or has been) adduced by the co-defendant, or

(b) which a witness is to be invited to give (or has given) in cross-examination by the co-defendant,

is admissible under section 101(1)(e).

## 105  'Evidence to correct a false impression'

(1) For the purposes of section 101(1)(f)—

(a) the defendant gives a false impression if he is responsible for the making of an express or implied assertion which is apt to give the court or jury a false or misleading impression about the defendant;

(b) evidence to correct such an impression is evidence which has probative value in correcting it.

(2) A defendant is treated as being responsible for the making of an assertion if—

(a) the assertion is made by the defendant in the proceedings (whether or not in evidence given by him),

(b) the assertion was made by the defendant—

(i) on being questioned under caution, before charge, about the offence with which he is charged, or

(ii) on being charged with the offence or officially informed that he might be prosecuted for it,

and evidence of the assertion is given in the proceedings,

(c) the assertion is made by a witness called by the defendant,

(d) the assertion is made by any witness in cross-examination in response to a question asked by the defendant that is intended to elicit it, or is likely to do so, or

(e) the assertion was made by any person out of court, and the defendant adduces evidence of it in the proceedings.

(3) A defendant who would otherwise be treated as responsible for the making of an assertion shall not be so treated if, or to the extent that, he withdraws it or disassociates himself from it.

(4) Where it appears to the court that a defendant, by means of his conduct (other than the giving of evidence) in the proceedings, is seeking to give the court or jury an impression about himself that is false or misleading, the court may if it appears just to do so treat the defendant as being responsible for the making of an assertion which is apt to give that impression.

(5) In subsection (4) 'conduct' includes appearance or dress.

(6) Evidence is admissible under section 101(1)(f) only if it goes no further than is necessary to correct the false impression.

(7) Only prosecution evidence is admissible under section 101(1)(f).

## 106  'Attack on another person's character'

(1) For the purposes of section 101(1)(g) a defendant makes an attack on another person's character if—

(a) he adduces evidence attacking the other person's character,

(b) he (or any legal representative appointed under section 38(4) of the Youth Justice and Criminal Evidence Act 1999 to cross-examine a witness in his interests) asks questions in cross-examination that are intended to elicit such evidence, or are likely to do so, or

---

* **Editor's Note:** Apply to 'corresponding offences' committed outside England and Wales.

(c) evidence is given of an imputation about the other person made by the defendant—
  (i) on being questioned under caution, before charge, about the offence with which he is charged, or
  (ii) on being charged with the offence or officially informed that he might be prosecuted for it.

(2) In subsection (1) 'evidence attacking the other person's character' means evidence to the effect that the other person—
  (a) has committed an offence (whether a different offence from the one with which the defendant is charged or the same one), or
  (b) has behaved, or is disposed to behave, in a reprehensible way;
and 'imputation about the other person' means an assertion to that effect.

(3) Only prosecution evidence is admissible under section 101(1)(g).

### 107 Stopping the case where evidence contaminated

(1) If on a defendant's trial before a judge and jury for an offence—
  (a) evidence of his bad character has been admitted under any of paragraphs (c) to (g) of section 101(1), and
  (b) the court is satisfied at any time after the close of the case for the prosecution that—
    (i) the evidence is contaminated, and
    (ii) the contamination is such that, considering the importance of the evidence to the case against the defendant, his conviction of the offence would be unsafe,
the court must either direct the jury to acquit the defendant of the offence or, if it considers that there ought to be a retrial, discharge the jury.

(2) Where—
  (a) a jury is directed under subsection (1) to acquit a defendant of an offence, and
  (b) the circumstances are such that, apart from this subsection, the defendant could if acquitted of that offence be found guilty of another offence,
the defendant may not be found guilty of that other offence if the court is satisfied as mentioned in subsection (1)(b) in respect of it.

(3) If—
  (a) a jury is required to determine under section 4A(2) of the Criminal Procedure (Insanity) Act 1964 whether a person charged on an indictment with an offence did the act or made the omission charged,
  (b) evidence of the person's bad character has been admitted under any of paragraphs (c) to (g) of section 101(1), and
  (c) the court is satisfied at any time after the close of the case for the prosecution that—
    (i) the evidence is contaminated, and
    (ii) the contamination is such that, considering the importance of the evidence to the case against the person, a finding that he did the act or made the omission would be unsafe,
the court must either direct the jury to acquit the defendant of the offence or, if it considers that there ought to be a rehearing, discharge the jury.

(4) This section does not prejudice any other power a court may have to direct a jury to acquit a person of an offence or to discharge a jury.

(5) For the purposes of this section a person's evidence is contaminated where—
  (a) as a result of an agreement or understanding between the person and one or more others, or
  (b) as a result of the person being aware of anything alleged by one or more others whose evidence may be, or has been, given in the proceedings,
the evidence is false or misleading in any respect, or is different from what it would otherwise have been.

## 108    Offences committed by defendant when a child

(1) Section 16(2) and (3) of the Children and Young Persons Act 1963 (offences committed by person under 14 disregarded for purposes of evidence relating to previous convictions) shall cease to have effect.

(2) In proceedings for an offence committed or alleged to have been committed by the defendant when aged 21 or over, evidence of his conviction for an offence when under the age of 14 is not admissible unless—

(a) both of the offences are triable only on indictment, and

(b) the court is satisfied that the interests of justice require the evidence to be admissible.

(2A), (2B) . . .*

(3) Subsection (2) applies in addition to section 101.

*General*

## 109    Assumption of truth in assessment of relevance or probative value

(1) Subject to subsection (2), a reference in this Chapter to the relevance or probative value of evidence is a reference to its relevance or probative value on the assumption that it is true.

(2) In assessing the relevance or probative value of an item of evidence for any purpose of this Chapter, a court need not assume that the evidence is true if it appears, on the basis of any material before the court (including any evidence it decides to hear on the matter), that no court or jury could reasonably find it to be true.

## 110    Court's duty to give reasons for rulings

(1) Where the court makes a relevant ruling—

(a) it must state in open court (but in the absence of the jury, if there is one) its reasons for the ruling;

(b) if it is a magistrates' court, it must cause the ruling and the reasons for it to be entered in the register of the court's proceedings.

(2) In this section 'relevant ruling' means—

(a) a ruling on whether an item of evidence is evidence of a person's bad character;

(b) a ruling on whether an item of such evidence is admissible under section 100 or 101 (including a ruling on an application under section 101(3));

(c) a ruling under section 107.

## 111    Rules of court

(1) Rules of court may make such provision as appears to the appropriate authority to be necessary or expedient for the purposes of this Act; and the appropriate authority is the authority entitled to make the rules.

(2) The rules may, and, where the party in question is the prosecution, must, contain provision requiring a party who—

(a) proposes to adduce evidence of a defendant's bad character, or

(b) proposes to cross-examine a witness with a view to eliciting such evidence,

to serve on the defendant such notice, and such particulars of or relating to the evidence, as may be prescribed.

(3) The rules may provide that the court or the defendant may, in such circumstances as may be prescribed, dispense with a requirement imposed by virtue of subsection (2).

(4) In considering the exercise of its powers with respect to costs, the court may take into account any failure by a party to comply with a requirement imposed by virtue of subsection (2) and not dispensed with by virtue of subsection (3).

(5) The rules may—

(a) limit the application of any provision of the rules to prescribed circumstances;

---

* **Editor's Note:** Apply to corresponding offences committed outside England and Wales.

(b) subject any provision of the rules to prescribed exceptions;

(c) make different provision for different cases or circumstances.

(6) Nothing in this section prejudices the generality of any enactment conferring power to make rules of court; and no particular provision of this section prejudices any general provision of it.

(7) In this section—

'prescribed' means prescribed by rules of court.

## 112 Interpretation of Chapter 1

(1) In this Chapter—

'bad character' is to be read in accordance with section 98;

'criminal proceedings' means criminal proceedings in relation to which the strict rules of evidence apply;

'defendant', in relation to criminal proceedings, means a person charged with an offence in those proceedings; and 'co-defendant', in relation to a defendant, means a person charged with an offence in the same proceedings;

'important matter' means a matter of substantial importance in the context of the case as a whole;

'misconduct' means the commission of an offence or other reprehensible behaviour;

'offence' includes a service offence;

'probative value', and 'relevant' (in relation to an item of evidence), are to be read in accordance with section 109;

'prosecution evidence' means evidence which is to be (or has been) adduced by the prosecution, or which a witness is to be invited to give (or has given) in cross-examination by the prosecution;

'written charge' has the same meaning as in section 29 and also includes an information.

(2) Where a defendant is charged with two or more offences in the same criminal proceedings, this Chapter (except section 101(3)) has effect as if each offence were charged in separate proceedings; and references to the offence with which the defendant is charged are to be read accordingly.

(3) Nothing in this Chapter affects the exclusion of evidence—

(a) under the rule in section 3 of the Criminal Procedure Act 1865 against a party impeaching the credit of his own witness by general evidence of bad character,

(b) under section 41 of the Youth Justice and Criminal Evidence Act 1999 on grounds other than the fact that it is evidence of a person's bad character.

(c) On grounds other than the fact that it is evidence of a person's bad character.

## 113 Armed Forces

. . .

# Chapter 2

## 114 Admissibility of hearsay evidence

(1) In criminal proceedings a statement not made in oral evidence in the proceedings is admissible as evidence of any matter stated if, but only if—

(a) any provision of this Chapter or any other statutory provision makes it admissible,

(b) any rule of law preserved by section 118 makes it admissible,

(c) all parties to the proceedings agree to it being admissible, or

(d) the court is satisfied that it is in the interests of justice for it to be admissible.

(2) In deciding whether a statement not made in oral evidence should be admitted under subsection (1)(d), the court must have regard to the following factors (and to any others it considers relevant)—

(a) how much probative value the statement has (assuming it to be true) in relation to a matter in issue in the proceedings, or how valuable it is for the understanding of other evidence in the case;

(b) what other evidence has been, or can be, given on the matter or evidence mentioned in paragraph (a);

(c) how important the matter or evidence mentioned in paragraph (a) is in the context of the case as a whole;

(d) the circumstances in which the statement was made;

(e) how reliable the maker of the statement appears to be;

(f) how reliable the evidence of the making of the statement appears to be;

(g) whether oral evidence of the matter stated can be given and, if not, why it cannot;

(h) the amount of difficulty involved in challenging the statement;

(i) the extent to which that difficulty would be likely to prejudice the party facing it.

(3) Nothing in this Chapter affects the exclusion of evidence of a statement on grounds other than the fact that it is a statement not made in oral evidence in the proceedings.

## 115 Statements and matters stated

(1) In this Chapter references to a statement or to a matter stated are to be read as follows.

(2) A statement is any representation of fact or opinion made by a person by whatever means; and it includes a representation made in a sketch, photofit or other pictorial form.

(3) A matter stated is one to which this Chapter applies if (and only if) the purpose, or one of the purposes, of the person making the statement appears to the court to have been—

(a) to cause another person to believe the matter, or

(b) to cause another person to act or a machine to operate on the basis that the matter is as stated.

*Principal categories of admissibility*

## 116 Cases where a witness is unavailable

(1) In criminal proceedings a statement not made in oral evidence in the proceedings is admissible as evidence of any matter stated if—

(a) oral evidence given in the proceedings by the person who made the statement would be admissible as evidence of that matter,

(b) the person who made the statement (the relevant person) is identified to the court's satisfaction, and

(c) any of the five conditions mentioned in subsection (2) is satisfied.

(2) The conditions are—

(a) that the relevant person is dead;

(b) that the relevant person is unfit to be a witness because of his bodily or mental condition;

(c) that the relevant person is outside the United Kingdom and it is not reasonably practicable to secure his attendance;

(d) that the relevant person cannot be found although such steps as it is reasonably practicable to take to find him have been taken;

(e) that through fear the relevant person does not give (or does not continue to give) oral evidence in the proceedings, either at all or in connection with the subject matter of the statement, and the court gives leave for the statement to be given in evidence.

(3) For the purposes of subsection (2)(e) 'fear' is to be widely construed and (for example) includes fear of the death or injury of another person or of financial loss.

(4) Leave may be given under subsection (2)(e) only if the court considers that the statement ought to be admitted in the interests of justice, having regard—

(a) to the statement's contents,

(b) to any risk that its admission or exclusion will result in unfairness to any party to the proceedings (and in particular to how difficult it will be to challenge the statement if the relevant person does not give oral evidence),

(c) in appropriate cases, to the fact that a direction under section 19 of the Youth Justice and Criminal Evidence Act 1999 (special measures for the giving of evidence by fearful witnesses etc.) could be made in relation to the relevant person, and

(d) to any other relevant circumstances.

(5) A condition set out in any paragraph of subsection (2) which is in fact satisfied is to be treated as not satisfied if it is shown that the circumstances described in that paragraph are caused—

(a) by the person in support of whose case it is sought to give the statement in evidence, or

(b) by a person acting on his behalf,

in order to prevent the relevant person giving oral evidence in the proceedings (whether at all or in connection with the subject matter of the statement).

## 117  Business and other documents

(1) In criminal proceedings a statement contained in a document is admissible as evidence of any matter stated if—

(a) oral evidence given in the proceedings would be admissible as evidence of that matter,

(b) the requirements of subsection (2) are satisfied, and

(c) the requirements of subsection (5) are satisfied, in a case where subsection (4) requires them to be.

(2) The requirements of this subsection are satisfied if—

(a) the document or the part containing the statement was created or received by a person in the course of a trade, business, profession or other occupation, or as the holder of a paid or unpaid office,

(b) the person who supplied the information contained in the statement (the relevant person) had or may reasonably be supposed to have had personal knowledge of the matters dealt with, and

(c) each person (if any) through whom the information was supplied from the relevant person to the person mentioned in paragraph (a) received the information in the course of a trade, business, profession or other occupation, or as the holder of a paid or unpaid office.

(3) The persons mentioned in paragraphs (a) and (b) of subsection (2) may be the same person.

(4) The additional requirements of subsection (5) must be satisfied if the statement—

(a) was prepared for the purposes of pending or contemplated criminal proceedings, or for a criminal investigation, but

(b) was not obtained pursuant to a request under section 7 of the Crime (International Co-operation) Act 2003 or an order under paragraph 6 of Schedule 13 to the Criminal Justice Act 1988 (which relate to overseas evidence).

(5) The requirements of this subsection are satisfied if—

(a) any of the five conditions mentioned in section 116(2) is satisfied (absence of relevant person etc.), or

(b) the relevant person cannot reasonably be expected to have any recollection of the matters dealt with in the statement (having regard to the length of time since he supplied the information and all other circumstances).

(6) A statement is not admissible under this section if the court makes a direction to that effect under subsection (7).

(7) The court may make a direction under this subsection if satisfied that the statement's reliability as evidence for the purpose for which it is tendered is doubtful in view of—

(a) its contents,

(b) the source of the information contained in it,

(c) the way in which or the circumstances in which the information was supplied or received, or

(d) the way in which or the circumstances in which the document concerned was created or received.

## 118  Preservation of certain common law categories of admissibility

(1) The following rules of law are preserved.

*Public information etc.*

1. Any rule of law under which in criminal proceedings—

   (a) published works dealing with matters of a public nature (such as histories, scientific works, dictionaries and maps) are admissible as evidence of facts of a public nature stated in them,

   (b) public documents (such as public registers, and returns made under public authority with respect to matters of public interest) are admissible as evidence of facts stated in them,

   (c) records (such as the records of certain courts, treaties, Crown grants, pardons and commissions) are admissible as evidence of facts stated in them, or

   (d) evidence relating to a person's age or date or place of birth may be given by a person without personal knowledge of the matter.

*Reputation as to character*

2. Any rule of law under which in criminal proceedings evidence of a person's reputation is admissible for the purpose of proving his good or bad character.

*Note*

The rule is preserved only so far as it allows the court to treat such evidence as proving the matter concerned.

*Reputation or family tradition*

3. Any rule of law under which in criminal proceedings evidence of reputation or family tradition is admissible for the purpose of proving or disproving—

   (a) pedigree or the existence of a marriage,

   (b) the existence of any public or general right, or

   (c) the identity of any person or thing.

*Note*

The rule is preserved only so far as it allows the court to treat such evidence as proving or disproving the matter concerned.

*Res gestae*

4. Any rule of law under which in criminal proceedings a statement is admissible as evidence of any matter stated if—

   (a) the statement was made by a person so emotionally overpowered by an event that the possibility of concoction or distortion can be disregarded,

   (b) the statement accompanied an act which can be properly evaluated as evidence only if considered in conjunction with the statement, or

   (c) the statement relates to a physical sensation or a mental state (such as intention or emotion).

*Confessions etc.*

5. Any rule of law relating to the admissibility of confessions or mixed statements in criminal proceedings.

*Admissions by agents etc.*

6. Any rule of law under which in criminal proceedings—

   (a) an admission made by an agent of a defendant is admissible against the defendant as evidence of any matter stated, or

   (b) a statement made by a person to whom a defendant refers a person for information is admissible against the defendant as evidence of any matter stated.

*Common enterprise*

7. Any rule of law under which in criminal proceedings a statement made by a party to a common enterprise is admissible against another party to the enterprise as evidence of any matter stated.

*Expert evidence*

8. Any rule of law under which in criminal proceedings an expert witness may draw on the body of expertise relevant to his field.

(2)  With the exception of the rules preserved by this section, the common law rules governing the admissibility of hearsay evidence in criminal proceedings are abolished.

### 119  Inconsistent statements

(1)  If in criminal proceedings a person gives oral evidence and—

    (a)  he admits making a previous inconsistent statement, or

    (b)  a previous inconsistent statement made by him is proved by virtue of section 3, 4 or 5 of the Criminal Procedure Act 1865,

the statement is admissible as evidence of any matter stated of which oral evidence by him would be admissible.

(2)  If in criminal proceedings evidence of an inconsistent statement by any person is given under section 124(2)(c), the statement is admissible as evidence of any matter stated in it of which oral evidence by that person would be admissible.

### 120  Other previous statements of witnesses

(1)  This section applies where a person (the witness) is called to give evidence in criminal proceedings.

(2)  If a previous statement by the witness is admitted as evidence to rebut a suggestion that his oral evidence has been fabricated, that statement is admissible as evidence of any matter stated of which oral evidence by the witness would be admissible.

(3)  A statement made by the witness in a document—

    (a)  which is used by him to refresh his memory while giving evidence,

    (b)  on which he is cross-examined, and

    (c)  which as a consequence is received in evidence in the proceedings,

is admissible as evidence of any matter stated of which oral evidence by him would be admissible.

(4)  A previous statement by the witness is admissible as evidence of any matter stated of which oral evidence by him would be admissible, if—

    (a)  any of the following three conditions is satisfied, and

    (b)  while giving evidence the witness indicates that to the best of his belief he made the statement, and that to the best of his belief it states the truth.

(5)  The first condition is that the statement identifies or describes a person, object or place.

(6)  The second condition is that the statement was made by the witness when the matters stated were fresh in his memory but he does not remember them, and cannot reasonably be expected to remember them, well enough to give oral evidence of them in the proceedings.

(7)  The third condition is that—

    (a)  the witness claims to be a person against whom an offence has been committed,

    (b)  the offence is one to which the proceedings relate,

    (c)  the statement consists of a complaint made by the witness (whether to a person in authority or not) about conduct which would, if proved, constitute the offence or part of the offence,

    (e)  the complaint was not made as a result of a threat or a promise, and

    (f)  before the statement is adduced the witness gives oral evidence in connection with its subject matter.

(8)  For the purposes of subsection (7) the fact that the complaint was elicited (for example, by a leading question) is irrelevant unless a threat or a promise was involved.

*Supplementary*

### 121  Additional requirement for admissibility of multiple hearsay

(1)  A hearsay statement is not admissible to prove the fact that an earlier hearsay statement was made unless—

(a) either of the statements is admissible under section 117, 119 or 120,

(b) all parties to the proceedings so agree, or

(c) the court is satisfied that the value of the evidence in question, taking into account how reliable the statements appear to be, is so high that the interests of justice require the later statement to be admissible for that purpose.

(2) In this section 'hearsay statement' means a statement, not made in oral evidence, that is relied on as evidence of a matter stated in it.

## 122   Documents produced as exhibits

(1) This section applies if on a trial before a judge and jury for an offence—

(a) a statement made in a document is admitted in evidence under section 119 or 120, and

(b) the document or a copy of it is produced as an exhibit.

(2) The exhibit must not accompany the jury when they retire to consider their verdict unless—

(a) the court considers it appropriate, or

(b) all the parties to the proceedings agree that it should accompany the jury.

## 123   Capability to make statement

(1) Nothing in section 116, 119 or 120 makes a statement admissible as evidence if it was made by a person who did not have the required capability at the time when he made the statement.

(2) Nothing in section 117 makes a statement admissible as evidence if any person who, in order for the requirements of section 117(2) to be satisfied, must at any time have supplied or received the information concerned or created or received the document or part concerned—

(a) did not have the required capability at that time, or

(b) cannot be identified but cannot reasonably be assumed to have had the required capability at that time.

(3) For the purposes of this section a person has the required capability if he is capable of—

(a) understanding questions put to him about the matters stated, and

(b) giving answers to such questions which can be understood.

(4) Where by reason of this section there is an issue as to whether a person had the required capability when he made a statement—

(a) proceedings held for the determination of the issue must take place in the absence of the jury (if there is one);

(b) in determining the issue the court may receive expert evidence and evidence from any person to whom the statement in question was made;

(c) the burden of proof on the issue lies on the party seeking to adduce the statement, and the standard of proof is the balance of probabilities.

## 124   Credibility

(1) This section applies if in criminal proceedings—

(a) a statement not made in oral evidence in the proceedings is admitted as evidence of a matter stated, and

(b) the maker of the statement does not give oral evidence in connection with the subject matter of the statement.

(2) In such a case—

(a) any evidence which (if he had given such evidence) would have been admissible as relevant to his credibility as a witness is so admissible in the proceedings;

(b) evidence may with the court's leave be given of any matter which (if he had given such evidence) could have been put to him in cross-examination as relevant to his credibility as a witness but of which evidence could not have been adduced by the cross-examining party;

(c) evidence tending to prove that he made (at whatever time) any other statement inconsistent with the statement admitted as evidence is admissible for the purpose of showing that he contradicted himself.

(3) If as a result of evidence admitted under this section an allegation is made against the maker of a statement, the court may permit a party to lead additional evidence of such description as the court may specify for the purposes of denying or answering the allegation.

(4) In the case of a statement in a document which is admitted as evidence under section 117 each person who, in order for the statement to be admissible, must have supplied or received the information concerned or created or received the document or part concerned is to be treated as the maker of the statement for the purposes of subsections (1) to (3) above.

## 125 Stopping the case where evidence is unconvincing

(1) If on a defendant's trial before a judge and jury for an offence the court is satisfied at any time after the close of the case for the prosecution that—

(a) the case against the defendant is based wholly or partly on a statement not made in oral evidence in the proceedings, and

(b) the evidence provided by the statement is so unconvincing that, considering its importance to the case against the defendant, his conviction of the offence would be unsafe,

the court must either direct the jury to acquit the defendant of the offence or, if it considers that there ought to be a retrial, discharge the jury.

(2) Where—

(a) a jury is directed under subsection (1) to acquit a defendant of an offence, and

(b) the circumstances are such that, apart from this subsection, the defendant could if acquitted of that offence be found guilty of another offence,

the defendant may not be found guilty of that other offence if the court is satisfied as mentioned in subsection (1) in respect of it.

(3) If—

(a) a jury is required to determine under section 4A(2) of the Criminal Procedure (Insanity) Act 1964 whether a person charged on an indictment with an offence did the act or made the omission charged, and

(b) the court is satisfied as mentioned in subsection (1) above at any time after the close of the case for the prosecution that—

(i) the case against the defendant is based wholly or partly on a statement not made in oral evidence in the proceedings, and

(ii) the evidence provided by the statement is so unconvincing that, considering its importance to the case against the person, a finding that he did the act or made the omission would be unsafe,

the court must either direct the jury to acquit the defendant of the offence or, if it considers that there ought to be a rehearing, discharge the jury.

(4) This section does not prejudice any other power a court may have to direct a jury to acquit a person of an offence or to discharge a jury.

## 126 Court's general discretion to exclude evidence

(1) In criminal proceedings the court may refuse to admit a statement as evidence of a matter stated if—

(a) the statement was made otherwise than in oral evidence in the proceedings, and

(b) the court is satisfied that the case for excluding the statement, taking account of the danger that to admit it would result in undue waste of time, substantially outweighs the case for admitting it, taking account of the value of the evidence.

(2) Nothing in this Chapter prejudices—

(a) any power of a court to exclude evidence under section 78 of the Police and Criminal Evidence Act 1984 (exclusion of unfair evidence), or

(b) any other power of a court to exclude evidence at its discretion (whether by preventing questions from being put or otherwise).

*Miscellaneous*

## 127  Expert evidence: preparatory work

(1)  This section applies if—

(a)  a statement has been prepared for the purposes of criminal proceedings,

(b)  the person who prepared the statement had or may reasonably be supposed to have had personal knowledge of the matters stated,

(c)  notice is given under the appropriate rules that another person (the expert) will in evidence given in the proceedings orally or under section 9 of the Criminal Justice Act 1967 base an opinion or inference on the statement, and

(d)  the notice gives the name of the person who prepared the statement and the nature of the matters stated.

(2)  In evidence given in the proceedings the expert may base an opinion or inference on the statement.

(3)  If evidence based on the statement is given under subsection (2) the statement is to be treated as evidence of what it states.

(4)  This section does not apply if the court, on an application by a party to the proceedings, orders that it is not in the interests of justice that it should apply.

(5)  The matters to be considered by the court in deciding whether to make an order under subsection (4) include—

(a)  the expense of calling as a witness the person who prepared the statement;

(b)  whether relevant evidence could be given by that person which could not be given by the expert;

(c)  whether that person can reasonably be expected to remember the matters stated well enough to give oral evidence of them.

(6)  Subsections (1) to (5) apply to a statement prepared for the purposes of a criminal investigation as they apply to a statement prepared for the purposes of criminal proceedings, and in such a case references to the proceedings are to criminal proceedings arising from the investigation.

(7)  The appropriate rules are Criminal Procedure Rules made by virtue of—

(a)  section 81 of the Police and Criminal Evidence Act 1984 (advance notice of expert evidence in Crown Court), or

(b)  section 20(3) of the Criminal Procedure and Investigations Act 1996 (advance notice of expert evidence in magistrates' courts).

## 128  Confessions

(1)  ...*

(2)  Subject to subsection (1), nothing in this Chapter makes a confession by a defendant admissible if it would not be admissible under section 76 of the Police and Criminal Evidence Act 1984.

(3)  In subsection (2) 'confession' has the meaning given by section 82 of that Act.

## 129  Representations other than by a person

(1)  Where a representation of any fact—

(a)  is made otherwise than by a person, but

(b)  depends for its accuracy on information supplied (directly or indirectly) by a person,

the representation is not admissible in criminal proceedings as evidence of the fact unless it is proved that the information was accurate.

(2)  Subsection (1) does not affect the operation of the presumption that a mechanical device has been properly set or calibrated.

---

* **Editor's Note:** Refers to Police and Criminal Evidence Act 1984 section 76A.

*General*

## 132 Rules of court

(1) Rules of court may make such provision as appears to the appropriate authority to be necessary or expedient for the purposes of this Chapter; and the appropriate authority is the authority entitled to make the rules.

(2) The rules may make provision about the procedure to be followed and other conditions to be fulfilled by a party proposing to tender a statement in evidence under any provision of this Chapter.

(3) The rules may require a party proposing to tender the evidence to serve on each party to the proceedings such notice, and such particulars of or relating to the evidence, as may be prescribed.

(4) The rules may provide that the evidence is to be treated as admissible by agreement of the parties if—

    (a) a notice has been served in accordance with provision made under subsection (3), and

    (b) no counter-notice in the prescribed form objecting to the admission of the evidence has been served by a party.

(5) If a party proposing to tender evidence fails to comply with a prescribed requirement applicable to it—

    (a) the evidence is not admissible except with the court's leave;

    (b) where leave is given the court or jury may draw such inferences from the failure as appear proper;

    (c) the failure may be taken into account by the court in considering the exercise of its powers with respect to costs.

(6) In considering whether or how to exercise any of its powers under subsection (5) the court shall have regard to whether there is any justification for the failure to comply with the requirement.

(7) A person shall not be convicted of an offence solely on an inference drawn under subsection (5)(b).

(8) Rules under this section may—

    (a) limit the application of any provision of the rules to prescribed circumstances;

    (b) subject any provision of the rules to prescribed exceptions;

    (c) make different provision for different cases or circumstances.

(9) Nothing in this section prejudices the generality of any enactment conferring power to make rules of court; and no particular provision of this section prejudices any general provision of it.

(10) In this section—

'prescribed' means prescribed by rules of court.

## 133 Proof of statements in documents

Where a statement in a document is admissible as evidence in criminal proceedings, the statement may be proved by producing either—

    (a) the document, or

    (b) (whether or not the document exists) a copy of the document or of the material part of it, authenticated in whatever way the court may approve.

## 134 Interpretation of Chapter 2

(1) In this Chapter—

'copy', in relation to a document, means anything on to which information recorded in the document has been copied, by whatever means and whether directly or indirectly;

'criminal proceedings' means criminal proceedings in relation to which the strict rules of evidence apply;

'defendant', in relation to criminal proceedings, means a person charged with an offence in those proceedings;

'document' means anything in which information of any description is recorded;

'oral evidence' includes evidence which, by reason of any disability, disorder or other impairment, a person called as a witness gives in writing or by signs or by way of any device;

'statutory provision' means any provision contained in, or in an instrument made under, this or any other Act, including any Act passed after this Act.

(2)  Section 115 (statements and matters stated) contains other general interpretative provisions.

(3)  Where a defendant is charged with two or more offences in the same criminal proceedings, this Chapter has effect as if each offence were charged in separate proceedings.

## Chapter 3  Miscellaneous and supplemental

### 137  Evidence by video recording

(1)  This section applies where—

(a)  a person is called as a witness in proceedings for an offence triable only on indictment, or for a prescribed offence triable either way,

(b)  the person claims to have witnessed (whether visually or in any other way)—

   (i)  events alleged by the prosecution to include conduct constituting the offence or part of the offence, or

   (ii)  events closely connected with such events,

(c)  he has previously given an account of the events in question (whether in response to questions asked or otherwise),

(d)  the account was given at a time when those events were fresh in the person's memory (or would have been, assuming the truth of the claim mentioned in paragraph (b)),

(e)  a video recording was made of the account,

(f)  the court has made a direction that the recording should be admitted as evidence in chief of the witness, and the direction has not been rescinded, and

(g)  the recording is played in the proceedings in accordance with the direction.

(2)  If, or to the extent that, the witness in his oral evidence in the proceedings asserts the truth of the statements made by him in the recorded account, they shall be treated as if made by him in that evidence.

(3)  A direction under subsection (1)(f)—

(a)  may not be made in relation to a recorded account given by the defendant;

(b)  may be made only if it appears to the court that—

   (i)  the witness's recollection of the events in question is likely to have been significantly better when he gave the recorded account than it will be when he gives oral evidence in the proceedings, and

   (ii)  it is in the interests of justice for the recording to be admitted, having regard in particular to the matters mentioned in subsection (4).

(4)  Those matters are—

(a)  the interval between the time of the events in question and the time when the recorded account was made;

(b)  any other factors that might affect the reliability of what the witness said in that account;

(c)  the quality of the recording;

(d)  any views of the witness as to whether his evidence in chief should be given orally or by means of the recording.

(5)  For the purposes of subsection (2) it does not matter if the statements in the recorded account were not made on oath.

(6)  In this section 'prescribed' means of a description specified in an order made by the Secretary of State.

## 138  Video evidence: further provisions

(2)  The reference in subsection (1)(f) of section 137 to the admission of a recording includes a reference to the admission of part of the recording; and references in that section and this one to the video recording or to the witness's recorded account shall, where appropriate, be read accordingly.

(3)  In considering whether any part of a recording should be not admitted under section 137, the court must consider—

(a)  whether admitting that part would carry a risk of prejudice to the defendant, and

(b)  if so, whether the interests of justice nevertheless require it to be admitted in view of the desirability of showing the whole, or substantially the whole, of the recorded interview.

(4)  A court may not make a direction under section 137(1)(f) in relation to any proceedings unless—

(a)  the Secretary of State has notified the court that arrangements can be made, in the area in which it appears to the court that the proceedings will take place, for implementing directions under that section, and

(b)  the notice has not been withdrawn.

(5)  Nothing in section 137 affects the admissibility of any video recording which would be admissible apart from that section.

## 139  Use of documents to refresh memory

(1)  A person giving oral evidence in criminal proceedings about any matter may, at any stage in the course of doing so, refresh his memory of it from a document made or verified by him at an earlier time if—

(a)  he states in his oral evidence that the document records his recollection of the matter at that earlier time, and

(b)  his recollection of the matter is likely to have been significantly better at that time than it is at the time of his oral evidence.

(2)  Where—

(a)  a person giving oral evidence in criminal proceedings about any matter has previously given an oral account, of which a sound recording was made, and he states in that evidence that the account represented his recollection of the matter at that time,

(b)  his recollection of the matter is likely to have been significantly better at the time of the previous account than it is at the time of his oral evidence, and

(c)  a transcript has been made of the sound recording,

he may, at any stage in the course of giving his evidence, refresh his memory of the matter from that transcript.

## 140  Interpretation of Chapter 3

In this Chapter—

'criminal proceedings' means criminal proceedings in relation to which the strict rules of evidence apply;

'defendant', in relation to criminal proceedings, means a person charged with an offence in those proceedings;

'document' means anything in which information of any description is recorded, but not including any recording of sounds or moving images;

'oral evidence' includes evidence which, by reason of any disability, disorder or other impairment, a person called as a witness gives in writing or by signs or by way of any device;

'video recording' means any recording, on any medium, from which a moving image may by any means be produced, and includes the accompanying sound-track.

# SCHEDULE 4

# QUALIFYING OFFENCES
# FOR PURPOSES OF SECTION 62

## PART 1  LIST OF OFFENCES

### Offences against the person

*Murder*
  1. Murder.

*Attempted murder*
  2. An offence under section 1 of the Criminal Attempts Act 1981 of attempting to commit murder.

*Soliciting murder*
  3. An offence under section 4 of the Offences against the Person Act 1861.

*Manslaughter*
  4. Manslaughter.

*Corporate manslaughter*
  4A. An offence under section 1 of the Corporate Manslaughter and Corporate Homicide Act 2007.

*Wounding or causing grievous bodily harm with intent*
  5. An offence under section 18 of the Offences against the Person Act 1861.

*Kidnapping*
  6. Kidnapping.

### Sexual offences

*Rape*
  7. An offence under section 1 of the Sexual Offences Act 1956 or section 1 of the Sexual Offences Act 2003.

*Attempted rape*
  8. An offence under section 1 of the Criminal Attempts Act 1981 of attempting to commit an offence under section 1 of the Sexual Offences Act 1956 or section 1 of the Sexual Offences Act 2003.

*Intercourse with a girl under thirteen*
  9. An offence under section 5 of the Sexual Offences Act 1956.

*Incest by a man with a girl under thirteen*
  10. An offence under section 10 of the Sexual Offences Act 1956 alleged to have been committed with a girl under thirteen.

*Assault by penetration*
  11. An offence under section 2 of the Sexual Offences Act 2003.

*Causing a person to engage in sexual activity without consent*
  12. An offence under section 4 of the Sexual Offences Act 2003 where it is alleged that the activity caused involved penetration within subsection (4)(a) to (d) of that section.

*Rape of a child under thirteen*
  13. An offence under section 5 of the Sexual Offences Act 2003.

*Attempted rape of a child under thirteen*

14. An offence under section 1 of the Criminal Attempts Act 1981 of attempting to commit an offence under section 5 of the Sexual Offences Act 2003.

*Assault of a child under thirteen by penetration*

15. An offence under section 6 of the Sexual Offences Act 2003.

*Causing a child under thirteen to engage in sexual activity*

16. An offence under section 8 of the Sexual Offences Act 2003 where it is alleged that an activity involving penetration within subsection (2)(a) to (d) of that section was caused.

*Sexual activity with a person with a mental disorder impeding choice*

17. An offence under section 30 of the Sexual Offences Act 2003 where it is alleged that the touching involved penetration within subsection (3)(a) to (d) of that section.

*Causing or inciting a person with a mental disorder impeding choice to engage in sexual activity*

18. An offence under section 31 of the Sexual Offences Act 2003 where it is alleged that an activity involving penetration within subsection (3)(a) to (d) of that section was caused.

## Drugs offences

*Unlawful importation of Class A drug*

19. An offence under section 50(2) of the Customs and Excise Management Act 1979 alleged to have been committed in respect of a Class A drug (as defined by section 2 of the Misuse of Drugs Act 1971).

*Unlawful exportation of Class A drug*

20. An offence under section 68(2) of the Customs and Excise Management Act 1979 alleged to have been committed in respect of a Class A drug (as defined by section 2 of the Misuse of Drugs Act 1971).

*Fraudulent evasion in respect of Class A drug*

21. An offence under section 170(1) or (2) of the Customs and Excise Management Act 1979 alleged to have been committed in respect of a Class A drug (as defined by section 2 of the Misuse of Drugs Act 1971).

*Producing or being concerned in production of Class A drug*

22. An offence under section 4(2) of the Misuse of Drugs Act 1971 alleged to have been committed in relation to a Class A drug (as defined by section 2 of that Act).

*Supplying or offering to supply Class A drug*

23. An offence under section 4(3) of the Misuse of Drugs Act 1971 alleged to have been committed in relation to a Class A drug (as defined by section 2 of that Act).

## Theft offences

*Robbery*

24. An offence under section 8(1) of the Theft Act 1968 where it is alleged that, at some time during the commission of the offence, the defendant had in his possession a firearm or imitation firearm (as defined by section 57 of the Firearms Act 1968).

## Criminal damage offences

*Arson endangering life*

25. An offence under section 1(2) of the Criminal Damage Act 1971 alleged to have been committed by destroying or damaging property by fire.

*Causing explosion likely to endanger life or property*
>26. An offence under section 2 of the Explosive Substances Act 1883.

*Intent or conspiracy to cause explosion likely to endanger life or property*
>27. An offence under section 3(1)(a) of the Explosive Substances Act 1883.

### War crimes and terrorism

*Genocide, crimes against humanity and war crimes*
>28. An offence under section 51 or 52 of the International Criminal Court Act 2001.

*Grave breaches of the Geneva Conventions*
>29. An offence under section 1 of the Geneva Conventions Act 1957.

*Directing terrorist organisation*
>30. An offence under section 56 of the Terrorism Act 2000.

*Hostage-taking*
>31. An offence under section 1 of the Taking of Hostages Act 1982.

### Hijacking and other offences relating to aviation, maritime and rail security

*Hijacking of aircraft*
>32. An offence under section 1 of the Aviation Security Act 1982.

*Destroying, damaging or endangering the safety of an aircraft*
>33. An offence under section 2 of the Aviation Security Act 1982.

*Hijacking of ships*
>34. An offence under section 9 of the Aviation and Maritime Security Act 1990.

*Seizing or exercising control of fixed platforms*
>35. An offence under section 10 of the Aviation and Maritime Security Act 1990.

*Destroying ships or fixed platforms or endangering their safety*
>36. An offence under section 11 of the Aviation and Maritime Security Act 1990.

*Hijacking of Channel Tunnel trains*
>37. An offence under article 4 of the Channel Tunnel (Security) Order 1994 (S.I.1994/570).

*Seizing or exercising control of the Channel Tunnel system*
>38. An offence under article 5 of the Channel Tunnel (Security) Order 1994 (S.I.1994/ 570).

### Conspiracy

*Conspiracy*
>39. An offence under section 1 of the Criminal Law Act 1977 of conspiracy to commit an offence listed in this Part of this Schedule.

## PART 2  SUPPLEMENTARY

>40. A reference in Part 1 of this Schedule to an offence includes a reference to an offence of aiding, abetting, counselling or procuring the commission of the offence.

>41. A reference in Part 1 of this Schedule to an enactment includes a reference to the enactment as enacted and as amended from time to time.

# SCHEDULE 5

## QUALIFYING OFFENCES
## FOR PURPOSES OF PART 10

### PART 1 LIST OF OFFENCES FOR ENGLAND AND WALES

#### Offences against the person

*Murder*

1. Murder.

*Attempted murder*

2. An offence under section 1 of the Criminal Attempts Act 1981 of attempting to commit murder.

*Soliciting murder*

3. An offence under section 4 of the Offences against the Person Act 1861.

*Manslaughter*

4. Manslaughter.

*Corporate manslaughter*

4A. An offence under section 1 of the Corporate Manslaughter and Corporate Homicide Act 2007.

*Kidnapping*

5. Kidnapping.

#### Sexual offences

*Rape*

6. An offence under section 1 of the Sexual Offences Act 1956 or section 1 of the Sexual Offences Act 2003.

*Attempted rape*

7. An offence under section 1 of the Criminal Attempts Act 1981 of attempting to commit an offence under section 1 of the Sexual Offences Act 1956 or section 1 of the Sexual Offences Act 2003.

*Intercourse with a girl under thirteen*

8. An offence under section 5 of the Sexual Offences Act 1956.

*Incest by a man with a girl under thirteen*

9. An offence under section 10 of the Sexual Offences Act 1956 alleged to have been committed with a girl under thirteen.

*Assault by penetration*

10. An offence under section 2 of the Sexual Offences Act 2003.

*Causing a person to engage in sexual activity without consent*

11. An offence under section 4 of the Sexual Offences Act 2003 where it is alleged that the activity caused involved penetration within subsection (4)(a) to (d) of that section.

*Rape of a child under thirteen*

12. An offence under section 5 of the Sexual Offences Act 2003.

*Attempted rape of a child under thirteen*

13. An offence under section 1 of the Criminal Attempts Act 1981 of attempting to commit an offence under section 5 of the Sexual Offences Act 2003.

*Assault of a child under thirteen by penetration*
14. An offence under section 6 of the Sexual Offences Act 2003.

*Causing a child under thirteen to engage in sexual activity*
15. An offence under section 8 of the Sexual Offences Act 2003 where it is alleged that an activity involving penetration within subsection (2)(a) to (d) of that section was caused.

*Sexual activity with a person with a mental disorder impeding choice*
16. An offence under section 30 of the Sexual Offences Act 2003 where it is alleged that the touching involved penetration within subsection (3)(a) to (d) of that section.

*Causing a person with a mental disorder impeding choice to engage in sexual activity*
17. An offence under section 31 of the Sexual Offences Act 2003 where it is alleged that an activity involving penetration within subsection (3)(a) to (d) of that section was caused.

## Drugs offences

*Unlawful importation of Class A drug*
18. An offence under section 50(2) of the Customs and Excise Management Act 1979 alleged to have been committed in respect of a Class A drug (as defined by section 2 of the Misuse of Drugs Act 1971).

*Unlawful exportation of Class A drug*
19. An offence under section 68(2) of the Customs and Excise Management Act 1979 alleged to have been committed in respect of a Class A drug (as defined by section 2 of the Misuse of Drugs Act 1971).

*Fraudulent evasion in respect of Class A drug*
20. An offence under section 170(1) or (2) of the Customs and Excise Management Act 1979 alleged to have been committed in respect of a Class A drug (as defined by section 2 of the Misuse of Drugs Act 1971).

*Producing or being concerned in production of Class A drug*
21. An offence under section 4(2) of the Misuse of Drugs Act 1971 alleged to have been committed in relation to a Class A drug (as defined by section 2 of that Act).

## Criminal damage offences

*Arson endangering life*
22. An offence under section 1(2) of the Criminal Damage Act 1971 alleged to have been committed by destroying or damaging property by fire.

*Causing explosion likely to endanger life or property*
23. An offence under section 2 of the Explosive Substances Act 1883.

*Intent or conspiracy to cause explosion likely to endanger life or property*
24. An offence under section 3(1)(a) of the Explosive Substances Act 1883.

## War crimes and terrorism

*Genocide, crimes against humanity and war crimes*
25. An offence under section 51 or 52 of the International Criminal Court Act 2001.

*Grave breaches of the Geneva Conventions*
26. An offence under section 1 of the Geneva Conventions Act 1957.

*Directing terrorist organisation*
27. An offence under section 56 of the Terrorism Act 2000.

*Hostage-taking*

28. An offence under section 1 of the Taking of Hostages Act 1982.

## Conspiracy

*Conspiracy*

29. An offence under section 1 of the Criminal Law Act 1977 of conspiracy to commit an offence listed in this Part of this Schedule.

# Domestic Violence, Crime and Victims Act 2004

(2004, c. 28)

## PART 1  DOMESTIC VIOLENCE ETC.

*Causing or allowing the death of a child or vulnerable adult*

**5   The offence**

(1)  A person ('D') is guilty of an offence if—

(a) a child or vulnerable adult ('V') dies or suffers serious physical harm as a result of the unlawful act of a person who—

(i)   was a member of the same household as V, and

(ii)  had frequent contact with him,

(b) D was such a person at the time of that act,

(c) at that time there was a significant risk of serious physical harm being caused to V by the unlawful act of such a person, and

(d) either D was the person whose act caused the death or serious physical harm or—

(i)   D was, or ought to have been, aware of the risk mentioned in paragraph (c),

(ii)  D failed to take such steps as he could reasonably have been expected to take to protect V from the risk, and

(iii)  the act occurred in circumstances of the kind that D foresaw or ought to have foreseen.

(2)  The prosecution does not have to prove whether it is the first alternative in subsection (1)(d) or the second (sub-paragraphs (i) to (iii)) that applies.

(3)  If D was not the mother or father of V—

(a) D may not be charged with an offence under this section if he was under the age of 16 at the time of the act that caused the death or serious physical harm;

(b) for the purposes of subsection (1)(d)(ii) D could not have been expected to take any such step as is referred to there before attaining that age.

(4)  For the purposes of this section—

(a) a person is to be regarded as a 'member' of a particular household, even if he does not live in that household, if he visits it so often and for such periods of time that it is reasonable to regard him as a member of it;

(b) where V lived in different households at different times, 'the same household as V' refers to the household in which V was living at the time of the act that caused the death or serious physical harm.

(5)  For the purposes of this section an 'unlawful' act is one that—

(a) constitutes an offence, or

(a) would constitute an offence but for being the act of—

(i)   a person under the age of ten, or

(ii)  a person entitled to rely on a defence of insanity.

Paragraph (b) does not apply to an act of D.

(6) In this section—

'act' includes a course of conduct and also includes omission;

'child' means a person under the age of 16;

'serious' harm means harm that amounts to grievous bodily harm for the purposes of the Offences against the Person Act 1861 (c. 100);

'vulnerable adult' means a person aged 16 or over whose ability to protect himself from violence, abuse or neglect is significantly impaired through physical or mental disability or illness, through old age or otherwise.

(7) A person guilty of an offence under this section of causing or allowing a person's death is liable on conviction on indictment to imprisonment for a term not exceeding 14 years or to a fine, or to both.

(8) A person guilty of an offence under this section of causing or allowing a person to suffer serious physical harm is liable on conviction on indictment to imprisonment for a term not exceeding 10 years or to a fine, or to both.

## 6   Evidence and procedure in cases of death: England and Wales

(1) Subsections (2) to (4) apply where a person ('the defendant') is charged in the same proceedings with an offence of murder or manslaughter and with an offence under section 5 in respect of the same death ('the section 5 offence').

(2) Where by virtue of section 35(3) of the Criminal Justice and Public Order Act 1994 (c. 33) a court or jury is permitted, in relation to the section 5 offence, to draw such inferences as appear proper from the defendant's failure to give evidence or refusal to answer a question, the court or jury may also draw such inferences in determining whether he is guilty—

(a) of murder or manslaughter, or

(b) of any other offence of which he could lawfully be convicted on the charge of murder or manslaughter,

even if there would otherwise be no case for him to answer in relation to that offence.

(3) The charge of murder or manslaughter is not to be dismissed under paragraph 2 of Schedule 3 to the Crime and Disorder Act 1998 (c. 37) (unless the section 5 offence is dismissed).

(4) At the defendant's trial the question whether there is a case for the defendant to answer on the charge of murder or manslaughter is not to be considered before the close of all the evidence (or, if at some earlier time he ceases to be charged with the section 5 offence, before that earlier time).

(5) An offence under section 5 of causing or allowing a person's death is an offence of homicide for the purposes of the following enactments—

sections 24 and 25 of the Magistrates' Courts Act 1980 (c. 43) (mode of trial of child or young person for indictable offence);

section 51A of the Crime and Disorder Act 1998 (sending cases to the Crown Court: children and young persons);

section 8 of the Powers of Criminal Courts (Sentencing) Act 2000 (c. 6) (power and duty to remit young offenders to youth courts for sentence).

## 6A   Evidence and procedure in cases of serious physical harm: England and Wales

(1) Subsections (3) to (5) apply where a person ('the defendant') is charged in the same proceedings with a relevant offence and with an offence under section 5 in respect of the same harm ('the section 5 offence').

(2) In this section 'relevant offence' means—

(a) an offence under section 18 or 20 of the Offences against the Person Act 1861 (grievous bodily harm etc.);

(b) an offence under section 1 of the Criminal Attempts Act 1981 of attempting to commit murder.

(3) Where by virtue of section 35(3) of the Criminal Justice and Public Order Act 1994 a court or jury is permitted, in relation to the section 5 offence, to draw such inferences as appear proper from

the defendant's failure to give evidence or refusal to answer a question, the court or jury may also draw such inferences in determining whether the defendant is guilty of a relevant offence, even if there would otherwise be no case for the defendant to answer in relation to that offence.

(4) The charge of the relevant offence is not to be dismissed under paragraph 2 of Schedule 3 to the Crime and Disorder Act 1998 (unless the section 5 offence is dismissed).

(5) At the defendant's trial the question whether there is a case for the defendant to answer on the charge of the relevant offence is not to be considered before the close of all the evidence (or, if at some earlier time the defendant ceases to be charged with the section 5 offence, before that earlier time).

# Coroners and Justice Act 2009

(2009, c. 25)

## PART 2  CRIMINAL OFFENCES

### Chapter 1  Murder, Infanticide and Suicide

#### 54  Partial defence to murder: loss of control

(1) Where a person ('D') kills or is a party to the killing of another ('V'), D is not to be convicted of murder if—

    (a) D's acts and omissions in doing or being a party to the killing resulted from D's loss of self-control,

    (b) the loss of self-control had a qualifying trigger, and

    (c) a person of D's sex and age, with a normal degree of tolerance and self-restraint and in the circumstances of D, might have reacted in the same or in a similar way to D.

(2) For the purposes of subsection (1)(a), it does not matter whether or not the loss of control was sudden.

(3) In subsection (1)(c) the reference to 'the circumstances of D' is a reference to all of D's circumstances other than those whose only relevance to D's conduct is that they bear on D's general capacity for tolerance or self-restraint.

(4) Subsection (1) does not apply if, in doing or being a party to the killing, D acted in a considered desire for revenge.

(5) On a charge of murder, if sufficient evidence is adduced to raise an issue with respect to the defence under subsection (1), the jury must assume that the defence is satisfied unless the prosecution proves beyond reasonable doubt that it is not.

(6) For the purposes of subsection (5), sufficient evidence is adduced to raise an issue with respect to the defence if evidence is adduced on which, in the opinion of the trial judge, a jury, properly directed, could reasonably conclude that the defence might apply.

(7) A person who, but for this section, would be liable to be convicted of murder is liable instead to be convicted of manslaughter.

(8) The fact that one party to a killing is by virtue of this section not liable to be convicted of murder does not affect the question whether the killing amounted to murder in the case of any other party to it.

#### 55  Meaning of 'qualifying trigger'

(1) This section applies for the purposes of section 54.

(2) A loss of self-control had a qualifying trigger if subsection (3), (4) or (5) applies.

(3) This subsection applies if D's loss of self-control was attributable to D's fear of serious violence from V against D or another identified person.

(4) This subsection applies if D's loss of self-control was attributable to a thing or things done or said (or both) which—

    (a) constituted circumstances of an extremely grave character, and

    (b) caused D to have a justifiable sense of being seriously wronged.

(5) This subsection applies if D's loss of self-control was attributable to a combination of the matters mentioned in subsections (3) and (4).

(6) In determining whether a loss of self-control had a qualifying trigger—

    (a) D's fear of serious violence is to be disregarded to the extent that it was caused by a thing which D incited to be done or said for the purpose of providing an excuse to use violence;

    (b) a sense of being seriously wronged by a thing done or said is not justifiable if D incited the thing to be done or said for the purpose of providing an excuse to use violence;

    (c) the fact that a thing done or said constituted sexual infidelity is to be disregarded.

(7) In this section references to 'D' and 'V' are to be construed in accordance with section 54.

## Chapter 2　Anonymity of Witnesses

*Witness anonymity orders*

### 86　Witness anonymity orders

(1) In this Chapter a 'witness anonymity order' is an order made by a court that requires such specified measures to be taken in relation to a witness in criminal proceedings as the court considers appropriate to ensure that the identity of the witness is not disclosed in or in connection with the proceedings.

(2) The kinds of measures that may be required to be taken in relation to a witness include measures for securing one or more of the following—

    (a) that the witness's name and other identifying details may be—

        (i) withheld;

        (ii) removed from materials disclosed to any party to the proceedings;

    (b) that the witness may use a pseudonym;

    (c) that the witness is not asked questions of any specified description that might lead to the identification of the witness;

    (d) that the witness is screened to any specified extent;

    (e) that the witness's voice is subjected to modulation to any specified extent.

(3) Subsection (2) does not affect the generality of subsection (1).

(4) Nothing in this section authorises the court to require—

    (a) the witness to be screened to such an extent that the witness cannot be seen by—

        (i) the judge or other members of the court (if any), or

        (ii) the jury (if there is one);

    (b) the witness's voice to be modulated to such an extent that the witness's natural voice cannot be heard by any persons within paragraph (a)(i) or (ii).

(5) In this section 'specified' means specified in the witness anonymity order concerned.

### 87　Applications

(1) An application for a witness anonymity order to be made in relation to a witness in criminal proceedings may be made to the court by the prosecutor or the defendant.

(2) Where an application is made by the prosecutor, the prosecutor—

    (a) must (unless the court directs otherwise) inform the court of the identity of the witness, but

    (b) is not required to disclose in connection with the application—

        (i) the identity of the witness, or

        (ii) any information that might enable the witness to be identified,

    to any other party to the proceedings or his or her legal representatives.

(3) Where an application is made by the defendant, the defendant—

    (a) must inform the court and the prosecutor of the identity of the witness, but

    (b) (if there is more than one defendant) is not required to disclose in connection with the application—

        (i)   the identity of the witness, or

        (ii)  any information that might enable the witness to be identified,

        to any other defendant or his or her legal representatives.

(4) Accordingly, where the prosecutor or the defendant proposes to make an application under this section in respect of a witness, any relevant material which is disclosed by or on behalf of that party before the determination of the application may be disclosed in such a way as to prevent—

    (a) the identity of the witness, or

    (b) any information that might enable the witness to be identified,

from being disclosed except as required by subsection (2)(a) or (3)(a).

(5) 'Relevant material' means any document or other material which falls to be disclosed, or is sought to be relied on, by or on behalf of the party concerned in connection with the proceedings or proceedings preliminary to them.

(6) The court must give every party to the proceedings the opportunity to be heard on an application under this section.

(7) But subsection (6) does not prevent the court from hearing one or more parties in the absence of a defendant and his or her legal representatives, if it appears to the court to be appropriate to do so in the circumstances of the case.

(8) Nothing in this section is to be taken as restricting any power to make rules of court.

## 88   Conditions for making order

(1) This section applies where an application is made for a witness anonymity order to be made in relation to a witness in criminal proceedings.

(2) The court may make such an order only if it is satisfied that Conditions A to C below are met.

(3) Condition A is that the proposed order is necessary—

    (a) in order to protect the safety of the witness or another person or to prevent any serious damage to property, or

    (b) in order to prevent real harm to the public interest (whether affecting the carrying on of any activities in the public interest or the safety of a person involved in carrying on such activities, or otherwise).

(4) Condition B is that, having regard to all the circumstances, the effect of the proposed order would be consistent with the defendant receiving a fair trial.

(5) Condition C is that the importance of the witness's testimony is such that in the interests of justice the witness ought to testify and—

    (a) the witness would not testify if the proposed order were not made, or

    (b) there would be real harm to the public interest if the witness were to testify without the proposed order being made.

(6) In determining whether the proposed order is necessary for the purpose mentioned in subsection (3)(a), the court must have regard (in particular) to any reasonable fear on the part of the witness—

    (a) that the witness or another person would suffer death or injury, or

    (b) that there would be serious damage to property,

if the witness were to be identified.

## 89   Relevant considerations

(1) When deciding whether Conditions A to C in section 88 are met in the case of an application for a witness anonymity order, the court must have regard to—

    (a) the considerations mentioned in subsection (2) below, and

    (b) such other matters as the court considers relevant.

is relevant to *paragraph 2.12* and *Note 2A,* which apply to identification procedures, to taking finger-prints, samples, footwear impressions, photographs and to evidential searches and examinations.

1.6 If a person appears to be blind, seriously visually impaired, deaf, unable to read or speak or has difficulty orally because of a speech impediment, they shall be treated as such for the purposes f this Code in the absence of clear evidence to the contrary.

1.7 'The appropriate adult' means, in the case of a:

(a) juvenile:

   (i) the parent, guardian or, if the juvenile is in the care of a local authority or voluntary organisation, a person representing that authority or organisation (see *Note 1B*);

   (ii) a social worker of a local authority (see *Note 1C*);

   (iii) failing these, some other responsible adult aged 18 or over who is *not*:

      ~ a police officer;

      ~ employed by the police;

      ~ under the direction or control of the chief officer of a police force; or

      ~ a person who provides services under contractual arrangements (but without being employed by the chief officer of a police force), to assist that force in relation to the discharge of its chief officer's functions,

     whether or not they are on duty at the time.

ee *Note 1F.*

rson who is mentally disordered or mentally vulnerable: See *Note 1D.*

a relative, guardian or other person responsible for their care or custody;

someone experienced in dealing with mentally disordered or mentally vulnerable people but who is not:

   a police officer;

   employed by the police;

   under the direction or control of the chief officer of a police force; or

   a person who provides services under contractual arrangements (but without eing employed by the chief officer of a police force), to assist that force in relaion to the discharge of its chief officer's functions,

   her or not they are on duty at the time;

these, some other responsible adult aged 18 or over other than a person ed in the bullet points in *sub-paragraph (b)(ii)* above.

res a person be given certain information, they do not have to be given it if ble of understanding what is said, are violent or may become violent or in ntion, but they must be given it as soon as practicable.

ody officer include any police officer who, for the time being, is perform- officer.

ires the prior authority or agreement of an officer of at least inspector or rity may be given by a sergeant or chief inspector authorised to perform under the Police and Criminal Evidence Act 1984 (PACE), section 107.

.12, this Code applies to people in custody at police stations in ot they have been arrested, and to those removed to a police sta-Mental Health Act 1983, sections 135 and 136, as a last resort (see solely to people in police detention, e.g. those brought to a police police station for an offence after going there voluntarily.

s to a detained person:

pplies because:

lowing arrest under section 41 of the Terrorism Act 2000 d; or

en given under section 22 of the Counter-Terrorism Act 2008 uestioning of terrorist suspects) to interview them.

(2) The considerations are—

(a) the general right of a defendant in criminal proceedings to know the identity of a witness in the proceedings;

(b) the extent to which the credibility of the witness concerned would be a relevant factor when the weight of his or her evidence comes to be assessed;

(c) whether evidence given by the witness might be the sole or decisive evidence implicating the defendant;

(d) whether the witness's evidence could be properly tested (whether on grounds of credibility or otherwise) without his or her identity being disclosed;

(e) whether there is any reason to believe that the witness—

   (i) has a tendency to be dishonest, or

   (ii) has any motive to be dishonest in the circumstances of the case,

having regard (in particular) to any previous convictions of the witness and to any relationship between the witness and the defendant or any associates of the defendant;

(f) whether it would be reasonably practicable to protect the witness by any means other than by making a witness anonymity order specifying the measures that are under consideration by the court.

### 90 Warning to jury

(1) Subsection (2) applies where, on a trial on indictment with a jury, any evidence has been given by a witness at a time when a witness anonymity order applied to the witness.

(2) The judge must give the jury such warning as the judge considers appropriate to ensure that the fact that the order was made in relation to the witness does not prejudice the defendant.

*Discharge and variation*

### 91 Discharge or variation of order

(1) A court that has made a witness anonymity order in relation to any criminal proceedings may in those proceedings subsequently discharge or vary (or further vary) the order if it appears to the court to be appropriate to do so in view of the provisions of sections 88 and 89 that apply to the making of an order.

(2) The court may do so—

(a) on an application made by a party to the proceedings if there has been a material change of circumstances since the relevant time, or

(b) on its own initiative.

(3) The court must give every party to the proceedings the opportunity to be heard—

(a) before determining an application made to it under subsection (2);

(b) before discharging or varying the order on its own initiative.

(4) But subsection (3) does not prevent the court hearing one or more of the parties to the proceedings in the absence of a defendant in the proceedings and his or her legal representatives, if it appears to the court to be appropriate to do so in the circumstances of the case.

(5) 'The relevant time' means—

(a) the time when the order was made, or

(b) if a previous application has been made under subsection (2), the time when the application (or the last application) was made.

### 92 Discharge or variation after proceedings

(1) This section applies if—

(a) a court has made a witness anonymity order in relation to a witness in criminal proceedings ('the old proceedings'), and

(b) the old proceedings have come to an end.

(2) The court that made the order may discharge or vary (or further vary) the order if it appears to the court to be appropriate to do so in view of—

(a) the provisions of sections 88 and 89 that apply to the making of a witness anonymity order, and

(b) such other matters as the court considers relevant.

(3) The court may do so—

(a) on an application made by a party to the old proceedings if there has been a material change of circumstances since the relevant time, or

(b) on an application made by the witness if there has been a material change of circumstances since the relevant time.

(4) The court may not determine an application made to it under subsection (3) unless in the case of each of the parties to the old proceedings and the witness—

(a) it has given the person the opportunity to be heard, or

(b) it is satisfied that it is not reasonably practicable to communicate with the person.

(5) Subsection (4) does not prevent the court hearing one or more of the persons mentioned in that subsection in the absence of a person who was a defendant in the old proceedings and that person's legal representatives, if it appears to the court to be appropriate to do so in the circumstances of the case.

(6) 'The relevant time' means—

(a) the time when the old proceedings came to an end, or

(b) if a previous application has been made under subsection (3), the time when the application (or the last application) was made.

### 93  Discharge or variation by appeal court

(1) This section applies if—

(a) a court has made a witness anonymity order in relation to a witness in criminal proceedings ('the trial proceedings'), and

(b) a defendant in the trial proceedings has in those proceedings—

    (i) been convicted,

    (ii) been found not guilty by reason of insanity, or

    (iii) been found to be under a disability and to have done the act charged in respect of an offence.

(2) The appeal court may in proceedings on or in connection with an appeal by the defendant from the trial proceedings discharge or vary (or further vary) the order if it appears to the court to be appropriate to do so in view of—

(a) the provisions of sections 88 and 89 that apply to the making of a witness anonymity order, and

(b) such other matters as the court considers relevant.

(3) The appeal court may not discharge or vary the order unless in the case of each party to the trial proceedings—

(a) it has given the person the opportunity to be heard, or

(b) it is satisfied that it is not reasonably practicable to communicate with the person.

(4) But subsection (3) does not prevent the appeal court hearing one or more of the parties to the trial proceedings in the absence of a person who was a defendant in the trial proceedings and that person's legal representatives, if it appears to the court to be appropriate to do so in the circumstances of the case.

(5) In this section a reference to the doing of an act includes a reference to a failure to act.

(6) 'Appeal court' means—

(a) the Court of Appeal,

(b) the Court of Appeal in Northern Ireland, or

(c) the Court Martial Appeal Court.

---

# Part II

# Criminal Proceedings—Codes, Rules[?] Guidelines

## Code of Practice for the Detention, Treatment a[nd?] of Persons by Police Officers (Code C)

(2017)

### 1  General

1.0  The powers and procedures in this Code must be used fair[ly?] the people to whom they apply and without unlawful discriminati[on?] section 149 (Public sector Equality Duty), police forces must, in due regard to the need to eliminate unlawful discrimination, other conduct which is prohibited by that Act, to advance equ[ality?] who share a relevant protected characteristic and people w[ho?] relations between those persons. The Equality Act *also* mak[es?] criminate against, harass or victimise any person on the g[rounds?] of age, disability, gender reassignment, race, religion or b[elief?] and civil partnership, pregnancy and maternity, when u[sing?]

1.1  All persons in custody must be dealt with exp[editiously?] for detention no longer applies.

1.1A  A custody officer must perform the functio[n?] officer will not be in breach of this Code if delay is j[ustified?] vent unnecessary delay. The custody record shall [?] See *Note 1H*.

1.2  This Code of Practice must be readily av[ailable to?]

- police officers;
- police staff;
- detained persons;
- members of the public.

1.3  The provisions of this Code:

- include the *Annexes*
- do not include the *Notes for* [?]

1.4  If an officer has any suspicion[?] tally disordered or otherwise menta[lly?] suspicion, the person shall be treate[d?]

1.5  Anyone who appears to b[e?] older and subject to *paragraph 1.* [?] other Code. See Note 1L

1.5A  *Paragraph 1.5 does n*[ot?] priate consent) which require[?]

In this Code, section 65(1) [?] *Annex K paragraphs 1(b) and* [?]

    (b) to whom the Code of Practice issued under paragraph 6 of Schedule 14 to TACT applies because they are detained for examination under Schedule 7 to TACT.

1.12 This Code does not apply to people in custody:

    (i) arrested by officers under the Criminal Justice and Public Order Act 1994, section 136(2) on warrants issued in Scotland, or arrested or detained without warrant under section 137(2) by officers from a police force in Scotland. In these cases, police powers and duties and the person's rights and entitlements whilst at a police station in England or Wales are the same as those in Scotland;

    (ii) arrested under the Immigration and Asylum Act 1999, section 142(3) in order to have their fingerprints taken;

    (iii) whose detention has been authorised under Schedules 2 or 3 to the Immigration Act 1971 or section 62 of the Nationality, Immigration and Asylum Act 2002;

    (iv) who are convicted or remanded prisoners held in police cells on behalf of the Prison Service under the Imprisonment (Temporary Provisions) Act 1980;

    (v) Not used.

    (vi) detained for searches under stop and search powers except as required by Code A.

The provisions on conditions of detention and treatment in *sections 8* and *9* must be considered as the minimum standards of treatment for such detainees.

1.13 In this Code:

    (a) 'designated person' means a person other than a police officer, who has specified powers and duties conferred or imposed on them by designation under section 38 or 39 of the Police Reform Act 2002;

    (b) reference to a police officer includes a designated person acting in the exercise or performance of the powers and duties conferred or imposed on them by their designation;

    (c) where a search or other procedure to which this Code applies may only be carried out or observed by a person of the same sex as the detainee, the gender of the detainee and other parties present should be established and recorded in line with Annex L of this Code.

1.14 Designated persons are entitled to use reasonable force as follows:

    (a) when exercising a power conferred on them which allows a police officer exercising that power to use reasonable force, a designated person has the same entitlement to use force; and

    (b) at other times when carrying out duties conferred or imposed on them that also entitle them to use reasonable force, for example:

      • when at a police station carrying out the duty to keep detainees for whom they are responsible under control and to assist any police officer or designated person to keep any detainee under control and to prevent their escape;

      • when securing, or assisting any police officer or designated person in securing, the detention of a person at a police station;

      • when escorting, or assisting any police officer or designated person in escorting, a detainee within a police station;

      • for the purpose of saving life or limb; or

      • or preventing serious damage to property.

1.15 Nothing in this Code prevents the custody officer, or other police officer or designated person (see *paragraph 1.13*) given custody of the detainee by the custody officer, from allowing another person (see *(a)* and *(b)* below) to carry out individual procedures or tasks at the police station if the law allows. However, the officer or designated person given custody remains responsible for making sure the procedures and tasks are carried out correctly in accordance with the Codes of Practice (see *paragraph 3.5* and *Note 3F*). The other person who is allowed to carry out the procedures or tasks must be someone who *at that time*, is:

    (a) under the direction and control of the chief officer of the force responsible for the police station in question; or

(b) providing services under contractual arrangements (but without being employed by the chief officer the police force), to assist a police force in relation to the discharge of its chief officer's functions.

1.16 Designated persons and others mentioned in *sub-paragraphs (a)* and *(b)* of *paragraph 1.15*, must have regard to any relevant provisions of the Codes of Practice.

1.17 In any provision of this or any other Code which allows or requires police officers or police staff to make a record in their report book, the reference to report book shall include any official report book or electronic recording device issued to them that enables the record in question to be made and dealt with in accordance with that provision. References in this and any other Code to written records, forms and signatures include electronic records and forms and electronic confirmation that identifies the person making the record or completing the form.

Chief officers must be satisfied as to the integrity and security of the devices, records and forms to which this *paragraph* applies and that use of those devices, records and forms satisfies relevant data protection legislation.

### Notes for Guidance

*1A Although certain sections of this Code apply specifically to people in custody at police stations, those there voluntarily to assist with an investigation should be treated with no less consideration, e.g. offered refreshments at appropriate times, and enjoy an absolute right to obtain legal advice or communicate with anyone outside the police station.*

*1AA In paragraph 1.0, under the Equality Act 2010, section 149, the 'relevant protected characteristics' are age, disability, gender reassignment, pregnancy and maternity, race, religion/belief and sex and sexual orientation. For further detailed guidance and advice on the Equality Act, see: https://www.gov.uk/guidance/equality-act-2010-guidance.*

*1B A person, including a parent or guardian, should not be an appropriate adult if they:*
- *are:*
  - ~ *suspected of involvement in the offence; the victim;*
  - ~ *a witness;*
  - ~ *involved in the investigation.*
- *received admissions prior to attending to act as the appropriate adult.*

*Note: If a juvenile's parent is estranged from the juvenile, they should not be asked to act as the appropriate adult if the juvenile expressly and specifically objects to their presence.*

*1C If a juvenile admits an offence to, or in the presence of, a social worker or member of a youth offending team other than during the time that person is acting as the juvenile's appropriate adult, another appropriate adult should be appointed in the interest of fairness.*

*1D In the case of people who are mentally disordered or otherwise mentally vulnerable, it may be more satisfactory if the appropriate adult is someone experienced or trained in their care rather than a relative lacking such qualifications. But if the detainee prefers a relative to a better qualified stranger or objects to a particular person their wishes should, if practicable, be respected.*

*1E A detainee should always be given an opportunity, when an appropriate adult is called to the police station, to consult privately with a solicitor in the appropriate adult's absence if they want. An appropriate adult is not subject to legal privilege.*

*1F A solicitor or independent custody visitor who is present at the police station and acting in that capacity, may not be the appropriate adult.*

*1G 'Mentally vulnerable' applies to any detainee who, because of their mental state or capacity, may not understand the significance of what is said, of questions or of their replies. 'Mental disorder' is defined in the Mental Health Act 1983, section 1(2) as 'any disorder or disability of mind'. When the custody officer has any doubt about the mental state or capacity of a detainee, that detainee should be treated as mentally vulnerable and an appropriate adult called.*

*1H Paragraph 1.1A is intended to cover delays which may occur in processing detainees e.g. if:*
- *a large number of suspects are brought into the station simultaneously to be placed in custody;*

## AN OFFER HE COULDN'T REFUSE

y were functional fangs, not just decorative, set in a
truding jaw, with long lips and a wide mouth; yet the total
ect was lupine rather than simian. Hair a dark matted mess.
d yes, fully eight feet tall, a rangy, tense-muscled body.

She clawed her wild hair away from her face and stared
him with renewed fierceness. Her eyes were a strange
ight hazel, adding to the wolfish effect. "What are you
really doing here?"

"I came for you. I'd heard of you. I'm . . . recruiting.
Or I was. Things went wrong and now I'm escaping. But
if you came with me, you could join the Dendarii
Mercenaries. A top outfit—always looking for a few good
men, or whatever. I have this master-sergeant who . . .
who needs a recruit like you." Sgt. Dyeb was infamous for
his sour attitude about women soldiers, insisting that they
were too soft . . .

"Very funny," she said coldly. "But I'm not even human.
Or hadn't you heard?"

"Human is as human does." He forced himself to reach
out and touch her damp cheek. "Animals don't weep."

She jerked, as from an electric shock. "Animals don't
lie. Humans do. All the time."

"Not all the time."

"Prove it." She tilted her head as she sat cross-legged.
"Take off your clothes."

". . . what?"

"Take off your clothes and lie down with me as humans do.
Men and women." Her hand reached out to touch his throat.

The pressing claws made little wells in his flesh. "Blrp?"
choked Miles. His eyes felt wide as saucers. A little more
pressure, and those wells would spring forth red fountains.
I am about to die. . . .

I can't believe this. Trapped on Jackson's Whole with a
sex-starved teenage werewolf. There was nothing about
this in any of my Imperial Academy training manuals. . . .

### BORDERS OF INFINITY by LOIS McMASTER BUJOLD
69841-9 • $3.95

planet-per-month schedule, and nearly seven hun-
dred planets were gone. There were epic battles in
space, but the Wholeth technical superiority pre-
vailed again and again, even when the Cloud was
able finally to meet the design of the golden ship
and more. The Cloud was weak, riddled by internal
bickering, fractionalized by growing conversions to
the Wholeth religion, its government lacking the
iron paranormal hand which the Whole enjoyed.
And paranormal spies from the Whole soon held the
Cloud in a tight intelligence network, made irresist-
ible by psionic power.

Word occasionally came regarding the Onn. The
Whole still dredged up the shibboleth of alien inva-
sion, despite what the Little Lord had denied and
revealed. There was a flurry of such claims around
the thirty-third year, the rumor flying that the
Whole had identified an infiltration network from the
aliens it had considered long extinct. Nothing came
of it, though; unless the rumors were true, and the
aliens themselves suppressed them. I found out the
truth on one of the suicidal missions Palla Belanger
forced me into, but that's not a part of this story.

That was the year that the black planet Institute
finally sent another mission to the Roil, this time in
a new class of starship whose power was, it was
believed, more than enough to overcome the inten-
sity of the gravitational chaos. It was a mission driven
by a Polarian desperation, a clutching at straws for
any chance, any wedge to use against the Whole. It
was also, though few knew it, a mission brought
about by the secret that I had revealed to Palla
Belanger, an inference I had made, a connecting of
disparate facts.

The Little Lord or Maja might have thought of it
if they had tried, but they had been too confident
in their psionics, too dismissive of what the spies
had done. Now, as the mission went out, they in

their empire in the galactic arm were aware of some of the desperate thinking behind the mission; what we let them know. Knowing as they did the events of Lee and my time, they simply looked on, amused. The spy ship had been cleaned out, as their Lord well knew.

And so the Roil opened up and swallowed the Institute ship, and only a few paid any real attention. Soon the shipful of the finest male scientists the Cloud could muster—male to avoid any possibility of a paranormal Wholeth spy aboard—found itself in wild orbit around the central peculiarity.

They reached the spy ship, and their disappointment was great. Hoping against hope that the Little Lord had left something behind, they found nothing, not in the ship's databanks, not in any secret hiding place inside or on her skin, though they virtually took the vessel apart. The ship had been wiped as clean as a newborn baby.

But the Polarian ship went on; why not? There was nothing to lose. They overtook and studied the ship of Crestor Falon; and they even reached the dusty hulk of the astronomer's son, *The Defiant*, whose age had brought it closer than any of the others to the deadly rings sweeping the sky.

And from that point, the expedition dropped from the ken of the Cloud and of the Whole. Both believed for a long time, one officially and the other absolutely, that the ship had been lost, as those before it, in the Roil of stars.

But in fact, something quite otherwise had occurred. The scientists had found all three ships functional when it came to their electronics, hard though time had been upon the people who had died inside. All ships were still sucking power out of the light around them. All had automatics turned on. All three shipcoms, two of them for centuries, had been monitoring the channels, electromagnetic and tachholo,

analyzing and rejecting the constant that the Roil threw between them an universe.

And two of them had caught the desp mission that the third had made when Le had despaired of surviving the grip of the caught, and recorded, the full details of pa genetics. After all, there was no Roil betwee and the spy ship's transmission; they were same swept-clean, closed-in space.

The scientists, well aware of the Wholeth i gence network and on admiralty instructions, to chance with their new and powerful ship emerging from the Roil in another direction fi their entry, sped away to an uncolonized plai which the Cloud had preselected, one of the fe known, lying far out on the rearmost fringes of th Cloud, too remote to have attracted settlers as yet. And there highly screened wives and lovers joined them, and they took the information that Lee's parents had forgotten, and used it.

And twenty years later, the Whole became aware that its spy network was no longer as reliable as it once had been. The pace of conquest slowed. There was paranormal interference coming from somewhere. But where. . . ?